Common Wild Flowers

of the
NORTHEASTERN
UNITED STATES

New York Botanical Garden

Carol H. Woodward
Harold William Rickett

BARRON'S / WOODBURY, NEW YORK

First U.S. Edition
Published in 1979 by
Barron's Educational Series, Inc.

All inquiries should be addressed to:
Barron's Educational Series, Inc.
113 Crossways Park Drive
Woodbury, New York 11797

Publication of the New York Botanical Garden
Library of Congress Catalog Card No. 77-18598
International Standard Book No. 0-8120-0937-1

PRINTED IN ENGLAND

Table of Contents

Foreword

This is the first of a series of handbooks devoted to the wild flowers of selected regions in the United States. The illustrations are taken from the comprehensive and definitive *Wild Flowers of the United States* by Dr. Harold William Rickett, published for the New York Botanical Garden by the McGraw-Hill Book Company. As author of the present text, Dr. Rickett has produced a field book which, when used in conjunction with the first of the six volumes of *Wild Flowers of the United States,* will offer the reader an ideal combination, since each book will then achieve its most effective usefulness.

The discovery of the kinds of living things in the world is some of our most urgent business. We still do not have a complete inventory of the plants and animals with which we share this planet, and on which we depend for our survival. Neither have we satisfactorily fitted the distribution of known species into environmental niches, for the diversity of environments remains incompletely understood. Thus, the dimensions of a serious dilemma become clear: to assess the characteristics of whole environmental units we must know the nature of the component species, living and nonliving. Put more bluntly, we cannot make intelligent decisions and choices about natural resources until we know at least what they are, where they occur, something of their plenitude and distribution, and with what they are associated.

The nature of human behavior with respect to the native herbaceous plants we call wild flowers depends upon the fabriclike relationship of objective reality and human perceptions. In such a fabric the warp is provided by taxonomic science applied to plants, utilizing our accumulated knowledge of species of plants, while the woof is socio-economic behavior, a field becoming known as human ecology, drawn from anthropology, sociology, geography, ethology, and psychology, among other disciplines.

Taxonomy is of the essence. Taxonomy exercises the naming habit and more, necessarily involving description and reflecting a search for order in the varied expressions of form and function in plants. In some parts of the world, especially in Europe and North America, plant inventories are well advanced, documented by preserved samples in plant-specimen museums or herbaria, upon which regional compendia or published floras are based and produced for the use of botanists, naturalists, foresters, agriculturists, geographers, physicians, pharmacists, and others who have mastered the technical language. A flora is more than an annotated list, however. The species and higher classificatory units are ordered according to an accepted taxonomic system, based on a scheme that is purported to reflect fact and informed opinion about evolution.

Most of us, unprepared to be drawn into the seemingly limitless and complex details of taxonomy, are nevertheless profoundly stamped by visual and other sensorial associations with plants—some of grand scale involving whole landscapes or sweeping forest scenes, others concentrating on a single leaf or petal or tuft of moss, spontaneously triggering environmental recognition in our inner imagery. It is hard to say how much this reflex is colored by scientific knowledge and how much by other aspects of experience, whether personal or vicarious. I have not found that my decades of professional work have diminished in any way the magic of the experience I still vividly recall, walking into the great conservatory of the New York Botanical Garden as a small boy and being overwhelmed not only by the towering palms silhouetted above but by the delicate emerald masses of pellitory among the rocks. I have since learned more about what I beheld, but the emotion has not faded.

Today the knowledge of botanists is out there and accessible in museums, in books, on television, on the screen—but it is not always presented in a way that relates to common experience. If it were, we might not be confronted with the dismaying fact that more than 1,000 of the 20,000 species comprising our native North American flora are threatened with extinction largely because of the unwitting ravages wrought by human endeavor. Appreciation and knowledge of wild flowers is an important way for people to weave elements of the natural world into their lives and broaden their horizons, preparing for the fuller accommodation of nature in the future rather than the heedless exploitation of it as in the past.

There are approximately 3,000 species of wild flowers within the area circumscribed by this book, exclusive of grasses, sedges, shrubs, trees, and a few unsightly weeds. These species include many with greatly restricted geographical distributions, and which represent a highly diverse series of floristic elements of several geographic origins. Among these, we can recognize the largely coniferous northern flora that extends as far south as the region considered here in deep shaded valleys where cold air prevails, as well as on the tops of higher hills. The seashore flora is an individual one, and in the New Jersey Pine Barrens and on Long Island, many species of tropical origin are to be found. Back of the coastal plain, one finds many representatives of the broad-leaved deciduous flora of the Allegheny Mountains, some of them at their northernmost limit.

Dr. Rickett (formerly of the staff of the New York Botanical Garden) is to be commended for creating a work that finally makes the identification of our local wild flowers easy and, equally important, certain. Also to be commended is Dr. William C. Steere, Senior Scientist and President Emeritus of the Garden, who served as editor of the full series, *Wild Flowers of the United States*, during the 10 years it was being written and who was instrumental in the development of the present volume.

HOWARD S. IRWIN
New York Botanical Garden

vi

Introduction

The object of this book is to enable the reader to identify any herbaceous wild flower that may be found within 50 miles of Manhattan. Flowering trees, shrubs, and vines are excluded, as are grass, sedges, pigweeds and ragweeds – though they are indeed flowering plants. Answering to our definition of wild flowers are about one thousand species in the specified area; all, we believe, described or at least mentioned in the following pages, and most of them illustrated. Identification, however, is not easy, and cannot be made easy. Plants are of more kinds than, for example, birds in the same area; and the differences between many of them are slight and technical. It is important, first, to turn the pages of the book, to read this Introduction and some of the descriptions, to examine the illustrations, perhaps with some plant in hand the name of which is known to the reader. Then, with an unknown plant, to search the color plates for something like it and to study carefully the corresponding descriptions, noticing not only the leading characteristics but also the type of situation and the season of flowering; and passing to the descriptions of closely related kinds not illustrated.

For an understanding – however elementary – of flowering plants, and for identifying them, some botanical terms must be made familiar. Not the elaborate terminology of the professional, which is like a foreign language; but a certain minimum of words by which to refer to the features that distinguish one plant from another – the parts of a flower, the shapes of leaves, and so on. For this purpose our common English speech is unfortunately inadequate – though it partly fulfills the need. With the addition of the small number of technical terms here presented and explained, a sufficient vocabulary is attained.

Flowers. Because of the constancy of their structure, flowers are more important in classifying plants – and therefore in identifying them – than leaves, stems, and other parts. Color, however, though the first choice of the uninstructed, is unreliable; many species have flowers of different colors (see, for instance, *Verbascum blattaria*); very many have albino forms. The following characteristics are relatively constant.

PARTS. A flower is on a *stalk* (anatomically like the stem), which may be so short as to be scarcely discernible. The most obvious part of the flower is the *perianth*, which typically consists of two circles: an outer circle of *sepals*, all together called the *calyx*; and an inner circle of *petals*, together composing the *corolla*. Petals may be lacking; or both may be absent. And though sepals are commonly green and petals of other colors, either set may be of almost any color, and the two may be alike (as in lilies). Sepals may be separate, or joined to form a cup or tube, only their tips being distinct as lobes or teeth. The same is true of petals. Petals may be all alike and *radially symmetric*; i.e. radiating from the center so that however one may divide them through the center, one gets two matching halves. Many flowers stand more or less horizontally and the petals may form *two lips*, an upper and a lower, generally different; so that one gets matching halves only by a vertical division; and they are said to be *bilaterally symmetric*. The *stamens* form one or more circles within the perianth. Each typically consists of a slender or flat *stalk* and a lobed *head* containing the male fertilizing bodies, the *pollen*. The center of the flower is occupied by one or more *pistils*, each consisting of a roundish *ovary* surmounted by one or several slender *styles* each of which bears one or more *stigmas*. Pollen, when deposited on the stigma, effects the fertilization of one or more *ovules* within the ovary; these become the *seeds*. Pollen is transferred to the stigmas by a great variety of agents, including wind and insects. The latter are attracted by color, odor, and the *nectar* secreted by *nectaries*, which may be found on petals, on stamens or pistils, or at the base of these organs.

The ovary of a pistil may be *superior*, i.e. visible in the midst of the stamens; or it may be embedded in the part beneath the flower – the tip of the flower-stalk or the united bases of calyx and corolla, or both; such an ovary is *inferior*. In other flowers the pistil may be hidden by but not embedded in a *floral tube* which bears perianth and stamens on its rim.

ARRANGEMENT. The origins and arrangements of flowers are generally characteristic of the kind of plant and therefore useful in identifying it. The flowers may be borne singly or clustered in the *axils* of leaves (see below for this term). Or they may be associated with scales or other leaflike bodies different from the foliage leaves; these are *bracts*. A number of flowers thus accompanied by bracts may constitute an *inflorescence*. The principal types of inflorescence are as follows. *Cyme :* typically a flower terminates a stalk, from the axils of bracts just below spring two more stalks bearing single flowers, from below *these* spring other flowers in the same way, and so on; in practice cymes are rarely so regular. *Raceme :* flowers are borne singly in the axils of bracts along a central stem; or smaller racemes or clusters may arise in these positions; flower-buds may still be opening at the tip while fruits are developing below. Some inflorescences commonly mistaken for racemes have two rows of flowers alternating on one side of the stem, *opposite* bracts (if present), not in their axils; these are termed *false racemes* (a form of cyme). *Umbel :* flowers are on stalks which radiate from the tip of a stem; as commonly understood, with buds opening from margin to center; but umbels of many genera are really cymes in which the flowers follow no such order; these may be termed *false umbels*. *Spike :* flowers are borne in a variety of ways along a central stem as in a raceme, but in all types with very short stalks; in the mint family and some other groups the flowers are in dense clusters – really condensed cymes – at intervals with bare stem between – an "interrupted spike." *Head :* flowers are in a dense spherical or short-cylindric mass, with very short stalks; some heads are umbels with practically no flower-stalks; others are condensed cymes. More complex inflorescences, known as *panicles*, may have a central stem from which spring various other types of inflorescences, as cymes.

Fruits. The kinds of fruits are numerous and even yet not differentiated by botanists with complete accuracy; botanically they are derived from pistils and concerned only with the production and dispersal of seeds, and may or may not be edible. We may distinguish the following: *Achene*, a small nut containing one seed and not opening to liberate it; often miscalled a seed. *Capsule*, a fruit which contains several or many seeds and splits open along several lines to liberate them. *Follicle*, a fruit with several seeds which splits along one side. *Berry*, a succulent fruit formed from a single ovary (excluding strawberries, raspberries, etc. which are the product of several pistils and other flower-parts). *Stone-fruit*, like a berry but with a hard shell or "pit" around the seed or seeds. Several other types of fruit have a less general occurrence and are described in the relevant text.

Leaves. Of all parts of plants, leaves have acquired perhaps the most extensive scientific jargon, which may be mostly dispensed with in this book. However, to avoid endless repetition of long descriptive phrases, a few unfamiliar terms are here retained.

ARRANGEMENT: Leaves may be borne singly on the stem, or in pairs or circles; or they may all be at or near the base of the stem and crowded together, perhaps forming a rosette on the ground; such terms explain themselves.

PARTS. A leaf may consist of a *stalk* and a *blade*; leaf-stalks are lacking on many plants, and blades on some. Anatomically the leaf-stalk is part of the leaf and differs from the *stem* to which it is attached. The angle between the upper side of the leaf-stalk (or blade if a stalk is lacking) and the stem to which it is attached is the *axil*. It is here that branches and flowers may originate.

SHAPE. Two very common shapes of leaf-blades are named *ovate* – having an outline like that of an egg; and *lanceolate* – like the head of a lance; both these are broadest between base and middle; but many leaves are broadest at or towards the other end. Both of these shapes may be sharp or blunt or even roundish at the tip, and tapering or roundish or even indented at the base; in the latter case the leaf may be *heart-shaped*. More extreme types are *narrow*, with parallel sides; and *round*, as broad as long.

MARGIN. Leaves are *toothed* in various ways. Some have a wavy outline, in some combined with teeth. Others are *scalloped*, with notches between roundish projections. Finally, the margin may be smooth or *plain*, with no teeth or notches or other features.

Underground parts: In general, the amateur naturalist does not dig plants to identify them. But since the underground stems and roots are important in making a plant perennial, they must be occasionally named even if not seen. The more important types are as follows. *Rhizome:* a horizontal underground stem (often miscalled a root). *Tuber:* an enlarged rhizome, as a potato. *Root-tuber*, an enlarged portion of a root. *Bulb:* a small circular flattish stem surmounted by leaves with circular bases in concentric rings, as in an onion. There is no very sharp line between rhizomes and bulbs, since a short scaly rhizome is close to being a bulb. *Corm:* a spherical, vertical underground stem, often miscalled a bulb.

Classification of Plants

In dealing with vast numbers of things, we create order by classifying them. What we recognize as the "kinds" of plants are *species* (often known to the layman as "varieties"). The plants of one species all agree in their more constant features, and their offspring resemble them in the same way. Among them, there may be some that differ in minor features – e.g. color – from the rest; these constitute what the botanist calls *varieties*; or, if they form a definite population, perhaps occupying a distinct territory, *subspecies*. The species, on the other hand, generally resembles in its less variable features – e.g. flower-structure – other species; as the various kinds of violets resemble each other. The group of species thus formed is a *genus* (plural *genera*). In the same way genera may be grouped in *families*: lilies, hyacinths, dog-tooth-violets, and others form the lily family. We thus create a hierarchy of groups of plants – family, genus, species, subspecies, variety.

Most persons do not appreciate the problems met with in naming the kinds of plants; many insist that the botanical (Latin) names are only for the scientist and unnecessary for the amateur. Two considerations dispose of this quite natural approach. First there are too many kinds: about a thousand in this book, many thousands in the United States, hundreds of thousands in the world. Second, most of this enormous variety of living things have never acquired vernacular names; most of the wild flowers of this country have no English – "common" – names. (Some have "made-up" names, translations of the Latin; but these are not "common" and not easy to remember or to use.)

In recognizing and naming plants, it is the species that comes readily to mind. Species, however, are so numerous that it would be impractical to give each an entirely distinctive name. Instead, we name each genus by a single word (*Lilium, Viola*, etc.); and each species by two words – the name of the genus followed by a qualifying word; the second word is often a descriptive Latin adjective (*lanceolata*), or commemorates the botanist who found it (*torreyi*, from John Torrey), or indicates the place where it was first collected by a botanist (*philadelphicum*). The subdivisions of species, though described, are not named in this book. Families are named by tacking on *-aceae* to the essential part of the name of a genus (*Liliaceae, Violaceae*).

The system is – when once mastered – simple and precise. Moreover, the botanical names of plants are standard all over the world, no matter in what language – German, Russian, or Japanese – the "common" names are formed.

The species in this book are arranged by families. Other arrangements have been suggested but are impractical for any complete presentation. The most frequent in books meant to be intelligible to the layman is arrangement by color: species with white flowers, species with blue flowers, and so on. But a great number of species have several color-forms, and many flowers change color as they age. The botanical characterization of families is technical, depending on distinctions in general not accessible to the amateur. But they may be *approximately* described in terms of easily visible features, such as number of petals, sepals, stamens, and pistils, and arrangement of flowers and leaves. The lily family, for instance, the first in this book, is generally recognizable by its six-parted perianth, its six stamens, its single pistil with three chambers in the ovary, and leaves with unbranched veins and smooth edges. While no general guide or key to the seventy-four families included is presented, each is characterized in a brief introductory statement which will satisfy any need to understand why certain genera are placed together.

WILD
FLOWER
FAMILIES

THE LILY FAMILY – LILIACEAE

Sepals three and petals three; in many species similar or identical, in some partly united. Stamens six. Ovary three-chambered and superior, or partially superior with the lower part joined to surrounding parts of the flower. Styles and stigmas one or three; if three, in several genera spreading out threadlike directly from the top of the ovary. Fruit of many species a pod (capsule) which splits into three parts when ripe; in other species a berry. (In a single genus, *Maianthemum*, the flower parts in twos and fours instead of threes and sixes.) Leaves undivided; with few exceptions lacking in marginal teeth. Veins unbranched except in *Trillium*. Plants growing mostly from bulbs or rhizomes, in a few genera from tubers or fibrous roots. Onions and asparagus among the well-known food plants in the family.

THE LILIES (LILIUM)

The outer and inner circles of the perianth (the sepals and petals) of our wild lilies are colored alike or nearly so: yellow or orange or red, mottled with darker color. At the base of each is a nectar-bearing gland. The flowers appear in midsummer and later. Each flower, when fertilized, is followed by a pod (a capsule) which splits along three lines when ripe, disclosing six columns of flat seeds. The lily plant grows from a scaly bulb. In mediaeval times, the bulbs of European lilies were credited with wonderful curative powers, but modern medicine denies them these attributes, and lilies today have no medicinal uses. In the New York City region, three native species.

WOOD LILY, L. PHILADELPHICUM (1–4 feet), has one or several erect reddish-orange flowers at the summit of the stem. The sepals and petals are separate and arch outward only slightly; at the base they are yellow with dark spots. Most of the slender leaves are borne in circles. The plant grows commonly in dry woodlands and on shady banks, flowering from June to August.

FIELD LILY, L. CANADENSE (2–7 feet), has up to twenty flowers which hang from long stalks arranged in an umbel at the tip of the stem, with others hanging singly from the leaf-axils directly below. The perianth-parts are halfway united from the base up, then outward-spreading. There are two color forms, red and yellow, both dark-spotted toward the center. Numerous narrow, lance-shaped leaves arch outward from the stem in circles. The plants grow in moist open ground. June to August.

TURK'S-CAP LILY, L. SUPERBUM (up to 8 feet), is the largest of our lilies and usually bears more flowers than the others. The sepals and petals, of orange or red and heavily spotted, are bent sharply back, exposing the stamens and pistil, which point more or less downward. It grows in moist meadows and woods, flowering from July to September, at its peak in early August.

TIGER LILY, L. TIGRINUM, the familiar garden plant (seldom more than 4 feet tall), is often found growing wild. Its perianth bends back sharply like that of the Turk's-cap lily. The stem is purplish and the leaves, slender but broad-based, are scattered on it. Small black bulbs are to be seen in the leaf-axils. Flowering from July to September.

ium philadelphicum *Johnson*

Lilium canadense *Johnson*

Lilium superbum *Gottscho*

MEDEOLA

INDIAN CUCUMBER-ROOT, M. VIRGINIANA, is the only species of *Medeola*. Halfway up the stem, which is 1–3 feet tall, is a circle of leaves, and at the summit three smaller leaves. The flowers also grow at the summit, but hang on curved stalks below the three leaves. The perianth, curled sharply backward, is greenish. Three long, thread-like, brown stigmas, projecting sideways and slightly curved backwards, are conspicuous. The fruit is a red berry; the stalks straighten so that several may be seen in the midst of the three uppermost leaves. The "root" – really a rhizome – is palatable. The plants grow in woods and on mossy banks, flowering in May and June.

DOGTOOTH-VIOLET or ADDER'S-TONGUE (ERYTHRONIUM)

These small plants of early spring, which are like miniature lilies, bear no relation to true violets, and the "dogtooth" part of their long-used common name refers to the small white underground bulb from which the leaves and flowers arise. These bulbs send out underground branches which form small new bulbs at their tips. The leaves and flowers mostly come directly from the soil, and the flowers hang singly on the stalks. The leaves are generally mottled. Only one species reaches the vicinity of New York, and different plants in this species vary considerably.

YELLOW DOGTOOTH-VIOLET, E. AMERICANUM, has yellow flowers with sepals and petals (six in all) separate and curving sharply upwards. They are generally spotted with brown on the inside. There are ordinarily two elliptic leaves accompanying the flower. Their blades merge inconspicuously at the base into their short stalks. In colonies of the plant, single leaves can often be seen. These appear for several years, either from seeds or from new bulbs, before a flower-stalk appears. The stamens in the flower occur in two circles of three each, one group often shorter than the other. When the pollen is ripe, the stamens turn brown. The ovary, in which the seeds develop, has three divisions. The flowers sometimes open in March, before any greenery appears in the woods; they may often still be seen in May.

BELLWORT (UVULARIA)

Bellworts, which start to flower in early spring, are easily recognized by their dangling yellow flowers on slender, leafy, arching stalks. The sepals and petals are separate and all alike – long and narrow, slightly twisted, always yellow. Flowers can be seen on all the species from April to June.

U. PERFOLIATA has leaves which surround the stem at the base; that is, the stem (and even the flower-stalk) seems to grow right through the leaf, which is ovate with a sharp point at the tip. The leaves are covered with a whitish bloom. The flowers, from ¾ inch to nearly 1½ inches long, are roughened inside with minute projecting glands. The stamens are shorter than the style. The plants, which grow to 2 feet high, are found in open woods, often in acid soil.

U. GRANDIFLORA is larger, growing up to 30 inches and bearing flowers to 2 inches long and of brighter yellow. The flowers are smooth inside and the stamens are longer than the style. The leaves are finely downy on the lower surface. As in *U. perfoliata*, they are "perfoliate"; that is, the stem appears to grow through the base of a leaf. These plants are likely to be found in woods in limestone regions.

MERRY-BELLS or WILD-OATS, U. SESSILIFOLIA, the kind most often seen near New York, is smaller in all its parts, and the flowers are of a paler yellow. The leaves are attached at their base and are elliptic in shape. They are whitish on the lower surface. The seed-pod is distinctly stalked. Woods and thickets.

Uvularia perfoliata   *D. Richards*

ythronium americanum   *Johnson*

Medeola virginiana   *Rhein*

THE TRILLIUMS (TRILLIUM)

The name for this group of spring-blooming woodland plants comes from the Latin word for "three"; flower parts and leaves are all in threes or a multiple of three: three green sepals, three separate petals, six stamens, a three-chambered ovary, with usually three or six angles to the berry that develops from it, and three stigmas, in most species seated directly on the ovary without supporting stalks, or styles. The single trillium flower of each plant grows directly above the three leaves, in some species with a short stalk, in others with none. The leaves of most species are broadly elliptic or ovate. The trilliums are one of the few members of the lily family that have noticeable cross-veins in their leaves in addition to the conspicuous lengthwise veins that characterize the family. The plants grow from horizontal underground stems, or rhizomes.

STINKING-BENJAMIN or SQUAWROOT, T. ERECTUM, normally a dark-red-flowered plant, 6–24 inches tall, with leaves extremely broad across the middle, is the commonest species here. There are varieties with greenish, yellow, or white petals. The flower is ill-scented. Sepals and petals are lance-shaped, from ½ to 2¼ inches long. The stalk, which is erect, often turned slightly to one side, averages 1¾ inches, but may be up to 4 inches long. The ovary is normally purple, the berry red and six-angled. Found chiefly in moist woods, flowering from April to June.

LARGE WHITE TRILLIUM, T. GRANDI-FLORUM, most frequently has wavy-edged white petals, broader than those in T. erectum and about 2 inches long. They may also be pink or green or green-and-white-striped, or they may undergo numerous other variations in color, size, shape, or number. The flower-stalk may be 2 inches long, the plant from 8 to 16 inches tall. A woodland plant, sometimes cultivated; considered the handsomest as well as the most variable species. Flowering time, from April to June.

PAINTED TRILLIUM, T. UNDULATUM, is a close rival to T. grandiflorum. The flowers, equally large, are white or pinkish with wavy margins to the petals, dark red or purplish markings at the base of each. Stamens are pink. The flower-stalk is erect and up to 2 inches long. The plant stands from 4 to 20 inches high. The red berry that develops from the ovary is obscurely three-angled. The leaves taper to a point. Flowering from April to June.

NODDING TRILLIUM, T. CERNUUM, has a sweet-scented flower whose arching stalk carries it below the leaves so that it "nods" – that is, it faces downward. The petals, which are white or pinkish (or in one variety deep rose), then curve sharply backward. They are relatively narrow and from ½ to 1 inch long. The tips of the stamens (the anthers) are pink and are longer than their stalks (the filaments). The ovary is either white or pink and the eventual berry is dark red. The leaves are about as broad as long and measure up to 6 inches. They are on short stalks. The plants grow mostly in damp woods with acid soil, flowering from April to July.

Farther west and south there are several species of *Trillium* with interestingly mottled leaves.

Trillium erectum *Rickett* Trillium grandiflorum *Gottscho*

Trillium undulatum *Johnson*

ONIONS (ALLIUM)

An onion seems a far cry from an Easter lily, yet *Allium* and *Lilium* are sister plants in the lily family. Onions have the same six identical or closely similar perianth-parts (sepals and petals) as lilies, the same six stamens, and the same three-chambered ovary. The leaves, however, are distinctive, being long and narrow; in most species they are flat, in some tubular, and all arise from the bulb in a cluster surrounding the long flowering stem. At the summit, one or more papery bracts conceal the buds. The flowers, each one on a stalk, open out in a more or less globular cluster of generally delicate appearance. Occasionally, or commonly in certain species, bulblets instead of flowers develop. The underground bulb is composed of non-green leaf-bases, which are fleshy and tightly compressed, one around another, seated on and concealing the thick dome-shaped basal stem from which they all arise. The bulbs and green leaves of the onions (which include garlic, chives, and leeks) are highly pungent. The cultivated species of *Allium* occasionally run wild. There are native species as well as weeds that have been introduced from Eurasia.

WILD LEEK, A. TRICOCCUM, grows from a bulb that in turn grows on a rhizome – which is a thick underground stem. The leaves range from 4 to 12 inches long and from ¾ to 2¼ inches wide, and they are smooth and fleshy. They are usually shriveled by midsummer, when the flowers appear. The flowering stem is up to 1 foot tall; the flowers, in a hemispherical cluster, are white or whitish; about ¼ inch long, on ½-inch stalks. Flowering in June and July.

FIELD GARLIC, A. VINEALE, is a disagreeable weed from Europe. It is from 1 to 4 feet tall, with gradually tapering hollow cylinders for leaves. The flowers, when present, are small and greenish or purplish; often they are replaced by a cluster of bulbs, each with a long green "tail." A single bract encloses the flower-buds or bulblets. This is roundish at the base, then is topped by a long spearlike point. (The name "garlic" comes from two Anglo-Saxon words meaning "spear" and "leek.") Field garlic is one of the alliums that imparts an unpleasant taste to the milk of cattle that feed where it grows. Flowering from May to July.

WILD GARLIC, A. CANADENSE, only half as tall as field garlic, is another obnoxious weed. In some of the meadows where this occurs it is so abundant as to appear like grass. It. also grows in open woods. The leaves, up to 2 feet long, are narrow, flat, soft, and smooth. While the bulblets which usually replace the flowers are developing, two or three papery bracts enclose the cluster. These bulblets may or may not have the tails that are characteristic of *A. vineale*. If flowers do appear, they are few, pink or white in color, and they open from May to July.

WOOD-LILIES (CLINTONIA)

The two northeastern species of *Clintonia* have small lily-like flowers, generally in an umbel, and, close to the ground, from two to four glossy leaves somewhat oval in outline, pointed at the tip.

CORN-LILY, BLUEBEAD, or DOGBERRY, C. BOREALIS, has from one to eight greenish-yellow flowers up to ¾ inch long dangling in a loose cluster. The flowering stems, 5 or 6 inches long, stand slightly above the leaves. The flowers are short-lived and are soon replaced by blue berries which last a longer time. The plants appear in moist, mossy woods, often in mountains, flowering between May and August.

SPECKLED WOOD-LILY, C. UMBELLULATA, is a slightly smaller plant with smaller flowers, up to thirty, somewhat more compactly arranged in an umbel. The perianth-parts (sepals and petals) spread outward and are roundish at the tip. They are white, speckled with green and purple. The berries are black. The plants grow in woods, flowering from May to July.

8

Clintonia borealis   *Johnson*

D. Richards

Allium vineale   *Rickett*   Allium canadense   Allium tricoccum   *Johnson*

SOLOMON'S-SEAL
(POLYGONATUM)

The marks of this genus are arching, unbranched stems with small flowers (followed by berries) hanging from the axils of the closely attached leaves, which occur singly in two ranks on the stem. In a colony the stems all arch in parallel curves. The leaves taper to a point. The flowers are mainly cylindrical with six spreading points at the tip, six stamens being attached at about the middle of the tube. The berries are dark blue. The ovary is three-chambered, the stigma obscurely three-lobed. The plants grow mostly in woods, arising from an underground stem (a rhizome), which was once considered efficacious for healing, or "sealing," wounds. Our species flower in May and June.

P. PUBESCENS has an arching stem from 1 to 3 feet long, with generally only one or two flowers hanging vertically from the point of attachment of each leaf. These flowers, yellowish-green and averaging ½ inch in length, are somewhat constricted at the base of the spreading points. The leaves, which are more or less elliptic, have minute hairs along the veins on the lower side. The rhizome is close to the soil surface.

P. BIFLORUM varies greatly in size, the larger plants, to 6 feet in length of stem (sometimes called *P. canaliculatum*), being more common in this area than the smaller ones, which may be less than 1 foot. An average length is 3 feet. Its extensive range in size has caused *P. biflorum* to be broken up into numerous species, each of course with a different name. These have also frequently been given different common names. It has been shown experimentally, however, that they are merely genetic variations of the one basic species, *P. biflorum*. While the name means "two-flowered," there are from one to three or more greenish flowers from ½ to 1 inch long on arching stalks in each leaf-axil. The leaves are somewhat ovate and generally more arching than on plants of *P. pubescens*. The rhizome of *P. biflorum* is deeply buried in the ground.

TWISTED-STALKS or
MANDARINS (STREPTOPUS)

The leaves of *Streptopus* are ovate, sharp-pointed, stalkless (it is the flower-stalks that are twisted), and borne singly along the stem, which is usually forked. Each flower-stalk arises on the opposite side of the stem from a leaf. It then doubles back under the leaf and bends sharply so that its single flower hangs downward. The tips of the petals and sepals of the somewhat bell-shaped pendent flower, which is about ½ inch long, are bent abruptly backwards. The fruit is a red berry. The plants of both species grow in cold, moist woods, flowering in different areas from May to July or even later.

WHITE MANDARIN, S. AMPLEXIFOLIUS, grows to 3 feet tall and has leaves that extend around the stem at the point of attachment. The flowers are most often greenish-white, but they vary to deep purple. The tips of the stamens, which bear the pollen, are much longer than the slender stalks that support them. The stigma that tops the ovary is conspicuously three-lobed. A red fruit containing many seeds develops from the ovary. The plant is sometimes called liverberry.

PINK MANDARIN, S. ROSEUS, to 2 feet, has tubular pink or purplish flowers, with the tips of the perianth-parts recurving only in age. The pollen-bearing tips of the stamens are shorter than their stalks and they bear two horns. The stigma is distinctly three-lobed. The leaves are tapered at the base and do not extend around the stem.

Polygonatum pubescens   *Scribner*

treptopus amplexifolius   *Thompson*

Polygonatum biflorum   *Justice*

FALSE SOLOMON'S-SEAL
(SMILACINA)

The two ranks of pointed, sessile leaves on the slightly arching stem of most plants of *Smilacina* provide a resemblance to the "true" Solomon's-seal (*Polygonatum*). The flowers, however, which have the lily family's usual six perianth-parts (sepals and petals combined), are borne in a cluster at the summit of the stem instead of dangling from leaf-axils all along the stem. Individual flowers are considerably smaller than in *Polygonatum*, but in their fairly large terminal cluster they become much showier. In both our species of *Smilacina* they are ivory-white, and are followed by a small, shiny berry. The rhizomes from which the flowering stems arise help the plants to spread in their woodland homes.

S. RACEMOSA, the largest and most common species of false Solomon's-seal, has stems that range from 16 to 40 inches long. The leaves are broadly elliptic and they extend outward from the stem. The flowers, each about ⅛ inch long (the stamens slightly longer), are borne at the tip in a much-branched, pointed raceme. They are seen in woods from May to July. The berries are at first brown-speckled, later bright red.

S. STELLATA, 2 feet tall or less, has ¼-inch flowers in an unbranched cluster, a simple raceme. They are followed by black or black-striped, small, shining berries. The tapering leaves, which are from 1 to 6 inches long, arch upward from around the stem. The plants grow in gravelly thickets and meadows, the flowers appearing from May to August.

BLAZING-STAR
(CHAMAELIRIUM)

Only one species grows in our area.

C. LUTEUM, also called DEVIL'S-BIT or FAIRY-WAND, has a 2-foot stem which bears small slender leaves at intervals and, at the tip, a long spike-like raceme of small white flowers with six identical perianth-parts (sepals and petals). The form of the spikes, however, differs according to sex – a long, tapering, and arching spike bearing only male flowers, with stamens; an erect, cylindric one bearing only female flowers, with pistils, the small, dry pods which develop from them splitting into three parts. On the ground is a tuft of leaves which are broadest near their tips. The plants are found chiefly in moist woods, the flowers appearing in June and July.

Smilacina racemosa   *Rickett*

milacina stellata   *Elbert*

Smilacina racemosa   *Johnson*

hamaelirium luteum   *Rickett*

MAIANTHEMUM

The only species known is a common woodland ground-cover.

CANADA MAYFLOWER or WILD-LILY-OF-THE-VALLEY, M. CANADENSE, has small white flowers with their parts in twos and fours instead of threes. They appear in a short raceme which becomes a cluster of berries, at first dark-speckled, eventually red. The plant's first leaf is a long-stalked narrow one, which is usually gone by flowering time. The foliage generally seen consists of two or three smooth, pointed, somewhat heart-shaped leaves, the basal lobes of which extend around the stem. Contrary to the habit in most members of the lily family outside of *Trillium* and *Smilax*, cross-veins can be seen connecting the lengthwise ones on most plants of *Maianthemum*. Spreading by means of slender underground stems (rhizomes), the plants often form dense mats in woods. Under cultivation they can also form an excellent ground-cover, especially in the shade, flowering in May and June.

The true lily-of-the-valley, *Convallaria majalis*, is a hardy Old-World plant that is widely cultivated and that has occasionally escaped into the wild. An almost identical plant, called *C. montana*, is native in the mountains from Virginia and West Virginia southward.

XEROPHYLLUM

The one eastern species of *Xerophyllum* barely touches the southern limits of the New York region, not extending north of the Pine Barrens of New Jersey.

TURKEY-BEARD, X. ASPHODELOIDES, is a spectacular plant, with a tremendous raceme of small white flowers rising up to 5 feet in the air. There is first a basal tuft of stiff, dry leaves about 6 inches long. (The name *Xerophyllum* means "dry leaf.") From the midst of this the flowering stem arises, beset with needle-like leaves which become mere bristles above. At the summit there develops a round-topped, foot-long raceme of small flowers on individual stalks several inches long. The perianth-parts (sepals and petals) are oval in shape, separate, and wide-spreading. They are of about the same length as the six stamens. The small seed-capsule is globular and three-lobed. The plant grows from a thick, tuberous rhizome. The only other species is on the West Coast.

YUCCA

Around old houses where it has long been cultivated, Adam's-needle (*Yucca*) has occasionally escaped into sunny spots in the wild. The stiff, leafless flowering stem rises up to 10 feet from a basal cluster of heavy, narrow leaves. The numerous flowers, in a large, branched raceme, are bell-shaped, white, and about 2 inches long. The leaves of *Y. filamentosa* are generally broader and often spoon-shaped at the tip; those of *Y. smalliana* taper to a sharp point. Flowering from July to September.

Xerophyllum asphodeloides   *Clark*

Maianthemum canadense   *Rickett*

BUNCHFLOWERS
(MELANTHIUM)

The branching spikes, or panicles, in this small group of plants bear stalked flowers that are at first cream-colored or greenish. Eventually, in accordance with the botanical name, which means "black flower," they turn purplish, then almost black. The six perianth-parts (sepals and petals) are identical and separate; they open out flat. The base of each is abruptly narrowed into a stalk-like part to which the six stamens are attached. With a hand-lens one can see two glands at the base of the blade of each sepal and petal. The seeds that are formed in the three-lobed ovary are flat and winged.

Both our species flower in June and July.

M. VIRGINICUM is the commoner species. Its rough-downy stem grows from 2 to 5 feet tall and bears narrow leaves its entire length. A thick rhizome sends up the stems in meadows and moist woods and thickets. The flowers are flattish.

M. HYBRIDUM is a slightly smaller plant with smaller flowers but with wider leaves – to 2½ inches. The flower-parts are wavy-edged. The plant is restricted to open woods, chiefly in upland regions. Called by some *Melanthium latifolium.*

FALSE HELLEBORE
(VERATRUM)

Large leaves that are strongly plaited lengthwise characterize this genus. These and all other parts of the plant are highly poisonous.

V. VIRIDE, also called INDIAN POKE, grows in wet places, from 2 to 7 feet high. The ovate leaves, long, broad, and pointed, which extend around the stem at their base, continue up the stem all the way to the flower-cluster. The flowers are yellowish-green, small, fringed, and densely arranged in numerous branching spikes that together form a branched inflorescence. They are seen from May to July.

SWAMP-PINK (HELONIAS)

The single species in this genus is very rarely seen. Within the New York area, it is doubtful if it can be found anywhere outside of southwestern Staten Island.

H. BULLATA grows in swamps, where numerous evergreen leaves 2 or 3 inches wide and about a foot long lie flat on the moist ground. Among them in spring rise hollow stems from 1 to 3 feet tall, each one topped by a dense cluster of pink flowers with blue-tipped stamens. The flowers have the usual six perianth-parts of the lily family and a three-chambered capsule for a fruit.

ALETRIS

Our only species grows in peaty or sandy soil in open woods and barrens. It sends up a spike-like raceme of small white flowers.

COLIC-ROOT or STAR-GRASS, A. FARINOSA, has tubular flowers close to ½ inch long with six slightly spreading points, mealy projections on the outside, and six stamens with bright orange anthers in evidence at the mouth of the tube. The flower-stalk rises from 1 to 3 feet from a cluster of basal leaves about ½ inch wide and 8 inches long. Flowers, shown opposite twice natural size, appear from May to August.

AMIANTHIUM

There is but one species, and this one is poisonous in all its parts, but particularly in its bulb.

FLY-POISON, A. MUSCAETOXICUM, has inch-wide leaves spreading out a foot or more at the base of the plant. The flower-stalk, naked except for a few bracts, rises 3 feet or more from the midst of these. At its summit is a cylindric raceme of initially white flowers that turn greenish or purplish. The sepals and petals, all alike, spread out nearly flat, each about ⅛ inch long. The fruit is a pod or capsule with three beaks, the seeds inside red-coated. Flowering June and July.

Melanthium virginicum   *Rhein*

Helonias bullata   *Gottscho*

Aletris farinosa   *Ryker*

Veratrum viride   *Elbert*

ZIGADENUS

The fact that several species of *Zigadenus* have the word "poison" in their common names – "crow-poison" and "poison-camass" (or "death-camass"), for example – indicates that all species are probably poisonous. Only one is likely to be found within the local range.

Z. LEIMANTHIOIDES is a tall plant, up to 8 feet, with its flowers, less than half an inch across, closely set around the wide-spreading branches of a long raceme. The sepals and petals, all alike, are separate and spread out quite flat. They are creamy or yellow with a darker spot and two small glands near the base. The leaves are long and narrow. The plant grows from a bulb in sandy soil and bogs near the coastline, flowering from July to September.

ORNITHOGALUM

Most species of *Ornithogalum* are tender plants from the southern hemisphere, many from South Africa. Of the few hardy species, one from the Old World has "escaped" from gardens in the New York area.

STAR-OF-BETHLEHEM, O. UMBELLATUM, has narrow, grasslike leaves that rise directly from a bulb, among them a branching flowering stem from 4 to 12 inches tall. The flowers, each about an inch across, are white with a green stripe down the back of each perianth-segment. The six stamens have flat white stalks. The style, which rises from the ovary, is three-sided, and the stigma at its tip is three-lobed. Seeds are borne in a roundish capsule. Flowers appear from April to June.

CARRION-FLOWERS and CATBRIERS (SMILAX)

SMILAX is a genus of vines, mostly woody, mostly troublesome. While one plant will have only stamens in its flowers, another will have only pistils. These will develop into berries. When species climb by means of tendrils, two appear at the base of a leaf-stalk.

CARRION-FLOWER, S. HERBACEA, often makes a tangled mass over other plants. The leaves are variable in shape, but veiny and usually broad at the base, pointed at the tip, pale green or whitish beneath. This species has no tendrils. Flower-stems several inches long stand erect from the axils of leaves. The small, white, ill-scented flowers are borne in large numbers in an umbel, from April to June. The berries have a bluish bloom.

S. PSEUDO-CHINA is also a carrion-flower, but it differs, particularly in its leaves and fruits, from *S. herbacea*. The leaf-margins tend to curve inward above the broad base, and there is generally a blunt tip bearing a small sharp projection. Three prominent veins run from the base of the leaf to the tip. The leaves are equally green on both sides. They vary in size and shape as the stem elongates, those at the base being smaller and narrower. The plant climbs by means of tendrils. The flowers are greenish and very small, loosely arranged in an umbel on rather long stalks, fewer in number than in the species illustrated, and later flowering (May–July). The berries are blue or black..... S. PULVERULENTA carries a streak of down on the five fine veins of the leaf's lower surface, and has a greener color there. The berries are black. Tendrils help the plant to climb. The flowers are greenish and small, in a loose umbel, appearing in late April and May.

DAYLILIES (HEMEROCALLIS)

Each daylily remains open just one day, but blossoms are abundant. The botanical name, in allusion to this trait, means "beautiful for a day." The flowers are large and colorful.

ORANGE DAYLILY, H. FULVA, is a common roadside sight, its flowers about 5 inches long on stalks up to 6 feet high from May to July..... LEMON DAYLILY, H. FLAVA, is smaller, fragrant, less common, and in bloom in May and June.

rnithogalum umbellatum *Rickett*

Zigadenus leimanthioides *Gottscho*

merocallis fulva *Johnson*

Smilax herbacea *Rhein*

THE DAFFODIL FAMILY – AMARYLLIDACEAE

Perianth six-parted as in the lily family, the sepals and petals all alike. Stamens six, the ovary inferior and three-chambered; leaves long and narrow, all rising from the base. Our garden daffodils do not usually appear in the wild around New York; the family's only local representative is a slender plant with small yellow flowers.

STAR-GRASS (HYPOXIS)

YELLOW STAR-GRASS, H. HIRSUTA, found in open woods and grassy places, bears long grasslike leaves that come directly from a corm and reach about a foot in height. In their midst (but not reaching above them) a stalk bearing a cluster of yellow flowers appears, each bloom a perfect six-pointed star. Flowering from April to September.

THE IRIS FAMILY – IRIDACEAE

Sepals three and petal-like, petals three, stamens three, ovary three-chambered and inferior, that is, below the sepals and petals and merging directly into the stem. Leaves more or less grasslike, but folded lengthwise along the midrib, each one enfolding the next younger leaf, which faces it.

THE IRISES (IRIS)

Wild iris flowers, like the cultivated ones, grow from a papery envelope (a spathe) of two or more bracts. The sepals, which generally curve downward, are furnished with a fringed or furry ridge (a "beard" or "crest"), often of a conspicuous color, or the sepal's base may be of a contrasting hue, often with dark markings. In horticultural language, the three perianth-parts in the inner circle (the petals), which are relatively narrow and usually erect, are known as "standards." Those in the outer circle (the sepals), which are broad and flat (occasionally drooping), are called "falls." The style is unusual in the way it branches into three flat parts resembling petals, the stigma on each branch appearing as a thin lip on the lower side of the apex. A stamen is concealed beneath each of these petal-like divisions of the style. Our native iris plants grow from more or less tuberous rhizomes.

YELLOW FLAG, I. PSEUDACORUS, an immigrant from Europe, grows in wet places. The bright yellow flowers, on stalks about 3 feet tall (the leaves mostly taller), are 3 inches or more across, their sepals with dark markings. Flowering from April to August.

BLUE FLAG or WILD IRIS, I. VERSICOLOR, decorates meadows and other moist, open places throughout the summer. Flowers 3 inches across grow on stalks about 3 feet tall. The sepals carry dark lines, the background toward the base becoming whitish with a yellow spot. Leaves rise above the flowers. The rhizome is poisonous. Flowering from May to August.

SLENDER BLUE FLAG, I. PRISMATICA, another inhabitant of wet places, has violet-colored flowers with dark veins and a white patch in the sepals. Leaves $\frac{1}{4}$ inch wide grow 2 feet tall. Flowers open above the leaves, from May to July.

poxis hirsuta *Johnson*   Iris versicolor *Gottscho*

prismatica *E. J. Miller*   Iris pseudacorus *Johnson*

BLUE-EYED-GRASSES (SISYRINCHIUM)

In contrast to the irises (though in the same family), the blue-eyed-grasses at first glance resemble lilies, for their three sepals and three petals are alike. Each is tipped with a sharp point. However, the ovary is inferior (that is, below the sepals and petals), and the stamens, forming a central column around the style, are three instead of six. Each leaf is folded edgeways to enclose the base of the next one above it. The flowering stems are flat. Our plants grow mostly in meadows, and flower from May to July.

S. MONTANUM, the most widespread species, is unbranched; a single cluster of two or three blue-violet flowers tips each stem. Usually only one flower an inch across opens at a time.

S. ANGUSTIFOLIUM is a branching plant, with flattened stems and leaves not more than ¼ inch wide. The pale blue or violet flowers, shown enlarged, are 1 inch across.

S. MUCRONATUM is a shorter plant with threadlike, unbranched stems and leaves, violet flowers less than an inch across, and pale seed-pods less than $\frac{1}{16}$ inch in diameter..... S. ARENICOLA is found in the sandy soil of the coastline. It resembles *S. angustifolium*, but grows in tufts composed largely of old leaves..... S. ATLANTICUM is branched, has narrow stems to 2 feet long, bearing violet flowers, and narrow leaves much shorter. Seed-pods are $\frac{1}{16}$ inch in diameter.

YELLOW-EYED-GRASS FAMILY – XYRIDACEAE

Sepals three, one disappearing as the flower opens, the other two boat-shaped; petals three, usually yellow; stamens six, of which three bear pollen and the three alternate ones end in a tuft of hairs; style three-cleft; flowers appearing one or two at a time in the axils of close-packed scales (bracts) that form a conelike head, or spike.

YELLOW-EYED-GRASS (XYRIS)

While this is mainly a southern or tropical genus of wetland areas, a few species have been found near the boundaries of the New York area. They have grasslike leaves to 2 feet tall, and flowering scapes at least half again as long. The conelike spikes or heads of small, sparse, yellow flowers can make an attractive sight when they cover an extensive area. July to September.

X. TORTA is the principal northern species. It has long, almost threadlike leaves that stand erect and slightly twisted. Their broad bases form a sort of bulb. The tips of the minute bracts in the half-inch "cones" that bear the flowers carry a tuft of red hairs in a terminal notch. The flowers are more nearly white than in the other species. The plants are seldom found near the coast.

X. CAROLINIANA grows in tufts; the leaves, at their base, are soft and chestnut-brown, and may be twisted. The half-inch spikes are covered with a reddish-brown fuzz. The bracts are yellowish or pale brown with a broad green center. They hide the calyx. This species grows in sandy places..... X. CONGDONI (or *X. smalliana congdoni*, as some prefer to call it) has tufted leaves, soft and brown (or reddish-brown) at the base and up to 2 feet long, similar to those of *X. caroliniana* but coarser in texture. The flowering spikes are nearly globose. The bracts are brown with a broad green center. The sepals are fully exposed..... X. FLEXUOSA rises from a tightly packed cluster of lustrous brown bulbs, often arranged spirally. The rigid, wiry leaves grow to 20 inches. The 1-inch flowering spike is slender. The lateral sepals are conspicuously fringed.

Sisyrinchium montanum   *J. J. Smith*

syrinchium angustifolium   *Uttal*

Sisyrinchium angustifolium   *Rickett*

Xyris torta   *Elbert*

WATER-PLANTAIN FAMILY – ALISMATACEAE

Three green sepals, three white (occasionally pink) petals, six or more stamens, several or many pistils, the stamens and pistils generally in different flowers. Flowering stem rising from among long-stalked leaves that grow directly from the base of the plant in wet sand or mud.

WATER-PLANTAINS (ALISMA)

Leaves in the spreading basal cluster are broadly elliptic, though some may have an indentation where the blade is attached to its long stalk. (Plants growing in deep water may, instead, have ribbon-like leaves.) The slender, leafless, flowering stem has one wide-spreading circle of branches after another, and each branch has similar series of branchlets in circles, until a flower develops at the end of each ultimate branchlet.

A. TRIVIALE (sometimes known as *A. plantago-aquatica*) has white flowers not more than $\frac{1}{4}$ inch across, appearing all summer long. The bulblike base of the plant, dried, was food for the American Indian..... A. SUBCORDATUM is similar but the flowers are much smaller and the leaf-blades almost heart-shaped. June to September.

ARROWHEADS (SAGITTARIA)

The shape of the leaves in most species gives both the common and botanical names from arrowheads to ribbons, or there may be mere spongy stalks. The tubers at their base were a staple food of the American Indian. The flowers consists of three white petals above three sepals, with many stamens or pistils. The number of stamens is diagnostic. All species flower all summer.

S. LATIFOLIA, the commonest, has leaves of arrowhead shape but with extreme variation. The petals average $\frac{2}{3}$ inch in length. There are from twenty-five to forty stamens.

S. GRAMINEA has grasslike leaves. The flowers are small, the petals only $\frac{1}{5}$ inch long.

S. RIGIDA, which has large petals – from $\frac{1}{2}$ to 1 inch long – may have long narrow leaves or slender arrowheads with short barbs. The flowering stem is often bent ot prostrate.

S. ENGELMANNIANA resembles *S. latifolia*, but with from fifteen to twenty-five stamens. ..... S. CUNEATA has a highly variable leaf: in deep water ribbonlike. From ten to eighteen stamens..... S. SPATULATA has fewer and smaller flowers than other species. Leaves have small narrow blades or only spongy stalks. The plant grows in tidal mud..... S. S)BULATA, also coastal, has two leaf types – ribbons of floating blades. Stamens less than twelve..... S. TERES has spongy stalks, no leaves; stamens twelve.

THE EEL-GRASS FAMILY – HYDROCHARITACEAE

Aquatic plants with flowers appearing all summer but rarely seen.

EEL-GRASS (VALLISNERIA)

Leaves of V. AMERICANA are long and grasslike. Thestems of the pistillate flowers may rise 10 feet through water. Staminate flowers float to the surface. After they have fertilized the pistillate flowers, the stems coil to let the fruit develop under water.

WATERWEED (ELODEA)

On E. CANADENSIS, long trailing stems are covered closely with leaves about $\frac{1}{4}$ inch long. The flowers, raised through the water on slender stalks, have three sepals and three roundish white petals $\frac{1}{8}$ inch across. Stamens and pistils are on separate plants.

Alisma triviale   *Rickett*

Sagittaria rigida   *Johnson*

Sagittaria latifolia   *Johnson*

Sagittaria graminea   *Rickett*

THE DAYFLOWER FAMILY – COMMELINACEAE

Sepals three, mostly green; petals three; stamens six, but in one genus pollen borne by only three of them; flowers appearing in clusters from an enveloping bract or pair of bracts. Leaves smooth-edged; veins running from base to tip without visible branches.

THE DAYFLOWERS (COMMELINA)

Two broad, erect blue petals with an inconspicuous third one of white or blue mark the dayflowers, each one of which is on display for one morning only, one flower in a cluster opening at a time. Three of the six stamens bear pollen; the other three, which are shorter, have cross-shaped heads.

C. COMMUNIS, the commonest species, is a persistent Asiatic annual. It creeps along the ground, rooting and re-rooting at the nodes. The two bright blue petals are about ½ inch long and somewhat broader, with a stalk-like base; the third petal, which is white, is much smaller. June–October.
C. ERECTA is a native perennial whose stems rise upward from a cluster of thick roots. It has very narrow leaves, the sheathing part a flange edged with hairs. The large blue petals appear to have blue stalks; the third is white and inconspicuous. June–October.

SPIDERWORT (TRADESCANTIA)

In this genus the three petals are alike and all six stamens bear pollen.

T. VIRGINIANA has three petals that are generally purple and about ¾ inch long and broad or slightly broader. The purple stalks of the six stamens are coated with long hairs. The leaves, 4–14 inches long, are slender and pointed and folded lengthwise; two upper ones envelop the flower-cluster. Flowers open only mornings, April–July.

THE PICKEREL-WEED FAMILY – PONTEDERIACEAE

Aquatic plants, mostly of warmer regions. Perianth (sepals and petals together) composed of six parts, all colored alike; stamens six, of which the three shorter ones may bear no pollen.

PICKEREL-WEED (PONTEDERIA)

P. CORDATA is the only species that reaches northern waters. The leaves are mostly heart-shaped, but some lack blades entirely. The deep blue flowers open in a dense spike a foot above the water. The perianth is composed of two lips, the three upper segments joined into one, the uppermost lobe showing two yellow spots; the three segments of the lower lip are separate. Only one of the ovary's chambers develops a seed. June–November.

HETERANTHERA

The three sepals and three petals are all alike in *Heteranthera*, forming a small star-like flower which emerges from a delicate bract. Plants grow in mud or shallow water.

WATER-STARGRASS, H. DUBIA, most often grows submerged. The leaves are long and narrow with slender pointed tips. The flowers are pale yellow and about ½ inch across. June–September.

Commelina erecta *Uttal*

Commelina
communis
Gottscho

Pontederia cordata *Rickett*

Tradescantia virginiana *Johnson*

THE ORCHID FAMILY – ORCHIDACEAE

Flowers markedly bilateral in symmetry, one of the three petals, usually the lowest one, differing from the two lateral petals in size, shape, or color – or in all three; this odd petal called the lip. Sepals in many species colored like the petals and, also like them, different from each other in their structure. Stamens and the style and stigma of the pistil united into a single column, in many orchids brightly colored and petal-like. Ovary inferior, embedded in the end of the stem that supports the rest of the flower; the future seeds (ovules) very minute and numerous. There are two subfamilies in the *Orchidaceae*, and these are easy to distinguish. One contains the lady's-slippers; the other, all the other orchids.

THE LADY'S-SLIPPERS (CYPRIPEDIUM)

Two fertile stamens on the column, instead of the usual single stamen, distinguish this north-temperate group from all other genera of orchids. The rudiment of a third, a sterile, stamen can also be seen in the glistening, shieldlike object in the center of the flower. The pouch-shaped lip, referred to as a "moccasin" or "slipper," is likewise characteristic of *Cypripedium*, although grass-pink (*Calopogon*, page 42) has a somewhat pouchlike lip. In *Cypripedium* the stigma projects downward from the column into the cavity of the lip. An insect that has entered this cavity, or pouch, through the opening at the top generally cannot get out that way. It brushes past the stigma, then the stamens, before it finds a point of exit at the base; thus, with the newly gathered pollen it is likely to pollinate the next lady's-slipper orchid that it visits, but not the one from which it has just acquired pollen.

The two lower sepals of *Cypripedium* plants are generally united. A bract, like a small foliage leaf, stands erect behind each flower. The main leaves are rather heavily veined from base to tip, fairly broad, and pointed at both ends.

PINK LADY'S-SLIPPER or MOCCASIN-FLOWER, C. ACAULE, is a "stemless" type, the two leaves and flower-stalk all arising from a stem that is concealed underground. The single flower (rarely two), about 2 inches long, has a large, veiny, pink pouch. (A white form is often seen.) The two lateral petals are long and narrow and greenish-brown, flat or slightly twisted; sepals are blended yellowish-green and purple. A woodland plant, flowering from April through July.

SHOWY LADY'S-SLIPPER, C. REGINAE, deserves the name *reginae* – "of the queen" – for it is a royal-looking flower, doubtless fit for Aphrodite, the goddess of love and beauty, who was born on the island of Cyprus. The large white pouch is so suffused with pink and so heavily streaked with rose-purple that it appears rich pink. Sepals and lateral petals are white and shorter than the lip. More than one flower may appear on a plant. An all-white form is sometimes seen. The stem, which may be 1–3 feet tall, bears several coarsely veined leaves. The entire plant is hairy, and the hairs sometimes cause a rash. The showy lady's-slipper grows in bogs and damp woods, where it may be in bloom from May to August.

WHITE LADY'S-SLIPPER, C. CANDIDUM, is rarely seen, and then mainly in damp meadows. It is smaller than the other species, the lip only about ¾ inch long, the stem not

Cypripedium acaule   *Gottscho*

Cypripedium reginae   *Mayer*

CYPRIPEDIUM (*cont.*)

more than 16 inches tall. The lip is white outside, but not to be mistaken for the white form of *C. acaule*; inside it is striped in crimson or purple. The sepals and lateral petals are greenish-yellow, often marked with crimson lines. Several leaves, less coarsely veined than in other species, grow on the flowering stem. May and June.

YELLOW LADY'S-SLIPPER, CYPRIPEDIUM CALCEOLUS, recognizable by its yellow pouch, has long, twisted, lateral petals that vary from greenish-yellow to purplish-brown. Sepals are similar in hue but shorter and broader. Because of its range in color, it has frequently been divided into two separate species, *C. pubescens* (the greenish-yellow form) and *C. parviflorum* (purplish-brown), but now these are more often referred to as varieties of *C. calceolus*. From three to five long leaves more than an inch broad grow upward from the base of the flowering stem, which bears one or occasionally two flowers. It grows in bogs and woods, flowering from April to July.

POGONIA

One species of *Pogonia* reaches eastern North America and the New York area. Others are scattered over warmer regions of other continents.

ROSE POGONIA or SNAKE-MOUTH, P. OPHIO-GLOSSOIDES, has rather narrow pink sepals and lateral petals an inch long, diverging in several directions, and a flat lip with a fringe around the edge and three rows of fleshy hairs tipped with yellow or brown. The single flower grows at the summit of a stem from 2 inches to 2 feet tall. Halfway up, at flowering time, there is an ovate or elliptic leaf about 4 inches long. Several narrow, long-stalked basal leaves are sometimes seen on new stems that emerge from the horizontal roots. The plants grow along wet shores and in bogs and peaty soil, flowering from May to August.

ISOTRIA

The two known species of *Isotria* are both eastern North American, and one, at least, can be found in the New York City area. In both, a single flower (sometimes two) stands on a fairly long stalk above a circle of five or more oblong or elliptic leaves. When not in bloom, the plant looks much like *Medeola* in the lily family.

FIVE-LEAVES or WHORLED-POGONIA, I. VERTICILLATA, has three very narrow, brown-purple sepals, at least twice as long as the petals. Face to, they give a flower the aspect of a dancing man. The lateral petals, about an inch long, are yellowish-green. The lip, about the same length, is also greenish, streaked with purple, and at the tip is white, lobed, and flaring. The leaves, which appear a foot or so above the ground, are about 4 inches long. This is a woodland plant which flowers in May and June.

I. MEDEOLOIDES is a smaller plant, about 10 inches high. The sepals are scarcely longer than the petals – about 1 inch. This species, also a resident of woods, is extremely rare. It blooms at about the same time as the other.

ARETHUSA

Sepals and lateral petals of *Arethusa* stand nearly erect, arching slightly over a petal-like column. The outer half of the lip bends sharply downward. One species grows in our region; one other in Japan.

SWAMP-PINK, A. BULBOSA, bears a single magenta-pink flower at the tip of a leafless stalk about a foot tall. The broad lip, which is crinkly-edged and hairy, is white, suffused with pink and streaked with a deeper tone than in the rest of the flower. A single slender leaf appears on the stem after the flower is gone. Botanically named for the Greek nymph Arethusa, the swamp-pink is sometimes given the common name of dragon's-mouth. It grows in bogs and peaty meadows, flowering from May to August.

Cypripedium calceolus   *Rhein*

Pogonia ophioglossoides   *Rhein*

Arethusa bulbosa   *Rhein*

Isotria verticillata   *Fogelson*

TIPULARIA

American woodlands provide a home for only one species of *Tipularia*, and that one is found but rarely, one other in Asia.

CRANE-FLY ORCHID, T. DISCOLOR, has flowers that resemble a certain insect. They are greenish, yellowish, or purplish, often mottled, and they hang on fairly long stalks in a loose raceme up to 10 inches long. Sepals and petals are barely ⅛ inch wide and about ¼ inch long. The inch-long lip is largely tubular at the base (the spur) and three-lobed at its tip. A single leaf with a plaited blade, purplish underneath, is formed in autumn from a small corm underground. It stays green but withers before flowering time in July and August.

APLECTRUM

The single species of *Aplectrum*, often called putty-root, is also named Adam-and-Eve because of the two underground tubers side by side.

A. HYEMALE bears one stalked, ovate, evergreen leaf 4–6 inches long, which withers before the flowers appear. The flowers, about half an inch long, are brownish or purplish except for the lip, which is white with purple markings. From seven to fifteen are in a raceme. Found in woods during May and June.

CORALROOTS (CORALLORHIZA)

Like toadstools, the coralroot orchids are dependent for their growth, not on green leaves, but on the dead remains of other plants in the soil. They are mainly woodland plants. The coral "root" is an underground stem, or rhizome, which resembles coral in being much branched, toothed, and coral-colored. A thick, colorful, leafless stem rises from this. In the flowers at its summit the two lower sepals are joined at their base and also joined to the stem.

SPOTTED or LARGE CORALROOT, C. MACULATA, may grow to 30 inches. The stem is brownish-purple or yellowish. The flowers, about ½ inch long in a raceme some 3 inches long, are crimson-purple with crimson-magenta spots on the white lip. June to August.

AUTUMN CORALROOT, C. ODONTORHIZA, grows to 20 inches. The stem, light brown or purplish, is bulblike at the base. Sepals and lateral petals, about ⅛ inch long, are purple or greenish. The lip, which is broad and notched at the tip and crinkled along the sides, is white with crimson-magenta spots. August to October.

TRIPHORA

THREE-BIRDS, T. TRIANTHOPHORA, has small ovate leaves clasping the stem separately. From the axil of each of the upper three (occasionally more or less), at a height approaching a foot, a single pink or white flower grows on a slightly curved stalk. Sepals, petals, and lip are slender, all about ¾ inch long. The lip is crinkled at the edge and has three toothed ridges. A woodland plant; August and September. Sometimes not seen a second time in one place for many years, the tuber remaining alive meanwhile.

MALAXIS

Very small greenish flowers in a raceme distinguish *Malaxis*.

GREEN ADDER'S-MOUTH, M. UNIFOLIA, has a single, somewhat oval leaf 1–3 inches long. It sheathes the stem, which may be 4–12 or more inches tall. Rarely, a second leaf appears. The raceme at the summit of the stem may be ½–4 inches long or longer. Petals are threadlike and curled; the lip is toothed or lobed at its tip. Woods, from May to August.

Triphora trianthophora   *Justice*

pularia discolor   *Luer*

rallorhiza maculata   *Elbert*   Aplectrum hyemale   *Horne*

ORCHIS

Sepals and lateral petals of *Orchis* form a hood over the column. At the base of the lip, which spreads out somewhat at its tip, is a long hollow tube (the "spur").

SHOWY ORCHIS, O. SPECTABILIS, usually has two broad, smooth leaves sheathing the base of the flowering stem. They may be from 1¼ to 4 inches long and blunt-tipped. In the raceme there are about six flowers, each one backed by a long, pointed, green bract, much like a foliage leaf. The flowers are mainly pink, lilac, or purplish, less than an inch long, with a conspicuous white lip. Flowers can be found from late April into June, largely in wooded areas.

THE TWAYBLADES (LISTERA)

The two leaves midway on the stem give the name of twayblade to members of this genus. (See also *Liparis* with this name, page 42.) A third leaf occasionally develops. The flowers, in a loose raceme, are very small.

HEART-LEAVED TWAYBLADE, L. CORDATA, has an indentation at the base of each of its paired, inch-long, stalkless leaves. The stem is not more than 1 foot high. Flowers are purple or greenish, the sepals and petals much alike, barely ⅛ inch long. The lip is slightly longer, slender and deeply cleft. Mossy woods; mainly July..... L. AUSTRALIS, the southern twayblade, has been occasionally reported in New York bogs. It is similar to *L. cordata* but a stouter plant with narrower, unindented leaves to 1½ inches long. The flowers are purplish; the lip is cleft. June.

FRINGED and REIN ORCHIDS (HABENARIA)

The lip of the fringed and rein orchids is the most useful identifying feature for them. Every *Habenaria* has, at the base of the lip, a long, thin, hollow tube (the spur) extending backward and/or downward. Within the genus the individual species can be readily distinguished by the tip of the lip. This tip seems to give the two common names to the group; also the botanical name, which comes from the Latin word "habena" meaning "rein." (The "rein" may likewise be the straplike appearance of the spur in certain species.) The flowers are all small and are mostly tightly packed in a raceme. In most species, the two lateral petals and the upper sepal together form a hood over the column. Plants of *Habenaria* grow largely in woods, thickets, bogs, and wet meadows. Both species shown opposite have a three-lobed lip that is cut into a fringe.

LESSER PURPLE FRINGED ORCHID, H. PSYCODES, has exquisite lilac or pinkish-purple flowers in a dense raceme that rises above four or five lance-shaped foliage-leaves to a possible height of 3 feet. Sepals and lateral petals are up to ⅓ inch long, the fringed lip about ½ inch. June–August..... A variety with flowers about twice as large, that blooms a little earlier, known as the large purple fringed orchid, sometimes goes under the separate specific name of *H. fimbriata*.

RAGGED FRINGED ORCHID, H. LACERA, growing to 30 inches, has greenish or yellowish flowers with several narrow leaves up to 8 inches long on its stem. Sepals and lateral petals are barely ¼ inch long, the lip is more than ½ inch, and the spur nearly an inch. Details of the flower are worth examining with a hand-lens. June–September.

benaria lacera   *Rickett*

Orchis spectabilis   *Johnson*

Habenaria psycodes   *Justice*

HABENARIA (*continued*)

Two of the *Habenaria* species shown opposite have a fringe but no other divisions or lobes on the lip. Leaves appear along the stem. On the other two species the lips have no fringes. The leaves, nearly round, lie on the ground.

WHITE FRINGED ORCHID, H. BLEPHARIGLOTTIS, grows to nearly 4 feet tall and bears a densely packed raceme of bloom. The flower-parts mostly measure less than half an inch, with a slightly longer lip and a 1-inch spur. The leaves vary from ovate to lance-shaped. Plants can be seen in flower in moist places from July to September.

ORANGE-PLUME or YELLOW FRINGED ORCHID, H. CILIARIS, closely resembles *H. blephariglottis* in all but color, with just a slightly longer lip and a longer flower-stalk – up to nearly an inch. The stem may reach a height of 40 inches; its leaves are lance-shaped, sharp-pointed, and to 1 foot in length. July–September.

ROUND-LEAVED REIN ORCHID, H. ORBICULATA, has greenish flowers with separate sepals and slightly shorter lateral petals (about ½ inch) and a very narrow, unfringed lip to 1 inch long, with a spur almost double that length. The flowers stand away from the stem on stalks ½–¾ inch long. Two wide, blunt-tipped leaves at the base are to 10 inches long by 8 inches wide. The stem rises some 2 feet above them. Flowers appear from June to August.

HOOKER'S ORCHID, H. HOOKERI, which does not grow beyond 16 inches, seems somewhat like a smaller version of *H. orbiculata*. The two leaves are 3 or 4 inches shorter and less wide than in the similar species, and the flower-parts, including the tapering spur, to an inch in length, are all smaller. The flowers are greenish or greenish-yellow and fragrant. May–August.

abenaria blephariglottis   *Luer*

Habenaria orbiculata   *Justice*

abenaria ciliaris   *Rhein*

Habenaria hookeri   *Johnson*

HABENARIA (*continued*)

If there are one or more lance-shaped leaves on the stem, and the lip of the flower is neither lobed nor fringed, one of the three species opposite is undoubtedly at hand. The flowers of all are fragrant.

LONG-BRACTED or FROG ORCHID, H. VIRIDIS, has green flowers with a strap-shaped lip nearly ½ inch long. Two or three teeth protrude at its tip. The spur is barely half the length of the lip. An exceptionally long slender green bract stands nearly erect behind each flower. Along the stem, which may reach 2 feet, several leaves develop, the lower ones ovate, the upper ones lance-shaped – one of the distinctions of the species. May–August.

BOG-CANDLE or TALL BOG ORCHID, H. DILATATA, is a 4-foot plant with white (sometimes yellow or greenish) flowers with a spicy fragrance that has given it also the common name of scent-bottle. The lip, about ¼ inch long, is broader at the base and has a smooth, blunt but narrow tip. The spur is about the same length as the lip. Green, leaflike bracts stand behind the flowers in the raceme. Foliage leaves that sheathe the lower part of the stem are narrow. This species interbreeds with *H. hyperborea*, a more northern species, when their flowering times and locations coincide, producing hybrid progeny. *H. dilatata* flowers here from June to August.

SOUTHERN REIN ORCHID, H. FLAVA, in a broader-leaved variety than in the south, is reported from the New York City area. There are usually only two leaves on the 2-foot stem (though sometimes three) and these are oblong or lance-shaped. Flowers are yellowish-green and a leafy bract shows behind each one. The lip is only ¼ inch long but broader; it has a tooth on each side near the base. The spur is longer than the lip. The flower is sweet-scented. June–September.

Habenaria viridis   *Elbert*

Habenaria dilatata   *Rhein*

enaria flava   *Johnson*

Habenaria flava   *Luer*

HABENARIA (*continued*)

Narrow leaves are characteristic of the remaining *Habenaria* species shown opposite.

FROG-SPIKE, SMALL GREEN ORCHID, or WOOD ORCHID, H. CLAVELLATA, has small flowers that are almost white with just a flush of yellow or green. The lip is ¼ inch long with three blunt teeth at its tip. The spur is longer, somewhat curved, and both extend sideways, giving the flower a distorted look. Usually only a single narrow tapering leaf appears midway on the stem, which may reach 18 inches. Relatively few flowers are in the raceme. July–September.

LADIES'-TRESSES (SPIRANTHES)

Two characteristics of ladies'-tresses are slender stems and a spike of very small white or whitish flowers, in some species spiraling around the stem. Of the several hundred species known, only a few reach the New York City area. Even these may require a hand-lens for identification.

NODDING LADIES'-TRESSES, S. CERNUA, carries a spike with individual flowers that appear to "nod," – each one curves downward on its very short stalk. The lip is usually constricted halfway back and crinkled around the tip. The stems may reach 2 feet in height; the narrow leaves – mostly at the base and broadest near the tip of the blade – are about 1 foot in length. The flowers, about ½ inch long, are apt to be off-white. They have the odor of vanilla. The flowering period is from July on.

SLENDER LADIES'-TRESSES, S. GRACILIS, has a spiral of exceedingly small white flowers, not more than ¼ inch long. While the sepals and lateral petals are white, the lip is marked with a central green stripe. The leaves are more or less elliptic, each on a short stalk, often appearing after flowering. June–October.

SPRING LADIES'-TRESSES, S. VERNALIS, grows to nearly 4 feet and is downy in its upper parts. The flowers are fragrant, spiraled, and either yellowish or white. Leaves are narrow, about a foot long, and appear at the base or just above..... S. LUCIDA has several crowded spirals of flowers. Leaves, on the lower part of the stem, are rather narrow and thick..... S. PRAECOX only occasionally occurs beyond its southern limits. The lip, ½ inch long or more, is green-veined and wavy. The spike of flowers may be either straight or spiraled. The plant may be slightly downy. It will sometimes reach 30 inches in height, bearing threadlike leaves 10 inches long, flowering March–September.

Habenaria clavellata   *Rhein*

Spiranthes vernalis   *Luer*

Spiranthes cernua   *Gottscho*

Spiranthes gracilis   *Elbert*

RATTLESNAKE-PLANTAIN (GOODYERA)

Only one of the northeastern species of *Goodyera* reaches the New York City area, and this happens to be the handsomest of them all.

G. PUBESCENS has a rosette of small, ovate, basal leaves that have an attractive network of white veins. The creeping rhizome that travels through the soil sends up new rosettes of leaves all around the original plant. The flower-spike bears flowers on all sides of it, each about ⅛ inch long. The lip is saclike; the upper sepal is joined at its edges to the two lateral petals to form a hood over the lip. Because the netted pattern of the leaves was thought to resemble snakeskin, it was once thought that to chew these leaves would be a remedy for snakebite, hence the first part of the common name. The flower-spike appears on a stem from 10 to 18 inches tall around July in the region of New York.

GRASS-PINKS (CALOPOGON)

The native orchids known as grass-pinks (which bear no relation to the true pinks of the pink family, *Caryophyllaceae*) are among the few orchids of the region in which the lip is the uppermost petal. Only one species reaches the northeastern states.

C. TUBEROSUS is a tall plant, sometimes reaching 4 feet, with a single grasslike leaf (rarely two) from the base to a height approaching 20 inches. In the flower, which may be 2 inches across, sepals, lateral petals, lip, and column are all colored alike, in pink, rose-purple, or magenta-crimson (very occasionally in white). The lip bears club-shaped hairs with light-colored stalks and orange tips. Several flowers are arranged in a long raceme. The plant grows mostly in wet areas, blooming any time from May to August.

TWAYBLADES (LIPARIS)

Two leaves at the base of the flower-stalk (not halfway up as in *Listera*, also called twayblade) are the first distinguishing mark of *Liparis*. Two different species are to be found in our area. The lateral petals in both are threadlike, the sepals also relatively narrow.

L. LILIFOLIA has a broad lip up to ⅝ inch long, usually colored like the petals, brownish-purple. Sepals, ½ inch long, are greenish-white and rolled up lengthwise. (The entire flower is sometimes greenish-white.) From five to forty flowers grow in a raceme, each on a stalk as long as the flower itself. The two leaves at the base of the stem, which may reach a foot in height, are ovate or elliptic, thick and lustrous, and about 6 inches long. The flowers appear from May to July in woods, on streambanks, and in clearings.

L. LOESELII has two longer, somewhat narrower, more yellowish-green leaves on a plant of about the same height as *L. lilifolia* – up to 12 inches. The flowers are yellowish-green. They are fewer in number and smaller than in the above species, and they have a narrow, concave-arching lip. Their stalks are short. These are plants of bogs, swamps, and shores, blooming in June and July.

paris lilifolia   *Allen*

Liparis loeselii   *Rhein*

lopogon tuberosus   *Gottscho*

Goodyera pubescens   *V. Richard*

THE CALLA FAMILY – ARACEAE

Very small flowers crowded over or around an erect, fleshy stem known as a spadix. Surrounding this or standing up at one side and sometimes bending over it, a large petal-like or leaf-like structure called a spathe. Sepals four or six or none; petals none. Stamens and pistils in separate flowers in some species, either in different places on the spadix or on different plants.

SKUNK-CABBAGE (SYMPLOCARPUS)

S. FOETIDUS, the only species, is marked at flowering time by a low, roundish, fleshy spathe that completely surrounds the spadix. The spathe is mottled in reddish-brown and has a twisted, pointed tip. On its spadix the plant bears flowers that were formed underground the preceding autumn. As they and the spathe push up, they often melt the snow and ice around them. Though reputed for their odor, they are found far more by sight than by smell. Each small flower on the dome-shaped spadix has four sepals, four stamens, and a pistil. As the spathe withers, the large foliage leaves appear – coarse and veiny and eventually up to 3 feet in length. The plant may be found in shallow water or in wet meadows. February to May.

WILD-CALLA or WATER-ARUM (CALLA)

The single existing species of *Calla* is only remotely related to the calla-lily of greenhouses, the South African *Zantedeschia*.

C. PALUSTRIS first sends up a group of long-stalked leaves, the blades of which are deeply indented at the base. The flower-stalk comes afterward, bearing a single spathe and spadix. The flowers around the spadix are exposed at its tip by the white, rather flat, pointed spathe at one side. Each flower has merely six stamens and a pistil. The plant is about a foot tall. April–August.

SWEET-FLAG (ACORUS)

Only one species of *Acorus* grows anywhere in America. One other is at home in Asia.

A. CALAMUS, found in wet places over much of the country, has been named sweet-flag because of the pleasant odor and flavor of both the leaves and the rhizome. The leaves are grasslike and 5 or more feet long. The tall flowering stem is flat like the leaves, with the spadix and spathe at its tip. The spadix displays a diamond-pattern of flowers below the spathe. Each has six sepals, six stamens, and a pistil. May–August.

GOLDEN-CLUB (ORONTIUM)

While *Orontium* plants have a conspicuous spadix – a long, erect club tipped with bright yellow flowers – the only sign of a spathe is a ring at its base.

O. AQUATICUM has elliptic leaves rising directly from the rhizome underground, the blades and stalks each about 6 inches long. Flowering stems, which also come up through the wet soil, are considerably taller and are colored somewhat orangey-brown. The lower half of the slender spadix at their tip is white, the upper half bright yellow with the flowers. Lower flowers have six sepals and six stamens, besides the pistil; upper flowers have four each. The fruits turn blue-green; each contains a single seed. April–June.

corus calamus *Johnson*

Calla palustris *DeVoe*

ymplocarpus foetidus *Rickett*

Orontium aquaticum *Gottscho*

ARISAEMA

The outstanding species of *Arisaema* is the familiar Jack-in-the-pulpit. In this genus flowers appear only around the base of the spadix.

JACK-IN-THE-PULPIT, A. TRIPHYLLUM, is an early spring flower whose three-parted green leaves last well into the summer. The spadix is Preacher Jack. His pulpit, formed by the spathe, arches over his head, hiding him completely. Green outside, the spathe inside is green marked with irregular purplish-brown lines. Stamens and pistils form separate flowers on the spadix, the pistillate ones around the base. The fruits are shiny red berries tightly clustered around the spadix. By the time they appear the spathe has fallen away, exposing them. Two leaves frequently develop on a single stem that rises from the corm along with the flowering stem. Each consists of three large elliptic segments that spread out above the spathe. The corm gives the plant its alternative name of Indian-turnip because it was cooked and eaten by the North American Indians. (Without cooking, the plant's needle-like crystals of calcium oxalate can cause a severe burning sensation in the mouth and throat.) The plant is most often a foot or so tall, but may reach 3 feet with comparable dimensions in its parts. It starts to flower in April and may continue through June.

GREEN-DRAGON or DRAGON-ROOT, A. DRACONTIUM, is less often seen than *A. triphyllum*, but is unmistakable with its leaf divided into many narrow segments – from five to fifteen. The spadix also is distinctive, protruding far beyond the pointed tip of the green spathe, which it seems to hold erect. Flowers are at the base of the spadix, the staminate and pistillate ones separate. The fruits in this arisaema also are bright red berries. The flowers may be seen in May and June.

ARROW-ARUM (PELTANDRA)

Leaves of most plants in this genus have the shape of long, narrow arrowheads, much like those of *Sagittaria* (page 24). Only one species reaches the swamps and stream borders of the northeast.

P. VIRGINICA has been named "tuckahoe," from the Algonquian Indian word for a tuberous root that is cooked and eaten. This particular arrow-arum is widespread in wet places. Its leaves take on many diverse forms. They stand erect or nearly so, rising directly from below ground, the flowering stem pushing up among them to a height of 8–14 inches. The spathe, long and narrow, tapers to an erect point. It has a constriction about one-fourth of the way up. Below this point, pistillate flowers cover the spadix; above it, the staminate flowers appear. No sepals or petals are present on either. The upper part of the spathe falls away in a relatively short time, exposing the staminate flowers. The heavier lower portion remains, later to surround the fruits, which may be green or amber. The flowers appear from April to July.

Arisaema triphyllum   *Rickett*

Arisaema triphyllum   *Rickett*

aema dracontium   *Johnson*

Peltandra virginica   *Roche*

THE CAT-TAIL FAMILY – TYPHACEAE

The tall brown "cat's-tail" seen on these familiar plants of wet meadows, swamps, and ditches made up of thousands of minute flowers, each composed of little more than a single pistil. Above them a more slender spike of staminate flowers, lighter in color and disappearing after the pollen is shed, leaving only the withered stem that bore them. Small seedlike fruits with long hairs then turning the brown cylinder into a downy mass.

CAT-TAIL (TYPHA)

This is the only genus in the cat-tail family. These two species occasionally hybridize. Both appear in flower from May to July.

T. LATIFOLIA, the commoner and larger species in the New York region, has grayish-green leaves up to 10 feet tall and 1 inch wide (*latifolia* means "wide-leaved"). The brown cylinder of pistillate flowers is up to 7 inches long and averages 1 inch in diameter when mature. The slender staminate spike directly above it is 1–8 inches long.

T. ANGUSTIFOLIA, the narrow-leaved species (*angustifolia* means "narrow-leaved"), has green leaves not more than ¼ inch wide and up to 5 feet tall. The two cylinders bearing the pistillate and staminate flowers are separated by several inches of stem. The female spike may be 3 inches long; the male spike above it is nearly twice as long.

THE BUR-REED FAMILY – SPARGANIACEAE

An aquatic family bearing minute flowers in globes on zigzag branches, the short-lived staminate ones at the top, the pistillate below, these becoming small, hard, seedlike fruits with sharp beaks, each mass of them forming a bur. The stems, rising directly from a rhizome, bearing long, slender leaves which sheathe them at the base.

SPARGANIUM EURYCARPUM is the only bur-reed in our area, and the only species with two stigmas on the pistil. The others have one stigma. This species grows from 1⅔ to 5 feet tall, with long, stiffish, grasslike leaves. Its prickly white globes of bloom develop at the angles of the leafy, zigzag stem and branches.

THE LIZARD'S-TAIL FAMILY – SAURURACEAE

Only one species in this largely Asiatic family occurs here.

LIZARD'S-TAIL or WATER-DRAGON, SAURURUS CERNUUS, is a plant of wet places. Its creeping stems send up branches bearing long-stalked leaves with rather thick, heart-shaped blades, and one or more slender, tapering spikes of minute flowers (the lizard's-tails), made white by the stalks of the stamens. The spikes droop at their tips (the meaning of *cernuus*). The flowers have no sepals or petals. Stamens and pistils are together in the flowers of some spikes, separated in others. June to September.

48

Typha latifolia   *Rickett*

Typha angustifolia   *Rickett*

Saururus cernuus   *Johnson*

Sparganium eurycarpum   *Rhein*

THE SANDALWOOD FAMILY – SANTALACEAE

A largely tropical family with only one herbaceous genus common in the northeastern states, and those plants partly parasitic.

BASTARD TOAD-FLAXES (COMANDRA)

The tip of the flower-stalk of *Comandra* flares into a small funnel. Within it is the ovary, and on its margin stand five minute white sepals. There are five stamens but no petals. The leaves, borne singly, are narrow, blunt, and without teeth. The plants are partly parasitic on the roots of woody plants.

C. UMBELLATA has a deep rhizome and leafy flowering stems 6–16 inches tall, the leaves pale underneath. Flower-clusters branch. April to July.

THE DUTCHMAN'S-PIPE FAMILY – ARISTOLOCHIACEAE

Sepals three and petal-like, joined or separate; petals lacking. Ovary embedded in tubular end of flower-stalk. Stamens six or twelve.

ASARUM

WILD–GINGER, A. CANADENSE, has two downy heart-shaped leaf-blades on shaggy stalks about 4 inches long. At their base is a single globular flower of three reddish-brown sepals with tips turned back and with twelve stamens within. The rhizome makes a fair substitute for true ginger. April and May.

ARISTOLOCHIA

VIRGINIA SNAKEROOT, A. SERPENTARIA, is a 2-foot plant bearing leaves shaped like arrowheads with blunt barbs. The brownish-purple flowers, less than an inch long, have a pipe-shaped calyx with three shallow terminal lobes. six stamens, and one broad stigma. They grow singly on short branches near the plant's base. May to July.

THE SMARTWEED FAMILY – POLYGONACEAE

For a description of the family, please turn the page.

SMARTWEEDS (POLYGONUM)

Most of the smartweeds, which carry several other names, have small, compact spikes of pink or white flowers in summer and autumn and slender, lance-shaped leaves.

PINKWEED, P. PENSYLVANICUM, is one of the tallest, reaching 4 feet in moist ground and bearing its flowers in erect, dense spikes.

LADY'S-THUMB, P. PERSICARIA, is similar but smaller. It is marked by bristles on its leaf-sheaths and a dark blotch on the leaf-blade.

mandra umbellata   *Johnson*

Polygonum persicaria   *Elbert*

ygonum pensylvanicum   *Johnson*

Asarum canadense   *Rickett*

SMARTWEED FAMILY – POLYGONACEAE (cont.)

Flowers, a fraction of an inch in size, generally numerous and tightly packed in a spike. Sepals from three to seven; petals none. Stamens from three to twelve. Pistil with either two or three styles, becoming a single one-seeded fruit, or grain – an achene. Stipules at base of leaves in most genera forming a sheath around the stem.

POLYGONUM CESPITOSUM is an immigrant from Asia which has made itself at home in waste places in the Atlantic states. Its spikes are slender and bright pink. Under a lens its leaf-sheaths are seen to be edged with long, conspicuous bristles.

CLIMBING FALSE BUCKWHEAT, P. SCANDENS, is a common weed which clambers in fence-rows among other plants. The leaf-blades are commonly heart-shaped, with a pointed tip and indented base. The flowers are in erect racemes. Their three outer sepals bear narrow projecting "wings" on their outer sides; these give the whole cluster the appearance of small fluttering leaves. It flowers later than others, August–November.

JUMPSEED or VIRGINIA KNOTWEED, P. VIRGINIANUM, has small flowers of greenish-white borne at intervals in a long slender spike, instead of being condensed in a tight mass. There are four sepals. It is a woodland plant with leaves broader than in most other members of the genus.

WATER SMARTWEED, P. AMPHIBIUM, grows in water or on land with equal ease. In water the leaf-stalks elongate and the leaf-blades float. On land the plant is likely to be hairy. The spikes of bright pink flowers are erect and dense, more than ½ inch thick, but little more than 1 inch long..... P. COCCINEUM, like *P. amphibium*, has different forms for its land and water habitats. On land the leaves have elliptic or lanceolate blades on short stalks. In water the blades tend to be broader and deeply indented at the base. The land form is downy. Both forms have rather slender but handsome spikes of pink or red..... The handsomest species is P. ORIENTALE, PRINCE'S-FEATHER (some say princess-feather), which was introduced from India as an ornamental annual and which has occasionally escaped from cultivation. Its large leaves are long-stalked and have heart-shaped blades. The wide-spreading branches bear drooping spikes of bright rose-colored flowers.

WATER-PEPPER, P. HYDROPIPER, is a native of Europe which has become naturalized in damp places here. It is peppery in taste; touching it causes smarting of sensitive skin. The stems may either stand erect or lean. The flowers are greenish-white, sometimes pink-tipped, in slender spikes which usually curve..... P. LAPATHIFOLIUM, a native American species, also grows in damp places and may reach 6 feet in height. Its spikes, about ¼ inch thick, droop at the tip. The flowers range from green or white to pink. .... WATER SMARTWEED, P. PUNCTATUM, reaches 3 feet in height, frequently grows as a perennial from a tough, branching rootstock. The leaves are heavy, short-stalked, deep green, usually spotted, and to 6 inches long. The flower-spikes may reach 6 inches in length. The flowers are white and green, very occasionally pinkish, usually spotted.

lygonum scandens   *Gottscho*

Polygonum cespitosum   *Rickett*

lygonum virginianum   *Rickett*

Polygonum amphibium   *Johnson*

JOINTWEED (POLYGONELLA)

The flowers of *Polygonella* are more loosely arranged than in most species of *Polygonum*. The calyx appears like a corolla of five petals. There are eight stamens.

P. ARTICULATA, which grows to 2 feet in dry sand, has narrow leaves that are jointed at the base. The very small flowers, of rose-color, white, dark purple or dark red, grow in slender racemes, all on short arching stalks that are also jointed. They seldom open before late summer or early fall.

RUMEX

RUMEX is a closely related genus of very weedy plants, most of which have originated in Europe. The small flowers have six sepals in two rings, the inner ones larger. Of the three that are mentioned here, SHEEP-SORREL, R. ACETOSELLA, is commonest, especially as a weed in gardens where it grows from 2 to 20 inches tall. Its stem is thin and somewhat lax; its leaves are slender, some of them elliptic, but the majority "hastate" – with sharp, outward-pointing lobes at the base of the blades. Long slender rootstocks carry the plant to great distances through the soil. The flowers, which are reddish to yellowish, hang loosely in their spike-like clusters. Most of them are seen rather late in the summer season; but they are inconspicuous even then..... YELLOW DOCK, R. CRISPUS, grows from 3 to 5 or more feet high. It can be recognized by the wavy margins on its slender leaves..... R. MARITIMUS is slightly smaller and has narrow, tapering leaves. The grainlike tubercle attached to the seed (achene) is bristly.

THE POKEWEED FAMILY – PHYTOLACCACEAE

Characteristics of the single species that is within our range the only ones that need concern us here. Most other species at home only in the tropics.

PHYTOLACCA

POKEWEED or POKEBERRY, PHYTOLACCA AMERICANA, is a widely branched, smooth plant which may reach a height of 10 feet but is more often 5 or 6 feet tall. The stem frequently turns crimson, especially late in the season. The small greenish-white or pinkish flowers are in erect racemes borne opposite the leaves. The five sepals could be mistaken for petals. The stamens vary in number, and the ovary is composed of several small, fleshy segments in a ring, each with its own style and stigma. The ovaries becomes purplish-black berries in a raceme which now hangs down. The crimson juice of the berries has been used as a red dye and as a pigment in painting. The macerated leaves will make a satisfactory tan coloring. The young shoots, before the crimson color appears, are palatable when cooked as greens. The large root, however, is dangerously poisonous. The plant blooms over a long period, from July to October.

Phytolacca americana   *Johnson*

ygonella articulata   *V. Richard*

Phytolacca americana   *Rickett*

THE SPURGE FAMILY – EUPHORBIACEAE

Individual flowers minute. Large appendages appearing with the flowers in certain species, as in *Euphorbia corollata*, general mistaken for petals. [The colorful poinsettia (*E. splendens*) from Mexico can be seen to be allied to this native species.]

THE SPURGES (EUPHORBIA)

In our local species there are no true petals or sepals. The single pistillate flower in the center of the cluster has a three-celled ovary with three two-cleft styles, surrounded in some species by a rudimentary three-parted calyx. This is accompanied by several staminate flowers of one stamen each. These all sit together within a sort of cup, to the edges of which four or five nectaries and petal-like appendages are usually attached. Each cluster thus looks like one flower. Like many others in the family, the species described here have milky juice.

FLOWERING SPURGE, E. COROLLATA, is a smooth plant that forms many branches. The flat-topped groups of flower-clusters at the branch tips, with their white petal-like appendages, look like masses of individual flowers. The leaves are narrow and blunt. The plant grows to 3 feet, thriving in dry places and flowering from June to October.

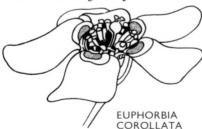

EUPHORBIA
COROLLATA

EYEBANE, E. MACULATA, is one of the weedy species, also growing in dry ground. It has creeping stems with small paired leaves, often forming mats, but also growing up to 3 feet high. The leaves frequently bear a crimson spot (*macula*). The flower clusters are small but numerous, each surrounded

by white or red appendages. The photograph, about four times enlarged, shows pistils (each constituting one flower) in various stages of development into fruits; here and there the two-lobed yellow tip of a stamen appears. June to October.

CYPRESS SPURGE, E. CYPARISSIAS, grows usually in dense masses, the stems about 2 feet tall, bearing great numbers of needle-like leaves. The tiny flowers at the summit of the stems are embraced by waxy, yellowish glands (see the photograph) and by one or more pairs of broad, pointed bracts colored a bright greenish-yellow. A field covered with these plants is carpeted with gold, and many a highway is gilt-edged. These bracts may turn red as they age. An immigrant from the Old World, this plant is now well established here, blooming from April to August.

LEAFY SPURGE, E. ESULA, resembles *E. cyparissias*, but is generally taller, with broader (but still narrow) and less numerous leaves. The glands around the flowers bear two distinct horns. This also is an immigrant, which has become in places a troublesome weed. April to August.

TARWEED (ACALYPHA)

ACALYPHA, a weedy genus in the spurge family, is occasionally seen in the New York City area. Its small staminate flowers are clustered in spikes, with pistillate flowers generally at the base. In *A. virginica* the bracts surrounding the pistillate flower-clusters are many-lobed palmate structures. In *A. gracilens* they are toothed and beset with glands. Stem and leaves in both are hairy. August to October.

Euphorbia cyparissias   *Rickett*

Euphorbia maculata   *Johnson*

phorbia esula   *Johnson*   Euphorbia corollata   *Justice*

THE WATER-LILY FAMILY – NYMPHAEACEAE

Aquatic plants; sepals and petals three or more; stamens numerous (except in *Cabomba*); ovary with many stigmas but no styles. Leaves and flowers long-stalked, rising to the water's surface or above it. Leaf-blades round or oval, attached to their stalks in the center or at the point of a notch in the margin.

WATER-LILIES (NYMPHAEA)

Only one species in this ornamental genus reaches the New York area.

FRAGRANT WATER-LILY, N. ODORATA, opens its white flowers, averaging 4 inches across, on three or four successive mornings. The flowers have four green sepals and many rows of petals – white or pink. There is no sharp distinction between inner petals and outer stamens. The ovary bears many stigmas radiating from the center; styles are absent. Sepals and leaves are red or purplish on the lower surface. June to September.

YELLOW POND-LILIES (NUPHAR)

The conspicuous part of the flower is the calyx, five or six sepals forming an open globe. The petals inside are mere scales. Stamens are numerous. The ovary bears many stigmas, no styles. May to October.

SPATTERDOCK or COW-LILY, N. ADVENA, thrusts leaf-blades and flowers above the water. The outer sepals are green, the inner ones yellow..... BULLHEAD-LILY, N. VARIEGATUM, is distinguished by its flat leaf-stalks. Many leaf-blades float on the surface. The sepals are generally red on the inner side..... N. MICROPHYLLUM has leaf-stalks like narrow ribbons and leaf-blades not more than 4 inches long. The flowers, about an inch across, have red stigmas..... N. RUBRODISCUM is presumably a hybrid between *N. microphyllum* and *N. variegatum*. It has leaves and flowers of intermediate size, flat leaf-stalks, red stigmas, and inner sepals suffused with red on the inner side.

LOTUS (NELUMBO)

In the rare aquatic genus *Nelumbo*, there is a broad, inverted cone in the center of the flower, its flat surface with a pistil inside each of several holes. Sepals and petals are numerous, with no sharp distinction. Round leaf-blades, 1–2 feet across, are attached to the stalk at their center.

WATER CHINQUAPIN, N. LUTEA, has pale yellow flowers 6–8 inches across. Flowers and leaf-blades are raised above the water. July to September.

WATER-SHIELD (BRASENIA)

The widespread genus *Brasenia* has one species, found in quiet waters.

B. SCHREBERI has roundish leaf-blades about 4 inches across, the stalk attached in the center, the lower surface coated with a jelly. The small purplish flowers have three sepals and three petals, all alike, from twelve to eighteen stamens, and about as many separate pistils. June to September.

CABOMBA

North America has only one species of *Cabomba*. Others are found in warmer areas.

FANWORT, C. CAROLINIANA, has submerged leaves cleft into fine, threadlike parts; a few leaves with small round blades on the surface; three sepals and three petals; not more than six each of stamens and pistils. Flowers are white with yellow spots at the base of the sepals and petals, which are similar. May to September.

uphar advena   *J. Smith*

Nymphaea odorata   *J. Smith*

elumbo lutea   *Rickett*

Nelumbo lutea   *Rickett*

asenia schreberi   *Johnson*

Cabomba caroliniana   *Johnson*

THE BUTTERCUP FAMILY–RANUNCULACEAE

Both sepals and petals present in some genera; petals lacking in others, the sepals colored like petals; when both are present the sepals sometimes falling as the flower opens, leaving only a single circle of parts; in some genera the petals so small as not to be recognized as such. Stamens usually numerous; pistils usually several or many; some becoming berries; others, pods that split down one side (follicles) or small seedlike fruits that do not open (achenes). Many species poisonous; some, such as aconite, deadly; some used in medicine. Larkspur (*Delphinium*) and aconite (*Aconitum*) familiar garden flowers. Buttercups (*Ranunculus*), anemones (*Anemone*), marsh-marigold (*Caltha*), and columbine (*Aquilegia*) among the native wild flowers. All genera of the New York region radially symmetric; that is, flowers are alike in every direction. Three genera in the New York area (*Ranunculus*, *Aquilegia*, and *Actaea*) bear flowers with both sepals and petals. The remainder (starting on page 66) have only sepals.

I.   *Flowers with both sepals and petals.*

BUTTERCUPS (RANUNCULUS)

The flowers have generally five green sepals and five yellow or white petals, but the number varies. The yellow petals have a curious waxy patina. There are numerous stamens and pistils, the pistils on a hump (receptacle) in the middle; these develop into small seedlike fruits called achenes.

WHITE WATER CROWFOOT, R. AQUATILIS, lives with its leaves all submerged, their blades, on short stalks, cut into innumerable hairlike parts. The white flowers, about ½ inch across, stand a little above the water. May to September..... *R. circinatus* is another white-flowered aquatic species. The fine leaf-divisions are more rigid, not collapsing so readily, and the leaves lack stalks.

YELLOW WATER CROWFOOT, R. FLABELLARIS, also has submerged leaves that are finely divided. The stem is stout and hollow. If plants get stranded on wet shores they develop thick, stalked, roundish leaves, with deeply cleft lobes. The flowers, an inch or so across, have broad petals of bright golden-yellow.

LESSER-CELANDINE, R. FICARIA, is a distinctive plant, low-growing, with fairly large yellow flowers of up to a dozen petals, each ¼ inch long. The leaf-blades are roundish, somewhat scalloped, and on long stalks from the base of the plant. April to June.

SEASIDE CROWFOOT, R. CYMBALARIA, has almost heart-shaped leaves growing in tufts at the base of erect, leafless stems, which bear up to ten yellow flowers each. The five petals are relatively narrow. The receptacle, on which the pistils are borne, becomes elongated in fruit. The pistils then may turn red.

SPEARWORT, R. FLAMMULA, grows on damp shores. It has a slender creeping stem, from which grow erect flowering branches with grasslike leaves mostly in tufts at the base. The stamens are not more than twenty..... *R. ambigens* has a stem that more or less lies on the ground, the tip finally growing

Ranunculus ficaria
Rickett

Ranunculus aquatilis
Rickett

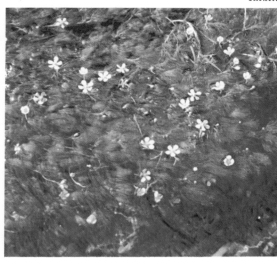

anunculus flabellaris
Johnson

Ranunculus cymbalaria
Johnson

RANUNCULUS (*continued*)

upward. The leaves have lanceolate blades on short stalks which sheathe the stem. The small flowers of these two and of the next are yellow.....*R. pusillus*, with petals shorter than sepals and not more than ten stamens, is a weak-stemmed plant with few branches and oblong leaves. It grows in shallow water.

RANUNCULUS RECURVATUS inhabits damp spots in woods, growing from 6 to 30 inches tall and bearing small, loose clusters of flowers, the green sepals longer than the narrow, pale yellow petals. The leaves are mostly deeply cleft (but not completely divided) into three or five lobes, the lobes coarsely toothed at and near the tips, their edges otherwise straight. Some leaves rise directly from the ground; these are long-stalked; others grow out from the upper half of the stem. All, along with the stem, are sparsely hairy. When the fruiting head is ripe, each achene will be seen to have a recurved hook (which was the style) at its tip. May to July.

SMALL-FLOWERED CROWFOOT, R. ABORTIVUS, has two different kinds of leaves. The blades of the stem-leaves are frequently divided to the base into narrow, blunt-tipped segments, and the blades of the basal leaves are often indented where they join their stalks. This plant is generally taller than *R. recurvatus*. It is a common garden weed..... R. MICRANTHUS resembles *R. abortivus*, but the plants are hairy and some of their roots are tuberous.

TALL BUTTERCUP, R. ACRIS, has an erect and branching stem up to 5 feet tall (but often shorter), with flowers at the ends of the branches. The leaves are in a rosette close to the ground. They are cleft and divided into many narrow, sharp-pointed lobes, teeth, and segments. Stem and leaves are more or less hairy. This is the common buttercup that has long made fields of gold in England and is conspicuous in eastern North America now. Unfortunately it is probably the most frequent cause of poisoning of cattle by buttercups. The poison is transmitted to the milk, which then becomes unpalatable. May to August.

BULBOUS BUTTERCUP, R. BULBOSUS, is another immigrant from Europe. It is recognized by the thick base of the stem which, with the enveloping broad leaf-bases, forms a sort of bulb. It grows up to 3 feet tall. The lobes and teeth of the leaves are rather blunt. It is a roadside plant, also found in fields and open woodlands. March to July.

SWAMP BUTTERCUP, R. SEPTENTRIONALIS, has a long creeping stem, the flowering branches growing upward. It is usually hairy. The larger leaves are mostly divided into three ovate, toothed segments on short stalks. The achenes are distinctive with a wide flange and a swordlike beak. April to July..... R. HISPIDUS resembles *R. septentrionalis* but it is generally taller. It flowers earlier and may often be found in drier places. Of the three ovate segments on the leaves, only the middle one is stalked. The two species often cross..... The CURSED CROWFOOT, R. SCELERATUS, is probably so

RANUNCULUS
SCELERATUS

called because its juice may cause blisters on the skin. (The name *sceleratus* means "cursed.") The leaves are rather succulent and fairly broad with numerous lobes and divisions. The flowers are insignificant-looking – very small and pale yellow. The pistils in the center of each flower are in a cylindrical mass. The plants grow in ditches and other wet places, averaging 1½ feet tall.

Ranunculus acris   *Rickett*   Ranunculus septentrionalis   *Gottscho*

Ranunculus recurvatus   *Rickett*

Ranunculus bulbosus   *Johnson*

RANUNCULUS (*continued*)

and blooming from May to August..... BRISTLY CROWFOOT, R. PENSYLVANICUS, has its pistils (and its eventual achenes) also around a cylinder. The plant can be distinguished, however, by its hairiness and by the sharper points on the lobes and divisions of the leaf-blades. It is found in similar wet places from July to September.

RANUNCULUS PENSYLVANICUS

EARLY BUTTERCUP, RANUNCULUS F CICU-LARIS, is a low plant, seldom growing more than 10 inches tall. The stems are silky; the roots are often tuberous. The petals are a rather pale yellow, about ½ inch long and half as broad. The lobes of the leaves are narrow and blunt. The plants flower generally in dry spots in open woods from March to May.

CREEPING BUTTERCUP, R. REPENS, has long trailing stems which send up flowering branches bearing leaves that are mostly divided into three stalked segments. Normally the flowers have from five to nine petals of bright yellow, but some forms have numerous petals. In these "double-flowered" forms this immigrant from Europe is often cultivated. Otherwise it is likely to be looked upon as a weed In the wild it most fre-

quently inhabits wet ground, flowering throughout the summer.

RANUNCULUS REPENS

COLUMBINES (AQUILEGIA)

The distinctive feature of the columbines is the tube, or "spur," attached to each of the five petals and extending upward or backward from the flower. The five sepals are brightly colored, either like the petals or of a contrasting color. There are five pistils, each of which becomes a small pod called a follicle, which opens down its inner side. The flower contains many stamens. The leaves are much divided into small, stalked segments which are usually rounded and notched. While *Aquilegia* is also called "honeysuckle," this name more properly belongs to the flowering shrubs and vines in the genus *Lonicera* of the honeysuckle family.

WILD COLUMBINE or ROCK-BELLS, A. CANA-DENSIS, has gracefully dangling flowers in red and yellow, the five red spurs all upright, the yellow blades of the petals and the red sepals facing downward. Variations in the coloring are recognized. The several divisions in the leaves are all in threes and the ultimate segments are three-lobed. The plant grows from ½ to 3 feet high, flowering from April to July..... The EUROPEAN COLUMBINE, A. VULGARIS, which is cultivated, sometimes escapes from gardens and may be seen in the wild in blue, purple, pink or white.

Aquilegia canadensis   *Rickett*

anunculus fascicularis   *Johnson*

Ranunculus repens   *Elbert*

ACTAEA

BANEBERRIES (ACTAEA) are unbranched plants, 2 or 3 feet tall, with a few large leaves which are much divided into small, ovate, sharp-toothed segments on long stalks, and a dense raceme of small white flowers terminating the stem. The short, broad sepals fall as the flower opens, and the narrow petals do not last long. The red baneberry described below has a white-fruited form; the white baneberry is known also in red. Criteria other than the color-name of the fruit are therefore best used in identification.

RED BANEBERRY, A. RUBRA, bears its flowers and fruits on slender stalks which are generally quite downy in the flowering stage. The berries are red or – to further add to the confusion – ivory-white. The segments of the leaves of *A. rubra* are generally downy along the veins on the lower side. August to October.

WHITE BANEBERRY, A. PACHYPODA, is easy to distinguish from the preceding species, not by the color of its berries but by the thickness of the stalks which bear them and, earlier, the flowers. (*Pachypoda* means "thick-footed.") Even in the flowering stage the stalks are as thick as the pistil. They may bear minute hairs. The red-berried form of the species has the same thick flower-stalks. The white berries are conspicuously marked with a dark dot (where the broad stigma was; there is almost no style); this has earned them the name of "doll's-eyes." The segments of the leaves are usually quite smooth. The plant is found in woods and particularly in wet thickets, flowering from July to October.

II. *Flowers that lack petals.*

(In these the sepals are generally colored and therefore may be taken for petals.)

CIMICIFUGA

In *Cimicifuga*, the four or five sepals fall off as soon as the flower opens. Several transformed stamens take on the appearance of petals, which are not otherwise present. The normal stamens are numerous.

BLACK SNAKEROOT, BLACK COHOSH, or BUGBANE, C. RACEMOSA, is an extraordinary plant, likely to become 8 feet tall, with enormous leaves divided usually into three parts and the parts divided pinnately into toothed blades or again divided into three and the three parts divided pinnately; the whole seems like a branch bearing many leaves. From among them rises a narrow raceme of small flowers, each of which will have a single pistil. When dry, the seeds inside the many pods (follicles) in the raceme justifiably give the plant the name of rattle-top. Its name of bugbane comes from its early use as a bug repellent, doubtless because of the unpleasant smell of the flowers, which appear from June through the summer.

66

Actaea rubra *Johnson*

taea rubra *Elbert*

taea rubra *Johnson*

Actaea pachypoda *Johnson*

VIRGIN'S-BOWER and LEATHER-FLOWERS (CLEMATIS)

Among our genera of the buttercup family, *Clematis* is unique in having its leaves in pairs on the stem. In most species they are pinnately divided; undivided in a few. Many of the species are vines. The leafstalks of these coil around any support, thus serving as tendrils.

VIRGIN'S-BOWER, C. VIRGINIANA, has clustered flowers with from six to twelve ivory-white sepals. It is the commonest species, climbing over other plants often to a height of 10 feet or even more. The leaf-blades are generally divided into three toothed segments. The feathery-tailed fruits are conspicuous in late summer and early fall, following the flowers that have been seen from July to September.

C. DIOSCOREIFOLIA is a similar-appearing native of Japan that has escaped to roadsides. It is distinguished by having four sepals averaging half an inch in length and by having five leaf-segments that are heart-shaped at the base and blunt at the tip; they are not toothed. Late summer...... PURPLE or MOUNTAIN CLEMATIS, C. VERTICILLARIS, is a rather woody climber, with leaf-blades divided into three segments. The four sepals are more than an inch long, blue or mauve, mostly hairy. Many of the stamens resemble narrow petals. May and June. .... CURLY-HEADS or LEATHER-FLOWERS, C. OCHROLEUCA, do not climb. The flowers occur singly at the ends of stalks. The four sepals are dull-yellow or purplish, the leaf-blades are undivided, and the entire plant, including the flowers, is covered with silky hairs. April to June.

MEADOW-RUES (THALICTRUM)

The meadow-rues are graceful plants with leaves divided into many small, round-edged segments much like those of columbine, and a crown of numerous small flowers in white or yellow or purple, usually in tassel-form. The color of the flowers is that of the many stamens, for the sepals fall as they open and there are no petals. There are several pistils, in most species on different plants from the stamens. They become achenes – small seedlike fruits that do not open. The genus is easily recognized, but to identify species a hand magnifier is needed.

TALL MEADOW-RUE, T. POLYGAMUM, may reach 7 feet or more in height. The stamens in staminate flowers stand erect, making a fine show with their broad white stalks. There are usually a few stamens also in the pistillate flowers. ("Polygamous" in the language of botany means having some flowers with both stamens and pistils, others with only stamens *or* pistils.) This plant is frequently seen in meadows, swamps, and ditches from June to August.

EARLY MEADOW-RUE, T. DIOICUM, is much smaller, seldom even 3 feet tall. In the plants that bear the stamens, small yellow tassels hang from the ends of the flower-stalks. The pistillate flowers have thread-like stigmas, colored purple when fresh. The main stalks of the leaves are long; the leaf segments are small. This is a woodland plant, blooming in April and May.

PURPLE MEADOW-RUE, T. DASYCARPUM, is almost as tall as *T. polygamum* and, like that plant, has some flowers with both stamens and pistils, others with stamens *or* pistils. The stem is often purple; the leaf-segments (and sometimes the stem) are covered with a fine down. May to July..... WAXY or PURPLE MEADOW-RUE, T. REVOLUTUM, has small, round, waxy bodies (glands) on the under side of the leaf-segments. In drier areas the stamens are attached to thin stalks. May to July.

...ematis virginiana *Johnson* Thalictrum polygamum *J. Smith*

Thalictrum dioicum *Johnson*

...ematis virginiana *Rickett*

CALTHA

A very early blooming plant, *Caltha* is especially well known in northern areas. Only one of the several species grows as far south as New York.

MARSH-MARIGOLD, C. PALUSTRIS, has a brittle, hollow stem that branches into a 2-foot mound of shining foliage interspersed with gleaming yellow flowers. The leaves are roundish and sharply toothed. The flowers are more or less globular, about ¾ inch across. The five or more sepals provide the color and shape; there are no petals. In the center the several pistils make a cluster of follicles (seed-pods that open down the inner side). Around them are numerous stamens. The flowers brighten wet meadows and similar places from April to June.

ANEMONE

Our species, some of which are known as windflowers, have white or greenish sepals (on occasions reddish); there are no petals. The principal leaves emerge from the base of the flowering stem; they are long-stalked with palmately lobed or divided blades. On the stem there are usually three or more leaves in a circle, forming what the botanist calls an involucre; this aids in identification. The flowers are arranged much as in the buttercups: one flower on a long stalk without leaves, rising from the involucre; then, from the same point, another stalk bearing a new involucre and another flower; and so on. The pistils become achenes. The plants are mostly residents of woods and meadows.

WOOD ANEMONE, A. QUINQUEFOLIA, is the earliest of our windflowers, a plant not more than a foot tall and usually less. There is commonly one basal leaf, the blade divided into three, and the side segments of the leaf on many plants so deeply cleft that there appear to be five segments.

The involucre below the flower consists of three stalked leaves. There is a single flower of five whitish sepals often tinged with pink. It appears mainly in open, moist woods from April to June.

THIMBLEWEED, A. VIRGINIANA, is one of the three *Anemone* species so named because the receptacle in the center of the flower becomes a thimble-shaped body as the pistils develop into achenes (seedlike fruits). This is a taller plant than the wood anemone, approaching 3 feet, but shorter than the other thimbleweeds. The leaves have three stalked divisions, then generally three further divisions or lobes, each segment with a slender, sharp tip and bulging sides with toothed edges. The sepals are greenish and somewhat leathery. The whole plant is rather hairy. It occupies rocky areas in woodlands, flowering from June to August. .... A. RIPARIA is another thimbleweed, the tallest one, growing to 4 feet or more. The "thimble" is oval at maturity. The three segments of the leaf-blades are more sharply and deeply divided than in *A. virginiana* and their sides are straight. The plant grows on rocky ledges and stream-banks, flowering from May to July..... A. CYLINDRICA, the third thimbleweed, with the tallest thimble of all (to 1½ inches), does not with certainty grow within the area covered in this book.

A. CANADENSIS has white flowers, the five sepals being white and up to an inch long. The three leaves circling the stem below each flower (the involucre) are stalkless, whereas the basal leaves have long stalks. The blades of these are broad and deeply cut into five or seven divisions, which in turn are sharply three-cleft into toothed segments. The veins are softly hairy on the lower surface. The plant grows about 2 feet tall, mostly in moist meadows, particularly in limy areas. May to July.

nemone quinquefolia *Johnson*

Anemone virginiana *Johnson*

Anemone canadensis
Johnson

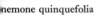

ltha palustris *Rickett*

ANEMONELLA

The one species in this genus is a delicate, anemone-like plant.

RUE-ANEMONE, A. THALICTROIDES, a flower of early spring, has leaves resembling those of rue (*Ruta*), a small woody plant, as does meadow-rue (*Thalictrum*), and flowers like anemones, hence both its common and botanical names. Early each spring, from the rue-anemone's cluster of small root-tubers rise several black, wiry leaf-stalks bearing blades divided into three and each segment again divided into three. The final small, round segments are notched at the outer margin. Among the leaves rise the slender black flowering stems, each bearing a small cluster of stalked flowers with an involucre below the group. The involucre is composed of two leaves, each divided into three; but since there is no main stalk to either leaf, they appear like six leaves, each with a thin stalk. The flowers have no petals but the sepals are white or pink. There are usually from five to ten, but "double" flowers with many more are not uncommon. The pistils form a cluster of achenes – seedlike fruits that do not open. In woods, from April to June.

COPTIS

Only one of four North American species of *Coptis* reaches the New York area.

GOLDTHREAD, C. GROENLANDICA, is a small plant, not 6 inches tall, with all its leaves growing from the thin yellow underground stem (rhizome), the several leafless stems bearing small white flowers. The leaves are evergreen. The roundish leaf-blades have three evenly-toothed divisions. The flowers have from five to seven sepals, no petals, numerous stamens, and several pistils. The plant can be found in mossy woods, bogs, and swamps from May to July.

LIVERLEAF or LIVERWORT (HEPATICA)

The stalks of the simple, three-lobed, smooth-edged leaves and the hairy flowering stems of the plants in this genus all rise directly from underground. Close beneath the flower is a circle of three small unlobed leaves, which comprise the involucre – not the calyx, as it appears to be. The actual calyx is the colored part of the flower – the petal-like sepals in white or pink or lavender, generally six in number. Each short stem bears a single flower above the recumbent brown leaves of last year. New leaves start to arise at about this time. As with anemones, the botanical name is more frequently used than any other as a common name.

H. AMERICANA has leaves with round-tipped lobes. (Its sister species, *H. acutiloba*, more likely to be found in limy soils just outside our range, has points on its three lobes.) In the flowers there are numerous stamens and pistils, the pistils developing into achenes. This is a woodland plant especially addicted to acid soils, flowering from March to June.

TROLLIUS

GLOBE-FLOWERS, TROLLIUS, are rarely seen outside of gardens, and then only as the species *T. laxus*, a resident of wet places, from a few inches to 2 feet high. The flower is not globular as in some of the garden species; the large, petal-like, greenish-yellow sepals (from five to fifteen) are outspread. Within them, first, are some insignificant stamen-like petals, then a mass of bright-yellow stamens surrounding the several pistils. The leaves are all palmately divided. Those at the base of the stem are long-stalked, those on the stem stalkless. The flowers appear in April and May.

Coptis groenlandica   *Johnson*

nemonella thalictroides   *Rickett*

Hepatica americana   *Johnson*

THE POPPY FAMILY – PAPAVERACEAE

Sepals two, falling as the flower opens; petals four or more; numerous stamens, one pistil, and a milky or colored juice.*

CELANDINE (CHELIDONIUM)

The only known species of *Chelidonium* is native in the Old World but it is now well established in the New. It has long been credited with both dyeing and medicinal attributes, from an orange-yellow juice.

C. MAJUS is called "greater celandine" in contrast to *Ranunculus ficaria* of the buttercup family, known as lesser-celandine. The leaf-blades are pinnately divided, the segments notched and lobed, with wavy edges. Beneath they are whitish and smooth. The flower, about an inch across, has four yellow petals. April to September.

BLOODROOT (SANGUINARIA)

S. CANADENSIS, the one species, a familiar and beautiful spring wild flower, displays eight white petals (often more or less), wide ones alternating with slightly narrower ones. The sepals are seldom seen. The single flower, nearly 2 inches across, over-tops the leaf, but eventually the leaf becomes taller than the seedpod, and may then be 6 or 8 inches wide. It is roundish, veiny, whitish beneath, and variously indented to make round-edged lobes. Both leaf and flower come directly from the rhizome (the horizontal stem underground). This contains an orange-red juice that can be used as a dye. March to May.

HORNED-POPPY (GLAUCIUM)

The Old-World genus *Glaucium* contains one species of which has become naturalized in North America.

G. FLAVUM is also known as sea-poppy. It grows to 3 feet, bearing a single large flower with four yellow petals. The foliage, which is whitened ("glaucous," hence the name *Glaucium*), is pinnately lobed or cleft. Leaves near the base of the plant have stalks; those higher up are stalkless and seem to surround the stem. The juice of the plant is yellowish. June to August.

PITCHER-PLANT FAMILY – SARRACENIACEAE

Water-holding pitchers formed by leaves catch and drown insects, the products of whose decomposition help to nourish the plant.

PITCHER-PLANT (SARRACENIA)

The curious pitcher-plants are mainly residents of peat bogs. Flowers of the one species which reaches the northeast are characteristic of the family as a whole.

S. PURPUREA has truly pitcher-shaped leaves, usually partly filled with water and drowned insects. It carries these pitchers upright from the ground in a sort of rosette. Smooth, bare flower-stalks rise from the center of the rosette, a single bloom hanging at the tip of each. This has five sepals (three small bracts below them), five red-purple petals, many stamens, and a curious pistil: the style spreads into a sort of umbrella with five small stigmas on the concealed surface underneath. There is also a form with yellow petals. May to August.

* Family descriptions here, it should be recalled, refer only to the species found in the area covered by this book.

Chelidonium majus   *Rickett*

laucium flavum   *V. Richard*

rracenia purpurea   *Gottscho*

Sanguinaria canadensis   *Gottscho*

THE ROSE FAMILY – ROSACEAE

Sepals five and petals five, with few exceptions. Stamens generally numerous. Pistils in most genera several or many, these on a mound in some plants, much as in the buttercups. The "receptacle" or base of the flower generally in the form of a cup or saucer, the perianth (sepals and petals combined) and the mass of stamens at or near the edge of this. The fruits of herbaceous species found in the wild are either follicles (small pods that open down their inner side) or achenes (small seedlike fruits that do not open at all). Leaves borne singly on the stem, generally with a pair of stipules – quite conspicuous appendages – at their base. Leaf-blades of many species divided into segments, some pinnately (feather-fashion), others palmately. Exception: *Sanguisorba* (see below).

BURNET (SANGUISORBA)

The first genus to be illustrated here is the one least like the others in the family. The two principal features which set *Sanguisorba* apart from other plants in the rose family are the lack of petals and the four instead of five sepals. The plants are tall (to 6 feet), with the flowers in a close-set spike at the summit of the main stem or branches.

S. CANADENSIS, the one American species, has long spikes of white flowers in which the filaments of the four stamens project so as to give a fuzzy appearance. The leaves, mostly at or near the base, are pinnately divided into numerous stalked segments with toothed edges. The plant favors marshy places and it flowers all summer..... SALAD BURNET, S. MINOR, a cultivated species from Europe, sometimes "escapes" from gardens. Its sepals are green or brown; its flowers are in a globe in which the upper ones contain only pistils, while the others have twelve stamens each.

CINQUEFOILS, FIVE-FINGERS, and SILVERWEEDS (POTENTILLA)

The genus *Potentilla* is easy to recognize.

The flowers always have five sepals; just below them, five alternating bracts which seem like an extra calyx. There are five petals, yellow in all except *P. palustris* in the New York area. Stamens and pistils are generally numerous, the pistils on a hump in the center of the flower. The cinquefoils may be mistaken for buttercups; but the five bracts, the "extra calyx," are sufficient distinction to assure identification. Pistils become achenes – small seedlike fruits.

P. CANADENSIS and P. SIMPLEX are very similar, for both have stems at first erect, then arching and lying on the ground. The two species may be fairly easily distinguished by the shape of their five leaf-segments. In *P. canadensis* they have teeth only towards the end. The sides that converge from there to the leaf-stalk are straight. In *P. simplex* the sides are convex, and they are toothed nearly to the base. The flowers are about ½ inch across. March and April to June.

P. RECTA has flowers about an inch across with pale yellow petals which are notched. It may become 2 feet tall. Stems and leaves are hairy; the lower leaves have five or seven toothed segments which are blunt at the tip. May to August.

Potentilla simplex   *Johnson*

anguisorba canadensis   *Gottscho*

Potentilla recta   *Rickett*

'otentilla canadensis   *Rickett*

POTENTILLA (*continued*)

SILVERWEED, P. ANSERINA, has very small leaf-segments alternating with the larger ones. Long silvery hairs are on the lower surface. The stems run along the ground, taking root at intervals. The flowers are up to an inch across. May to September.

SILVERY CINQUEFOIL, P. ARGENTEA, like *P. recta* (*Plate* 38), also comes from the Old World. Its five leaf-segments are narrow and so deeply toothed as to be almost lobed. Underneath, silky hairs give them a silvery effect. The plants are widely branched and grow nearly 2 feet tall. The flowers are less than ½ inch across. May to August..... P. REPTANS is another Old-World native with five or seven leaf-segments. Its stems are creeping – which is the meaning of *reptans*. The flowers, to an inch across, appear from May to August..... P. NORVEGICA is a bushy-appearing, hairy plant to 3 feet tall, the leaves with three coarsely toothed segments, the flowers with petals somewhat narrow and shorter than the sepals. June to October..... P. INTERMEDIA, also from Europe, is similar except for the five segments of the palmate leaves..... P. PACIFICA, a western species occasionally seen on Long Island, is similar to *P. argentea* but its leaves are woolly rather than silky underneath.

P. FRUTICOSA closely resembles other species treated here, but is actually a shrub. The name *fruticosa* comes from *frutex*, meaning "shrub" in Latin; it bears no relation to "fruit." The five or seven narrow leaf-segments are silky, like those of other species, but lack teeth. The flowers are about an inch across. June to October.

P. PALUSTRIS, which grows chiefly in or close to water, is the only species treated here that does not have yellow flowers. Its petals are red-purple, long-lasting, and shorter than the calyx. The five or seven leaf-segments are slender, often elliptic, and they may be either silky or smooth. They are finely toothed and the upper three segments are close together as if palmate. The flowers are nearly an inch across. June to August.

POTENTILLA REPTANS

Potentilla anserina   *Scribner*

otentilla argentea   *Uttal*

otentilla fruticosa   *Johnson*

Potentilla palustris   *Johnson*

THE AGRIMONIES
(AGRIMONIA)

The small yellow flowers of *Agrimonia* are spaced a bit apart in a long, narrow spike. There are five petals, each little more than ⅛ inch long, and from five to fifteen stamens. The end of the short flower-stalk is cup-shaped. Within this hollow, two seed-like fruits (achenes) are formed. Around it, enveloping the achenes, is a ring of hooked bristles, making a sort of bur. The plants themselves are relatively tall. The leaves are mostly pinnately divided, small segments alternating with the larger ones. All the agrimonies grow principally in woods, flowering in July and August.

A. PUBESCENS will reach 5 feet in height. The leaves have from five to nine of the larger segments. Both stem and leaves bear long curling hairs.

A. GRYPOSEPALA may become even taller, its hairy stem sometimes reaching 6 feet. These leaves, too, have from five to nine of the larger segments. A hand lens will reveal glands, especially on the lower surface. This area is also hairy on the veins.

A. PARVIFLORA sometimes grows even taller than 6 feet. Its stem is densely covered with long hairs. In the leaves the larger segments number from eleven to twenty-three. Through a hand lens many glands can be seen on their lower surfaces. These plants favor moist areas in woods.

A. STRIATA is another extra-tall species, sometimes exceeding 6 feet. The leaves have up to eleven large segments, with long-pointed tips and with numerous glands on their lower surfaces. The stem that bears the flowers is densely hairy..... A. ROSTELLATA is the pygmy of the group, not exceeding 3 feet in height. The leaves have five or seven main segments with very large, blunt teeth. The flower's name, which means

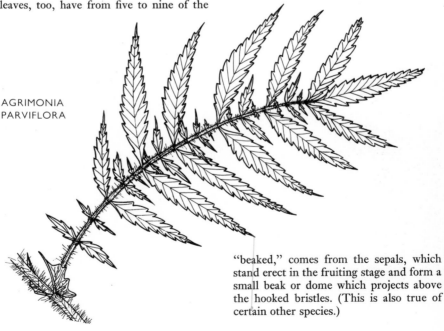

AGRIMONIA
PARVIFLORA

"beaked," comes from the sepals, which stand erect in the fruiting stage and form a small beak or dome which projects above the hooked bristles. (This is also true of certain other species.)

eum canadense   *Rickett*

Geum
canadense
Rickett

Geum rivale   *Johnson*

Geum aleppicum   *Johnson*

um vernum   *Pollock*

AVENS (GEUM)

The curious name, "avens," comes from *avence*, the old French name of a species native in Europe (*G. urbanum*), which was believed to have certain magical properties. The flowers have five petals, five sepals with five small bracts between them like an extra calyx, many stamens, and numerous pistils. In the species treated here, each style has a sharp crook near the tip. (In many other species the style is straight, also hairy.) As the fruits ripen into achenes the styles adhere to them, thus forming a bur-like globe after the petals have fallen. The leaves of most species are divided pinnately, with the terminal segment much larger than the others.

G. CANADENSE is a variable plant, the stems and leaf-stalks either smooth or slightly hairy, the leaf-stalks of varying lengths or lacking altogether, the leaves with or without divisions. Mostly, however, the upper ones have three segments, the lower ones five, the three at the tip being larger. The plant straggles through thickets with stems nearly 4 feet long. Its white flowers have petals about ¼ inch long. May to August..... G. LACINIATUM is a sturdier-appearing, hairier plant, up to 3 feet tall, also with white flowers but with petals about ³⁄₁₆ inch long, smaller than the sepals. The upper leaves are divided into three, the lower often into more than three, the segments on all being generally sharply toothed or jaggedly

cut. June to July..... G. VIRGINIANUM, also a hairy plant, has cream-colored or greenish-yellow flowers with petals shorter than the sepals. The leaf-segments are rather blunt and shallowly toothed. The plant grows in rocky places and dry woods, flowering from June to August.

G. VERNUM is a slightly smaller plant than *G. laciniatum*, with yellow flowers. Some of the lower leaves have undivided but lobed blades. Some leaves are pinnately divided with deeply toothed or lobed segments. The flowers are ¼ inch across. April to June.

G. ALEPPICUM, which was originally known in Syria and thereabouts, is represented with us by a variety. It is a hairy plant which may reach 5 feet in height, growing in thickets and meadows. The leaves vary greatly, but have a general tendency to mix small segments with large ones, all sharply toothed. The flowers, which are yellow, look much like those of *Potentilla*. May to August.

PURPLE AVENS, G. RIVALE, has reddish-purple coloring in stems as well as flowers. The flowers droop, but the fruiting "bur" stands more or less erect. The leaves on the stem have generally only three segments; those at the base have five or more. The bracts outside the sepals are longer than the sepals themselves. This plant is virtually world-wide in distribution, growing chiefly in wet meadows and bogs. May to August.

grimonia parviflora   *McDowell*

Agrimonia pubescens   *Elbert*

Rickett

grimonia gryposepala   *Rickett*   Agrimonia gryposepala

DUCHESNEA

INDIAN-STRAWBERRY, D. INDICA, the only species in the genus, looks like a *Potentilla* when in flower but like a strawberry in fruit. It has creeping stems from which the leaves and flowers rise at intervals. The leaf somewhat resembles that of strawberry, having a blade divided into three segments. The yellow flowers are distinguished from those of *Potentilla* by the bracts that alternate with the sepals; these are both longer and broader than the sepals and three-toothed at the broad outer end. April to August.

STRAWBERRIES (FRAGARIA)

Strawberries scarcely need description; but it is perhaps necessary to point out that the edible "berry" is not a berry at all in the usual botanical sense – a succulent fruit developed from an ovary – but the central part of the stem tip, the receptacle of the flower, enormously enlarged. The "seeds" on its surface are seedlike fruits (achenes), each developed from a pistil and each containing one seed. The flowers are much like those of *Potentilla*, except that the petals are white, with the same circle of small bracts below the sepals and alternating with them. The short stem sends up long-stalked leaves, with blades divided palmately into three segments, and erect branches with flowers in terminal clusters on stems that bear no ordinary leaves but do have bracts.

WILD STRAWBERRY (F. VIRGINIANA) is our most widely distributed species. It is characterized by the sinking of the achenes ("seeds") in small pits on the surface of the fruit. The flower-cluster is flattish and usually beneath the leaf-blades. This species is one of the parents of today's cultivated forms. April to July.

WOOD STRAWBERRY, F. VESCA, differs from *F. virginiana* in having its achenes ("seeds") on the surface of the fruit, not sunken in it. The flowers form a taller cluster which may rise above the leaves. April to August.

GILLENIA

Five narrow petals in white or pale pink and many stamens help to distinguish *Gillenia*. The five pistils become small pods (follicles) which split open along their inner side. The leaves are without stalks and are divided into three segments that look like separate leaves. At their base are stipules, the size of which may determine the species, only one of which reaches eastern New York.

BOWMAN'S-ROOT, G. TRIFOLIATA, is one of the two species that contain a bitter substance (obtained from the root) with emetic properties. It was used medicinally by Indians and colonists. Its leaves have finely toothed margins, and the stipules at their base are tiny. The petals are from $\frac{1}{2}$ to 1 inch long. May to July.

RUBUS

This tremendously large genus contains all the raspberries and blackberries and their relatives. Most of them are shrubs or woody vines. A very few, however, are essentially herbaceous (non-woody), hence they belong among the wild flowers as here defined.

The DWARF BLACKBERRY, R. PUBESCENS, creeps into our area from farther north. This has erect, generally spineless branches, rising from creeping stems. The leaves have three divisions, the flowers have five petals, the fruit is dark red. May to July.

Duchesnea indica   *Elbert*

agaria virginiana   *J. Smith*

Gillenia trifoliata   *Rickett*

agaria vesca   *D. Richards*

MEADOW-SWEETS and HARDHACK (SPIRAEA)

The meadow-sweets and their kin are really shrubs, but their woody stems are not conspicuous – and their spires of bright flowers are. The common native species are therefore included. Each of the small flowers has a shallow cup at the tip of its stalk, in which are seated (usually) five pistils. Around the margin stand numerous stamens, five pink or white petals, and five sepals. The leaves are without stipules (appendages at the base of the leaf-stalk). They are also undivided, and toothed but not lobed or cleft.

MEADOW-SWEET, S. LATIFOLIA, grows up to 4 feet tall, with purplish-brown branches. The leaves are coarsely and sharply toothed. The flowers, white or pink-tinged, are in tapering inflorescences, the lower ones springing from the axils of the upper leaves. June to September..... S. ALBA, another meadow-sweet, is similar to *S. latifolia*. The stem and its branches are yellowish, the leaves more finely toothed. The branches of the inflorescence are downy or woolly. The flowers are white. June to September.

HARDHACK, S. TOMENTOSA, has dense wool on the lower surface of its leaves, coloring them white or yellowish. The flowers, in a branched, spire-shaped inflorescence, are bright pink (but there is a white-flowered form). July to September.

THE MALLOW FAMILY – MALVACEAE

Sepals and petals each five, the sepals united at the base; in some genera a sort of exterior calyx formed by an involucre directly outside of the real calyx. Stamens numerous, their tips projecting sideways from a five-toothed cylinder formed around the style; in *Hibiscus*, stamens occurring in clusters the length of the tube, but those on the points lacking anthers; in other genera the stamens massed around the upper half of the tube and also on its five points. The style divided into five branches which extend beyond the staminal tube, each one bearing a round stigma, except in *Malva*. The ovary composed of five or more parts that may separate at maturity.

THE ROSE-MALLOWS (HIBISCUS)

Most species of *Hibiscus* grow in wet places, furnishing some of America's handsomest wild flowers.

SEA-HOLLYHOCK or SWAMP-ROSE, H. PALUSTRIS, has ovate leaf-blades, sometimes lobed, tapering to a sharp point. It often grows to 8 feet. The upper stem and the lower leaf surfaces are whitened by a fine down. The flowers are generally pink, otherwise purple or white, sometimes 6 inches across. July to October.

FLOWER-OF-AN-HOUR, H. TRIONUM, is a very different-appearing plant. It sometimes trails along the ground and at most reaches 2 feet in height. The leaf-blades, which are on long stalks, are divided into three segments, deeply cut into several narrow, blunt-tipped lobes. The flowers, about 3 inches across, are yellow with a purplish-black center. They remain open for only a few hours. July to September.

86

Spiraea tomentosa *Rickett*

Spiraea latifolia *Rickett*

Hibiscus trionum *Johnson*

Hibiscus palustris *Gottscho*

THE MALLOWS (MALVA)

The true mallows are all immigrants from abroad. While the musk mallow has become a garden ornament, others, like so many plant wanderers, have become weeds around dwellings and in waste places. They may be recognized by their petals, which are indented, either shallowly or deeply, at the outer edge. The leaves have roundish blades, more or less lobed or cleft palmately. Three bracts surround the flower-stalk just beneath the calyx. The flowers grow singly or in clusters from the axils of leaves. The stigmas are threadlike and receptive to pollen down their inner side.

MUSK MALLOW, M. MOSCHATA, is a handsome species with pink, lavender, or white flowers about 2 inches across, possessed of a faint musky odor. The leaves generally have deeply cleft blades, the lobes themselves cleft or toothed. The bracts beneath the flowers are narrow. June to September.

CHEESES, M. NEGLECTA, known as "common mallow," is a familiar weed, lying nearly flat on the ground. The leaves have long stalks and roundish blades, shallowly lobed and scalloped at the edges. The small flowers (about ¼ inch across) are clustered in the axils; the petals are pale lavender or white, about twice as long as the sepals. The fruit consists of a flattish ring of segments together simulating a Cheddar cheese – and often eaten by children. April to October. .... M. ROTUNDIFOLIA is similar to *M. neglecta*, but the petals are smaller and they are hairy near the base.

SIDA

This is principally a genus which is found in warm regions.

PRICKLY-MALLOW, S. SPINOSA, is a widespread tropical plant that has become naturalized northward. Its common and botanical names both come from the small spine at the base of each leaf. The leafstalks are short and the leaves themselves are finely toothed and narrow. It is a softly downy, branching plant 2 or 3 feet tall. The flowers are pale yellow, with dark lines and darker coloring toward the center. They are about ½ inch across, on short stalks in bunches in the axils of the leaves. June to October.

ABUTILON

The warmer parts of the world are home to most species of *Abutilon*. The only one that reaches our range is a native of Asia.

VELVET-LEAF, A. THEOPHRASTI, is "velvety" all over with finely branched hairs. The leaf-blades are heart-shaped; the plant is tall, up to 5 feet. The flowers, which grow on stalks in the axils of the leaves, are yellow and about an inch across. The fruit is the usual ring of segments, in this species ridged and with outward-curving horns, and opening across the flat top while still attached. By some called "butter-print" or "pie-marker." July to October.

Abutilon theophrasti
D. Richards

Sida spinosa
D. Richards

Malva moschata   *Elbert*

Malva neglecta   *Johnson*

ST.-JOHN'S-WORT FAMILY – HYPERICACEAE

Flowers of most species yellow and with five petals (of others with four); the same in number of sepals; many stamens; a pistil with several styles, the ovary becoming a small pod (capsule), generally with one or more beaks at the tip. On the leaves, oil-bearing glands which appear as black dots on the surface or, against a source of light, as translucent spots. Similar dots on the petals of some species. Leaves mainly without stalks and without teeth; in most of our species in pairs (in the others, in circles). Our three genera distinguished by five yellow petals on *Hypericum*, four yellow petals on *Ascyrum*, and pink flowers on *Triadenum*.

THE ST.-JOHN'S-WORTS (HYPERICUM)

The numerous species of *Hypericum* are much alike, except for a group with very small flowers and almost no leaves. Most are herbaceous, but several are shrubby. The stamens are typically numerous except in the small-flowered group. In some species they are arranged in several bunches. The pistils have from three to five styles. Most of the species are native, but the commonest is a weed from the Old World. To identify the species one may need to use a hand lens and a small ruler with fine divisions. The larger-flowered species (all those described on this page) have petals at least ¼ inch long.

H. PERFORATUM is the widespread, weedy species from the Old World. It is a branching plant that grows to 3 feet tall. Its leaves are narrow, those on the branches about ½ inch long, those on the main stem 1 inch. The plant bears numerous flowers. The petals, which measure ½ inch, are slightly one-sided and have black dots running along the margin on the shorter side. The bright yellow flowers can be seen along roadsides and in fields all summer.

H. PUNCTATUM, true to its name ("punctate" means dotted), is copiously marked with black dots, also with lines on both leaves and petals. The leaves are elliptic, roundish at the ends, and from 1 to 2 inches long. The petals are about ⅔ inch long. The plant grows to 4 feet tall in fields and woods, flowering from June to September.

H. ADPRESSUM has many flowers crowded together, the petals not more than ⅓ inch long, and without black dots. The sepals are wide at their base, rather blunt at their tip. The leaves are narrow, those on the branches about 1 inch long, those on the main stem 2 inches. The plant's erect stems grow to 2½ feet from a horizontal rhizome just below ground level. The plant is seen in flower in bogs and wet meadows and at the margins of ponds from July to September.

Hypericum adpressum   *Allen*

Hypericum punctatum   *Elbert*

Hypericum perforatum   *Johnson*

HYPERICUM (*continued*)

HYPERICUM MUTILUM, like other St.-John's-worts on this page, is one of the smaller-flowered species, all having petals less than $\frac{1}{4}$ inch long. In this species, petals are scarcely $\frac{1}{8}$ inch long and of a rather pale yellow. The paired leaves are broadly elliptic or ovate, an inch or more long, with three or five main veins. The plant, which grows about 30 inches tall, lives in moist ground and is noticeable from July to September.

H. BOREALE takes to wet ground, especially if it is peaty. Its stems tend to lie flat, only the tips turning upward to reveal the flowers, which have pointed petals about $\frac{1}{12}$ inch long in a very pale yellow. The leaves, about $\frac{1}{2}$ inch long, are elliptic and stalkless, paired, rounded at the tip, and with three or five main veins. The flowers, though inconspicuous, may generally be seen from July to September.

H. GENTIANOIDES, known as "orange-grass" or "pineweed," is a totally different-appearing plant. In its 2 feet of growth it exhibits little evidence of leaves – only minute narrow scales. The wiry green stem (sometimes reddish toward the base) is repeatedly forked, but not with spreading branches. Numerous tiny yellow flowers (these in the general style of other *Hypericum* species) open from red buds at the ends of these branches and along their sides. The plant likes sandy and rocky places in full sun, where it will flower from June to October. It is sometimes given the botanical name of *Sarothra gentianoides*.

H. ELLIPTICUM has petals about $\frac{1}{3}$ inch long, without dots. The sepals are widest near their tips. The leaves are broadly elliptic, to 1 inch long. The plants grow in moist places, to 20 inches tall, flowering from June to August..... H. DENTICULATUM also has petals about $\frac{1}{8}$ inch long and without dots but with toothed ("denticulate") edges. They are coppery-yellow. The leaves are broad, less than an inch long, and without stalks. They stand nearly erect. The stems are square, the plants 1 to 2 feet high. They grow chiefly in wet and sandy areas, flowering from June to August.

H. MAJUS (growing to 2 feet) has blunt, lanceolate leaves an inch or longer with five or seven main veins. The petals are about $\frac{1}{8}$ inch long. July–September..... H. CANADENSE (to 2 feet) has narrow, sharp-pointed leaves scarcely an inch in length, with three main veins. The petals are about $\frac{1}{8}$ inch long. July–September..... H. GYMNANTHUM (to 3 feet) has nearly triangular leaves that partly encircle the stem with their broad base. They are about $\frac{1}{2}$ inch long and have three or five main veins. The flowers, with petals only $\frac{1}{12}$ inch long, rise on naked stalks above the leaves. June to September.

Hypericum gentianoides   *Ryker*

Hypericum gentianoides   *Johnson*

Hypericum boreale   *Elbert*

Hypericum mutilum   *Scribner*

MARSH-ST.JOHN'S-WORTS (TRIADENUM)

Triadenum is the only member of the St.-John's-wort family that does not have yellow flowers; its flowers are of a decided pink. There are generally only nine stamens, these in three bunches alternating with three large orange glands.

T. VIRGINICUM grows 2 feet tall or more in wet sandy and boggy places. The leaves are ovate or elliptic and blunt; at the base they are broad and embrace the stem. The flowers are clustered at the ends of branches from the axils of leaves, or in the axils of the uppermost leaves. July and August.

ASCYRUM

This is the odd genus of the *Hypericaceae*; it has four sepals and four petals instead of five. The sepals are of two sizes, two large outer ones enclosing two small inner ones. These sepals remain attached in the fruiting stage, enclosing the capsule. Both species favor sandy soil, and bloom from July to September.

St.-PETER'S-WORT, A. STANS, has flowers with three or four styles above the ovary and with narrowly elliptic petals of pale yellow, ½ inch long or more, at the tip of the stem and in the axils of leaves. The plant stands 3 feet tall or taller. The leaves are pale green, somewhat crowded, from 1 to 1½ inches long, elliptic or ovate, and they often have an indented base.

St.-ANDREW'S-CROSS, A. HYPERICOIDES, is a variable species, bushy-branched, growing 2 feet tall or taller. The leaves are narrow, often widest towards the tip, tapering at the base. The petals are somewhat less than ½ inch long and, like the leaves, are broad across the outer end. The two inner sepals are sometimes missing. The ovary supports two erect styles. It is a plant of dry sandy soil. July to September.

Triadenum virginicum   *Gottscho*

scyrum hypericoides   *D. Richards*   Ascyrum stans   *Allen*

THE ROCKROSE FAMILY – CISTACEAE

Sepals five – two very small ones and three larger, inner ones that enclose the fruit; petals five in the American species, these all shed in a day; stamens numerous; the pistil forming a pod (capsule) which splits into three parts when mature. Leaves narrow and pointed. Most species European.

ROCKROSES or FROSTWEEDS (HELIANTHEMUM)

The name of "frostweed" comes from the fact that in late autumn the bark of the stem splits and strings of ice crystals may emerge through the cracks. The flowers, an inch or so across, have five broad, slightly overlapping yellow petals. Later in the season there are flowers that have no petals and that do not open, but that form fruit nevertheless. The plants grow in dry soil. May to July.

H. CANADENSE grows a foot or two tall. Its stems and leaves are covered with branched hairs. The narrow, pointed leaves are more or less stalkless and they taper at the base. The under-surface of the leaves is pale. The flowers are borne singly. Though a bud may be terminal, new growth soon rises above it so that the flower itself is over-topped by young branches. May to July.....
H. BICKNELLII bears its flowers generally in a cluster atop the stem, new growth not developing above them. The leaves, which are wider than those on *H. canadense* and also have short stalks, bear their branched hairs mainly on the upper surface. June and July.

HUDSONIA

Our two species of *Hudsonia* are heather-like plants characteristic of beaches, dunes, and other sandy places, with bushy stems sprawling on the ground, small scale-like or needle-like leaves, and many yellow flowers borne singly at the ends of short branches. Both flower from May to July.

BEACH-HEATHER or POVERTY-GRASS, H. TO-MENTOSA, has scale-like leaves up to ⅛ inch long which adhere quite closely to the hoary stem and branches.

FALSE HEATHER, H. ERICOIDES, has needle-like leaves about ¼ inch long. The plant is largely coated with a greenish down.

PINWEED (LECHEA)

Numerous species and varieties of *Lechea* enter our area but are seldom noticed. The plants do not grow large, the leaves are small, and the flowers still smaller, the sepals exceeding the three reddish petals in size. As in *Helianthemum*, the three inner sepals are much larger than the two outer ones. The ovary has three sections and three dark red, feathery stigmas. The flowers themselves are apt to be reddish or brownish, barely ⅛ inch across, and borne largely in short, broad panicles. There are usually overwintering basal shoots. The plants grow almost entirely in open, sandy woods.

Hudsonia tomentosa   *V. Richard*

Ielianthemum canadense   *Rickett*   Hudsonia ericoides   *Allen*

THE CACTUS FAMILY – CACTACEAE

Stems thick and succulent, of various shapes, mostly beset with prickles and lacking in foliage (except for small leaves that drop as they reach maturity). Sepals and petals numerous and similar to each other. Many stamens on the inner surface of the cup-shaped receptacle at the base of the perianth. Ovary inferior.

PRICKLY-PEAR (OPUNTIA)

Only one species of this large western genus reaches the vicinity of New York. This one can be found on Staten and Long Islands and in sandy areas of New Jersey.

O. COMPRESSA consists of thick oval sections joined end to end, the surface marked by small spots containing minute reddish-brown barbed hairs. These are much more dangerous than spines, for when detached they work into the skin tissues and cause painful inflammation. In early summer the end joints bear small, narrow, thick leaves. The flowers, 1¼–2 inches across, are yellow, often with a red center. May to July. (By some called *Opuntia humifusa*.)

THE BARBERRY FAMILY – BERBERIDACEAE

Sepals six in the species treated here, small bractlets at their base; petals usually six or nine, stamens as many or twice as many. These herbaceous relatives of the familiar thorny, red-berried shrubs known as barberries only remotely resembling them.

CAULOPHYLLUM

The only other species is Asiatic.

BLUE COHOSH or PAPOOSE-ROOT, C. THALIC-TROIDES, is a stout plant 1–3 feet tall. It grows in moist, deep woods. The single leaf is so large and so divided into segments which are themselves divided and redivided that it gives the impression of many leaves. The ultimate segments somewhat resemble those of meadow-rue (*Thalictrum*, whence the botanical name). The flowers are in a large, branched inflorescence. Individually they are small and greenish-yellow, with six pointed petals and six stamens. The "berries" are simply the seeds, which split the ovary as they develop, and form a blue, fleshy outer layer. There are two such seeds from each flower. April to June.

PODOPHYLLUM

In *Podophyllum* as in *Caulophyllum*, there is only one North American species.

MAY-APPLE or MANDRAKE, P. PELTATUM, lives from year to year as a horizontal underground stem, a rhizome. This sends up either a single leaf having a round, toothed blade on a long stalk, or a flowering stem with two such leaves and a single flower between them. The flower has either six or nine large petals, twice as many stamens, and a large pistil with no style, the stigma sitting on the ovary, which becomes a yellowish berry, sweetish and mildly acid, sometimes made into a preserve. Other parts of the plant are reputedly poisonous. The plant grows in open woods, on hillsides, and in meadows. April to June.

Caulophyllum thalictroides   *Johnson*

odophyllum peltatum   *Gottscho*

Opuntia compressa
V. Richard

THE MUSTARD FAMILY – CRUCIFERAE

Sepals four and petals four in a radially symmetric flower in which the petals generally spread out flat to form a cross (*crucifer* means "cross-bearer"). Stamens six in almost every species, two shorter than the other four and placed on opposite sides of the pistil from each other. Seed-pods generally divided into two chambers by a central lengthwise partition. Flowers of most genera in the elongated clusters called racemes, with the older flowers forming fruits while upper ones at the tip are still showing buds. Hairs on the plants (seen through a magnifier) all simple or some or all of them branched.

I. *Plants with yellow (or occasionally white) petals.*

THE MUSTARDS (BRASSICA)

The mustards are distinguished by the stout beak on the seed-pod and by the characteristic foliage: the end lobe on the leaves is larger than the side lobes. They all have yellow petals about ½ inch long.

CHARLOCK, BRASSICA KABER, has a prominent, angled beak, a third the length of the pod and usually containing one or two seeds. The stem, close to 3 feet tall, is apt to be bristly. May to July..... B. JUNCEA, called Chinese, Indian, brown, or leaf mustard, is smooth and whitened with a waxy bloom. Mature pods are up to 1¾ inches long. June to September..... B. CAMPESTRIS (or *B. rapa*) also has a bloom. Its upper leaves clasp the stem with a pair of "ears." Mature pods, 2 or 3 inches long, have a slender beak..... WHITE MUSTARD, B. HIRTA, has bristly pods with a flat beak the length of the seed-bearing portion. June to August.

BLACK MUSTARD, B. NIGRA, from Eurasia, has a hairy stem up to 5 feet tall. The mature pods, less than 1 inch long, stand erect, close against the stem. The beak is straight. June to October.

WINTER CRESSES (BARBAREA)

The winter cresses in *Barbarea* resemble the mustards, except for their minute beak.

All are smooth. At least the upper leaves "clasp" the stem by two basal lobes.

YELLOW ROCKET, B. VULGARIS, often 3 feet tall, has somewhat fan-shaped upper leaves which are deeply cleft. April to August..... EARLY WINTER CRESS, B. VERNA, differs chiefly in having from four to ten pairs of side lobes on the basal leaves. Mature pods may be 3 inches long. March to May.

YELLOW CRESSES (RORIPPA)

Most leaves are deeply cleft pinnately. The petals, also the pods, are very small.

R. ISLANDICA may be smooth or hairy, and leaves range from deeply indented to merely toothed. Pods, to ⅝ inch in length, vary from elliptic to almost circular. Sepals, ⅛ inch long, slightly exceed the petals. Late spring to late autumn..... CREEPING YELLOW CRESS, R. SYLVESTRIS, sends up erect branches to 2 feet tall. The leaves may have lobes cut into narrow divisions. The petals are longer than the sepals. Pods are about ½ inch long. May to September.

RAPHANUS

WILD RADISH, R. RAPHANISTRUM, also known as jointed-charlock, has yellow petals ½ inch long. The lower leaves are up to 2 inches long and pinnately cleft, the end lobes the largest. The plants, to 2 feet tall or more, are somewhat bristly-hairy. The pod, about 3 inches long, is constricted between the seeds. April to November.

rippa islandica *Rickett*

Brassica nigra *Marler*

rbarea vulgaris *Johnson*

Raphanus raphanistrum *Johnson*

ERYSIMUM

ERYSIMUM CHEIRANTHOIDES, known as treacle-mustard or wormseed-mustard, a species introduced from Europe, is a 4-foot plant with few branches or none. The leaves are narrow, sometimes slightly toothed, but undivided and unlobed. They bear three-forked hairs. The yellow flowers have petals about ⅛ inch long with a stalk-like base. The pods, four-angled, long and narrow, with a flattened tip, stand almost erect on stalks that extend at right angles from the main stem. June to September.

DIPLOTAXIS

DIPLOTAXIS closely resembles *Brassica*. The leaves, pinnately cleft, are mostly near the base of the stem. The petals are yellow. May to September.

WALL ROCKET, D. MURALIS, so called because it is often found on walls in Europe, is generally smooth and grows up to 20 inches tall. Petals are about ⅓ inch long, pods 1½ inches..... SAND ROCKET, D. TENUIFOLIA, is larger and has more leaves on the stem. Petals may reach an inch in length.

OTHER YELLOW MUSTARDS

ERUCASTRUM GALLICUM resembles a mustard, except that the leaf end-lobe is not enlarged and the beak on the pod is less conspicuous. Stem and leaves are downy; lower flowers spring from axils of leaves; the petals are pale yellow. May to October.

DESCURAINIA SOPHIA, tansy-mustard, is a weedy plant with pinnate leaves finely divided somewhat like those of *Tanacetum* (page 290). The flowers are small and yellow. The pods, about an inch long, extend outward and have no beak..... SISYMBRIUM ALTISSIMUM, tumble-mustard, has pods up to 4 inches long, not close to the main stem, pale yellow flowers, and long, narrow leaf-segments..... S. OFFICINALE, hedge-mustard, a weed from Europe, has pods pressed close against the stem. The racemes of flowers are long and thin; the basal lobes

of leaves point backward..... CAMELINA SATIVA, false flax, was once cultivated for its oily seeds. The stem, which grows to 3 feet, is fairly smooth. The slender leaves "clasp" the stem by two basal lobes. The pods, which are pear-shaped, standing erect on their small end, are about ⅓ inch long..... The slightly smaller sister species, C. MICROCARPA, is rough-hairy. Its pods are likewise pear-shaped, about ⅕ inch long. Both species of *Camelina* have come from the Old World.

II. *Plants with white, pink, lavender, or purple petals.*

TOOTHWORTS (DENTARIA)

The toothworts are distinguished by their leaves being palmately cleft or divided. From one to three such leaves, with short stalks, are borne about halfway up the flowering stem. The flowers, generally in a short, loose raceme, are white or pale purple, the petals averaging ½ inch. The pod is long, narrow, and flat. The flowering stems, 6 inches to a foot or more tall, grow from succulent white or yellowish rhizomes – underground stems – which are toothed (presumably the "teeth" of the name). All spring woodland plants (March to June).

D. HETEROPHYLLA has leaves (-*phylla*) different (*hetero*-) at the base and on the stem. The basal ones have three oval segments, variously toothed or lobed. The two or three leaves on the stem (usually at the same level) are divided into narrow segments which may or may not be toothed.

D. LACINIATA bears three stem-leaves, each cleft or divided into generally five narrow lobes or segments. These are jagged, toothed, or lobed in varying degrees. Basal leaves are usually lacking.

CRINKLEROOT, D. DIPHYLLA, has two leaves at nearly the same level on the stem, each divided into three broad, toothed segments. The flowers are slightly smaller than in the other species.

Dentaria diphylla   *Johnson*

ntaria laciniata   *Gottscho*   Dentaria heterophylla   *Uttal*

THE BITTER CRESSES
(CARDAMINE)

It is difficult to characterize the genus *Cardamine*, for it includes a group of very diverse plants. The leaves of some are pinnately divided; those of others are round-bladed and undivided. Some plants have minute flowers; others have comparatively large ones. Most, but not all, are found in wet places. They are held in one genus on the basis of certain details of fruit and seed. None have yellow petals. They are most likely to be confused with *Arabis*, but the species of *Arabis* more frequently have branched hairs (page 106).

SPRING CRESS, C. BULBOSA, is a smooth plant up to 2 feet tall. The basal leaves have long stalks bearing round blades. The stem leaves are narrow and without stalks, sometimes with a few teeth. The petals are white, about $\frac{1}{2}$ inch long. The species takes its botanical name from the cluster of small round corms (not true bulbs) at the base of the stem. March to June.

C. DOUGLASSII is about a foot tall, with a hairy stem. The petals are purple or pink; otherwise it is much like *C. bulbosa*. March to May.

CUCKOO-FLOWER or LADY'S-SMOCK, C. PRATENSIS, grows 2 feet tall or taller. The slender, generally unbranched stem bears many pinnately divided leaves, the segments varying from very narrow to round. The flowers are pink or white, the petals about $\frac{1}{2}$ inch long. Pods are often not formed, the plants reproducing mainly by short branches which spring from the base. April to July.

C. PENSYLVANICA is rather like a small "edition" of *C. pratensis*, seldom reaching 2 feet in height. It has pinnately divided or deeply cleft leaves, the end lobe or segment the largest. The pods are very narrow, and the flowers only about $\frac{1}{8}$ inch across. A common and very variable species. It is said to be an excellent substitute for water cress. March to August.

C. PARVIFLORA is a low plant that prefers dry soil. The leaves are pinnately divided into very short, narrow segments, the end segment no larger than those along the sides. The petals are $\frac{1}{8}$ inch long or less; the pods about an inch long and less than $\frac{1}{25}$ inch wide. April to August.

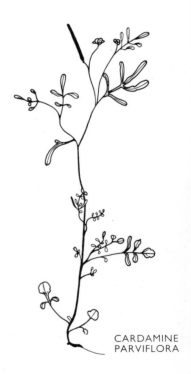

CARDAMINE
PARVIFLORA

rdamine pensylvanica *McDowell*

Cardamine bulbosa *Scribner*

rdamine pratensis *Rickett*

Cardamine douglasii *D. Richards*

ARABIS

Some species of *Arabis* are scrawny weeds, while others are grown in rock gardens. Of the six that reach the vicinity of New York City, only the first one described below has any horticultural possibilities.

A. LYRATA appropriately carries the name of rock cress, for it thrives among rocks – but so do many other species of *Arabis*. This one has several stems, a foot tall or taller, rising from a tuft of pinnately lobed leaves that have a large end lobe. There are a few scattered leaves on the stems, mostly narrow and not lobed. The petals are generally white, up to $\frac{1}{3}$ inch long. The pods, nearly straight, about $1\frac{1}{2}$ inches long, point upwards. April and May.

A. CANADENSIS reaches to 3 feet, carrying its long, open racemes of flowers on long stalks. The cream-colored petals are barely $\frac{1}{4}$ inch long. The pods are hairy, slightly curved downward, and up to 4 inches long. This is in the group called sicklepods. The leaves are long and narrow, often (but not always) toothed, and at least the lower ones are hairy. The upper part of the plant is smooth. April to June.

A. LAEVIGATA, another sicklepod, is conspicuously smooth and whitened with a bloom. The stem, up to 3 feet tall, bears long narrow leaves, often toothed, with sharp basal lobes extending around the stem. The petals are white, about $\frac{1}{5}$ inch long. The pods are up to 4 inches long and $\frac{1}{10}$ inch wide. March to July..... A. VIRIDIS, a plant of rocky woods, is like a smaller version of *A. laevigata*, being smooth and whitened. The basal leaves, however, may be pinnately lobed; those on the stem have pointed lobes at the base. The cream-colored petals, up to $\frac{3}{8}$ inch long, are twice as long as the sepals. May and June..... A. GLABRA is called tower-mustard, probably because it sometimes reaches 4 feet in height. Stem and upper leaves are smooth; lower leaves bear branched hairs. Stem leaves are lance-shaped and embrace the stem. Petals are cream-white or yellowish and up to $\frac{1}{4}$ inch long. Slender pods almost 4 inches long stand upright close to the stem. May to July..... A. HIRSUTA is similar but shorter and with pods only 2 inches long. Petals are white. May to July.

DRABA

Plants in this genus seldom reach a foot in height. Most of them have a tuft of small, smooth-edged leaves at the base with a few additional leaves on the stem. The petals are small and white. The short pods are oval or elliptic.

WHITLOW-GRASS, D. VERNA, is one of the earliest flowers of spring, its deeply cleft white petals appearing above the basal mat of foliage on stems that are only an inch tall. These will increase to 3 or 4 inches by the time the plant is in fruit. February to June. .... D. REPTANS resembles whitlow-grass but is much taller when in fruit and it carries two or three leaves on its flowering stems. Furthermore, the petals (if present) are barely notched, not deeply cleft. March to June.

BERTEROA

One species of this Old-World genus has become distributed in North America.

HOARY-ALYSSUM, B. INCANA, is a not unattractive white-flowered lawn weed with deeply cleft petals, somewhat like a tall *Draba* without basal foliage. The pod, about twice as long as wide, carries a short beak. Leaves on stem and branches are 2 inches long, narrow, smooth-edged, and stalkless. Branched hairs cover the entire plant. June to September.

raba verna   *D. Richards*

Berteroa incana   *Rickett*

abis canadensis   *Johnson*

Arabis lyrata   *Johnson*

HESPERIS

The one existing species of the Old-World genus *Hesperis* is a large and handsome plant that has made itself a more welcome immigrant than most.

DAME'S ROCKET, also known as DAME'S-VIOLET and MOTHER-OF-THE-EVENING, H. MATRONALIS, is a plant often 3 feet tall or taller. The leaf-blades are lanceolate, short-stalked, toothed. The flowers make a handsome show, with petals up to an inch long varying from white through pink to purple. The pods may be 5 inches long and are quite narrow, scarcely wider than the stalks on which they stand.

An old-fashioned garden flower originally, the dame's rocket is now mainly a roadside escape in this country. The supplemental name of damask rocket comes as a corruption, not of Damascus, but of "dame's," from the early Roman matrons who grew it. May to August.

ARABIDOPSIS

One European species of *Arabidopsis* has become established in some of the dry soils of North America.

MOUSE-EAR CRESS, A. THALIANA, carries its minute flowers in white or purplish tones up to 18 inches high. When pods appear they are narrow and less than an inch long. At the base of the plant there are several downy leaves about 2 inches long. On the stem itself a few very narrow leaves can be found. March to June.

NASTURTIUM

The demure-looking genus *Nasturtium* in the mustard family bears no relation to the bright-colored annual called nasturtium (*Tropaeolum majus*) grown in flower gardens.

WATER CRESS, N. OFFICINALE, grows in flowing water, generally spring water, partly or wholly submerged. The flowers are small and white. The leaves, which are smooth all around and pinnately divided, have a pleasantly pungent taste, for which they are frequently gathered. (In England they are widely cultivated but only the plants' young tips are used in salads.) April to October.

ALLIARIA

GARLIC-MUSTARD, A. OFFICINALIS, is unmistakable, both from the odor of garlic emitted when the leaves are crushed and from the large ovate or even triangular leaf-blades, deeply toothed. In Europe, where it was used for many years as a condiment, mostly by poor people who had no other seasoning, it is known as "sauce-alone." The petals are white, about ¼ inch long; the pods are up to 2 inches long. April to June.

ARMORACIA

One European native and one American are among the most pungent of the numerous cresses found in the American wild. These two are in the genus *Armoracia*.

HORSE-RADISH, A. RUSTICANA, which has spread from cultivation, grows up to 4 feet tall and bears long-stalked basal leaves besides a few stalkless or short-stalked ones on the stem. The leaf-blades have blunt teeth and some of the stem-leaves may be pinnately cleft. The seasoning comes from the root. The plant is topped by several racemes of small white flowers. May to July. .... LAKE CRESS, A. AQUATICA, growing in water, has both submerged and open-air leaves. Those growing beneath the quiet surface are divided into numerous hairlike segments. Those above are narrow – either lanceolate or elliptic – and toothed on the edges. The petals are ¼ inch long and white. June to August.

Arabidopsis thaliana   *Rickett*

esperis matronalis   *Johnson*

asturtium officinale   *Johnson*   Alliria officinalis   *Scribner*

CAKILE

Sea Rocket, C. edentula, is essentially a seacoast plant whose succulent stems bear their many spreading branches along sandy sea beaches. (A few plants appear at the edge of the Great Lakes.) The leaves are small and broadest near their tip. The edges may be wavy, toothed, scalloped, or even pinnately lobed. The pods consist of two fleshy sections, each as thick as it is wide, but the upper one much larger. This one contains the single seed; occasionally the pod is surmounted by a long beak. The flowers are minute and pale purple. July to September.

LEPIDIUM

The spikes of small flat seed-pods of *Lepidium*, round in outline, are more conspicuous than the flowers, for many of these have no petals to brighten them. Most species have invaded here from Europe.

L. densiflorum has two stamens and no petals. Its basal leaves are either coarsely toothed or pinnately cleft..... L. campestre, cow cress, is a densely hairy plant found in fields. The leaves "clasp" the stem between their pointed lobes..... L. virginicum, pepper-grass or poor-man's-pepper, the only native American species in the genus, like *L. densiflorum* has two stamens. The petals and sepals are of about equal length. The round, flat seed-pods, up to ¼ inch long, are deeply indented at the tip. The plant may be smooth or very finely hairy. The basal leaves range from being toothed to being pinnately divided. The leaves along the stem differ in being narrow with edges either entire or toothed, and they stand almost erect. June to November.

THLASPI

Small, flat, circular pods with a notch in the end and two or three seeds on each side of the partition mark the two species of this European genus that have settled in waste places in America. The flowers of both are white and very small.

Penny Cress, T. arvense, may grow to nearly 3 feet tall. It is a smooth plant with stalkless leaves shaped like an arrowhead where they meet the stem. Petals are not more than $\frac{1}{16}$ inch long. April to August. .... T. perfoliatum has ⅛-inch petals. Its seed-pods are somewhat asymmetric. Though the leaf-blades are ovate in outline, they have the same arrowhead base as *T. arvense*. March and April.

CAPSELLA

Shepherd's-purse, C. bursa-pastoris, is an all-too-familiar weed, especially in lawns. Its clusters of small white four-petaled flowers at the tips of branches give way to heart-shaped seed-pods, like a shepherd's purse of medieval days. The plant's basal leaves are pinnately cleft or divided into segments. A few leaves shaped like arrowheads grow out from the stem. In acceptable weather the plant is a year-round bloomer, though not a desirable one.

akile edentula   *Gillis*   Cakile edentula   *Rollins*

Thlaspi arvense   *Scribner*

:pidium densiflorum   *Johnson*

BLEEDING-HEART FAMILY – FUMARIACEAE

Sepals two and scale-like; petals four, of two different sizes and shapes, two outer enclosing two inner ones, which are narrower, and the outer petals – one or both of them – extended into a saclike base called a "spur," the inner ones united by their tips over the stigma; stamens six. Leaves several times finely divided.

DICENTRA

The two spurs that dangle upside-down on every flower are just what the name *Dicentra* signifies (*di*, "two"; *kentron*, "spur") in the Greek from which it was taken. The stem of the raceme of flowers bends in an arch. The leaves of all are finely divided and redivided into narrow segments.

DUTCHMAN'S-BREECHES, D. CUCULLARIA, bears white flowers shaped like a pair of baggy breeches. The leaves are of a frosty bluish tone; their delicate segments are narrow and more or less straight-sided. For its attractive foliage as well as for its appealing flowers, this is one of the most beloved plants of spring. Its leaf-stalks and flower-stems rise from a cluster of small white grainlike tubers. April to June..... SQUIRREL-CORN, D. CANADENSIS, is a similar species but one that is rarely seen near New York. The flower, with the fragrance of hyacinths, is heart-shaped and the inner petals are more conspicuous than those of *D. cucullaria*. The English name refers to the many small grainlike tubers that are scattered along the underground stem. April and May.

WILD BLEEDING-HEART, D. EXIMIA, closely resembles the pink bleeding-heart of gardens (*D. spectabilis*), but both flowers and leaf-segments are smaller. The stem rises from a short, scaly, underground stem, a rhizome, and grows to a height of nearly 2 feet. It likes rock ledges and also grows in woods. April to September.

ADLUMIA

ALLEGHENY-VINE, A. FUNGOSA, climbs by its leaves, which are many times divided into small, roundish, toothed segments on thin stalks; these stalks coil around their supports. The flowers hang in branched clusters at the ends of branches. Their spurs are merely a pair of rounded lobes at the top (near the point of attachment) of their slender white or purplish petals. After the flower is fertilized the petals become spongy and enclose the developing seed-pod. This plant is mainly a resident of woods and mountains. June to October.

CORYDALIS

While both outer petals of *Corydalis* have vertical flattish projections near the tip, only one of them has a spur.

YELLOW-HARLEQUIN, C. FLAVULA, is a yellow-flowered species (others grow farther west). Its flowers are small – less than $\frac{1}{2}$ inch long – and pale in color, and they generally hang singly from the branches. The spur on the upper petal is very short. The outer petals each carry a crest of three or four teeth. The plant grows to 20 inches. The lower leaves are long-stalked and finely divided. March to May..... PALE CORYDALIS or ROCK-HARLEQUIN, C. SEMPERVIRENS, is the only pink-flowered species. The pink petals have yellow tips and a very short spur. The leaves appear whitish with a bloom. The plant grows erect up to 4 feet tall with its racemes of flowers carried in loose panicles. It thrives best in rocky places and in recently cleared woodlands. May to September.

Dicentra eximia   *Johnson*

llumia fungosa   *Gottscho*

icentra cucullaria   *Gottscho*   Corydalis flavula   *Leeson*

THE PINK FAMILY – CARYOPHYLLACEAE

Flowers arranged in the candelabrum style known as a cyme; that is, at the tip of the central stem there is a flower; ideally, two flower-stalks spring from directly below it, and from the stem below each of these flowers, two other flowers arise, and so on (but not always that regularly). Flower-parts usually in fours or fives. From two to five styles on the ovary; ovules attached all over a central stalk.

I. *Sepals forming a cup, tube, or bladder.*

THE CAMPIONS and CATCHFLIES (SILENE)

Campion is a name given also to some species of *Lychnis* in this family. "Catchfly" comes from the sticky stems of some. There are five petals on narrow stalks, three or four styles, ten stamens. The capsule opens at the top, usually show six teeth.

STARRY CAMPION, S. STELLATA, about ¾ inch across, is readily identified by its five white petals, irregularly cut into narrow lobes. Most of the leaves are in circles of four. July to September.

BLADDER CAMPION, S. CUCUBALUS, from Europe, can be recognized by the widely expanded calyx. The five white petals are notched. The flower-clusters are long-stalked. The plant grows up to 3 feet tall. April to September..... S. CSEREI is similar but the leaves are thicker and the inflorescence narrower. May to September.

STICKY COCKLE or NIGHT-FLOWERING CATCHFLY, S. NOCTIFLORA, has an inflated calyx with a network of veins. The flowers, with cream-white petals, pinkish at the base and notched, open at night and are fragrant. The stem is sticky-hairy, the leaves mostly lance-shaped. May to September.

Silene noctiflora is often confused with *Lychnis alba*. In the *Silene* the leaves (bracts) just below the flowers are long and narrow; in the *Lychnis* they are short and elliptic. In the *Silene* each flower generally contains both stamens and pistil; in the *Lychnis* they are in separate flowers.

SLEEPY CATCHFLY, S. ANTIRRHINA, bears its pairs of narrow leaves at rather wide intervals, between which small insects are usually trapped in dark sticky zones. The petals, if present, are pink or white, less than ½ inch long, and more or less cleft. May to September..... SWEET-WILLIAM CATCHFLY or NONE-SO-PRETTY, S. ARMERIA, Eurasian, is a smaller plant, about a foot tall, its ovate leaves whitened with a bloom. The flowers, generally pink, grow close together. June to October..... S. CONICA, up to 20 inches tall, has narrow, pointed leaves. Its petals, white or rose-colored, are ¼ inch long. The calyx is strongly ribbed, covered with short stiff hairs, and tipped with five long, pointed teeth. May to July.

MORE CAMPIONS (LYCHNIS)

The brilliant flowers of some resemble those of *Silene* but they usually have five styles instead of three and they frequently carry their male and female elements on different plants. Most species have come from Europe.

WHITE CAMPION, L. ALBA, bears flowers that open only at night or when the sky is clouded. The five white petals, about ½ inch long, expand on the corolla-tube, with a ruffled crown, or "corona," at their base. Each petal is deeply cut into two lobes. The flowers are fragrant. Each holds stamens or pistil, not both. All are alike on one plant. The male flowers have a slender calyx, frequently with reddish ribs and veining, the female, a greatly expanded calyx, less often with reddish coloring. Some plants may be glandular and downy, but not sticky. May to September.

Silene stellata   *Johnson*

ychnis alba (male)   *Gottscho*

Silene cucubalus   *Elbert*

ychnis alba (female)   *Johnson*

LYCHNIS (*continued*)

RED CAMPION, LYCHNIS DIOICA, has rose-red petals deeply cut into two lobes like those of *Lychnis alba* (page 114). Also like this sister species, *L. dioica* has either stamens or a pistil in a flower, not both together (*dioica* means "of two households"). The calyx is hairy and somewhat inflated and tipped with long-pointed teeth. The flowers have little odor. The plants grow up to 3 feet high and bear soft hairs on stem and leaves, the leaves being from oval to lance-oblong and averaging 3 inches in length. The plants are common weeds in England.

RAGGED-ROBIN or CUCKOO-FLOWER, L. FLOS-CUCULI, has four long, narrow, and unequal lobes on each of its five pink petals. The calyx is not inflated. At the base of the plant there are leaves with more or less parallel sides, whereas the few stem-leaves have slightly curved sides, though they are very narrow. The stem is mostly free of hairs but is somewhat sticky. The plant may reach 4 feet in height. In open fields it often forms large colonies. May to July.

AGROSTEMMA

CORN COCKLE, A. GITHAGO, the only species, has invaded our country from the grain fields of Europe, where it has been a dangerous weed. The seeds, if harvested with the grain crop, add a poisonous element to the flour. It is a slender plant up to 3 feet tall or taller, with a silky-downy stem and very narrow leaves. The petals are rose-red with black spots showing near the base. June to September.

PINKS (DIANTHUS)

Carnations are one of the several garden forms of the genus *Dianthus*, the botanical name of which indicates that it was once considered Jove's own flower (*Di-* for *Dios* – Jupiter or Jove; *anthos* – flower). The calyx is more or less cylindrical and five-toothed, with two or more small, overlapping leaves (bractlets) directly beneath it. There are ten stamens and two styles. The seed-capsule is four-valved at the apex. All species found in the wild in North America came from Europe and have spread through cultivation.

DEPTFORD PINK, D. ARMERIA, is tall (up to 3 feet) with very narrow leaves standing upright, close to the stem. One or more tight clusters of small pink flowers, only one usually open at a time, appear at the tip of the stem. Beneath each cluster there is a pair of narrow bracts; beneath each flower another bract, longer than the flower-stalk. The petals are slightly toothed and are lightly spotted in white. The visible part is only about $\frac{1}{5}$ inch long. May to July. Deptford is now a part of industrial London. The Deptford pink once colored the fields of the region..... SWEET-WILLIAM, D. BARBATUS, most often seen in gardens, occasionally "escapes" to fields and roadsides. The flowers are crowded in a somewhat flat-topped inflorescence, in colors ranging from red through rose and pink to white, and often in combinations. June to August.

BABY'S-BREATH (GYPSOPHILA)

G. MURALIS is an 8-inch, small-flowered weed that comes from Europe. The leaves are very narrow and about $\frac{1}{3}$ inch long. The flowers arise from their axils on threadlike stalks. The petals are rose-color, their blades about $\frac{1}{4}$ inch long. June to October.

Lychnis dioica   *Gottscho*

Lychnis flos–cuculi   *Rickett*

Agrostemma githago   *LaJara*

Dianthus armeria   *Gottscho*

SAPONARIA

Both species of *Saponaria* present in America have been introduced from the Old World. The abundant one called bouncing-Bet, the flowers of which are fragrant and frequently are "doubled," was originally cultivated. The calyx in both species is shaped like a narrow flask. The petals are shallowly notched, not forked. There are two styles, and the pod (a capsule) opens to make four teeth. An extract from either species forms a lather with water (the Latin for "soap" is *sapo*; hence the botanical name). The action is due to substances called "saponins," which are poisonous.

BOUNCING-BET or SOAPWORT, S. OFFICINALIS, is a smooth plant, up to 3 feet tall, with ovate or lanceolate leaves which have three veins branching out from the base. The flowers, which are white or pale pink, are fairly large and are in close clusters in the axils of the leaves and at the tip of the stem. June to October..... COWHERB or COW COCKLE, S. VACCARIA, is less frequently seen than *S. officinalis*. It is a shorter and more slender plant with smaller flowers on longer stalks. The petals are pink; the calyx has five sharp angles. June to September.

II. *Sepals separate* (most of the plants small with insignificant flowers).

CHICKWEEDS (CERASTIUM)

Cerastium is one of two genera of plants known as chickweeds because of their use as food by small birds. Wild birds pick the seeds from lawns; caged birds accept entire plants. Chickweeds found in wet places are most likely to be *Stellaria* (page 120); those of dry areas are more probably *Cerastium*. Flowers of *Cerastium* usually have five styles, and the seed-pod opens so as to make ten teeth. The five white petals are notched.

MOUSE-EAR CHICKWEED, C. VULGATUM, creeps through lawns and fields, forming mats with its wide-spreading branches. Its hairy leaves are an inch in length, its sepals and white petals from ⅛ to ¼ inch or slightly longer. April to October.

FIELD CHICKWEED, C. ARVENSE, most often found in gravelly soil, is also a trailing plant, but its flowering branches may rise to a foot or more. The sepals average ¼ inch in length, the narrow petals ½ inch or more. The leaves are variable but mostly very narrow and from a fraction of an inch to 2½ inches long. They occupy mainly the lower two-thirds of the branch. April to August.

C. VISCOSUM is a sticky species found in waste places. It is also hairy or downy, and has erect stems up to a foot tall bearing leaves to 1 inch long. It is an invader from Europe, flowering from March to July..... C. NUTANS, an American native, is also both sticky and hairy. Its stems are up to 2 feet long but they are sprawling. The narrow leaves may be 3 inches long. This is a woodland plant. March to June.

PEARLWORTS (SAGINA)

The pearlworts are low plants, some species forming mats, with threadlike leaves and tiny flowers on rather long stalks. A magnifier reveals that the sepals, petals, stamens, and styles usually number four or five (the petals may be lacking).

BIRDSEYE, S. PROCUMBENS, is a small, matted plant with its flower-parts generally in fours (but occasionally fives), the petals, if present, much shorter than the sepals. On the ground and along the branches (to 6 inches long) there are tightly packed rosettes of bristle-tipped leaves to ¼ inch in length. April to November..... S. DECUMBENS is a more or less erect plant with a threadlike stem up to 6 inches tall and flower-parts in fives. It grows largely in sandy fields, where it flowers over a long season.

Sagina procumbens   *Scribner*

Cerastium vulgatum   *Scribner*

aponaria officinalis   *Johnson*

Cerastium arvense   *Scribner*

CHICKWEEDS (STELLARIA)

The starry appearance of the chickweeds in the genus *Stellaria* has given them their botanical name; *stella* is the Latin for "star." Their petals, if present, are so deeply notched as to appear double their number. The petal count is variable, as is the number of stamens. The styles are usually three. The seed-pod splits into three or six parts.

S. MEDIA is the common little white-flowered weed of lawns, most often a smooth plant branching out close to the soil. The petals, when present, are shorter than the calyx. The leaf-blades average ¾ inch in length. The flowers appear at almost any time..... STAR CHICKWEED, S. PUBERA, in contrast, is a woodland plant a foot tall with leaves up to 3 inches long. The petal divisions are narrow and sharp. March to May.

STITCHWORT is the name given to several species, notably S. GRAMINEA, from Europe, once used to relieve the sudden sharp pains known as "stitches." S. *graminea* is tall, it has four-angled stems, grasslike leaves, and a loose terminal cluster of small white flowers..... S. LONGIFOLIA, American, is similar but has flowers in long-stalked clusters from the upper leaf-axils..... S. HOLOSTEA, once cultivated, has petals nearly an inch across, split halfway. May and June.

THE SANDWORTS (ARENARIA)

Arena is the Latin word for "sand," and the species of *Arenaria* are most at home in sandy situations. They are small, generally bushy plants, mostly with tiny leaves and small white flowers, the petals not cleft. There are usually ten stamens, three styles.

GROVE SANDWORT, A. LATERIFLORA, a foot tall, has a threadlike creeping stem (rhizome), leafy branches, and elliptic leaves about 1 inch long. The flowers, with petals to ⅛ inch long, are in small, long-stemmed clusters. May to August.

PINE-BARREN SANDWORT, A. CAROLINIANA, forms dense tufts with forking stems that lie on the ground. The flowering stems may rise 8 inches; their upper parts are glandular. Most of the leaves are near the base. The flowers are on long stalks in branched clusters. Their narrow petals are about ⅖ inch long. May to July..... THYME-LEAVED SANDWORT, A. SERPYLLIFOLIA, has slender, much-branched, 8-inch stems bearing ovate leaves about ⅕ inch long. Minute, short-petaled flowers are in clusters at the branch tips. April to August..... SEA-CHICKWEED, A. PEPLOIDES, has a thick, succulent stem and leaves, five or six very small petals and eight or ten stamens. May to September.

SAND-SPURREYS (SPERGULARIA) are small plants resembling *Arenaria*, with threadlike leaves. There are five sepals and five petals (these not divided), three styles, and from two to ten stamens. They grow principally in sandy soil. Both species are about a foot tall and much branched. S. RUBRA usually has ten stamens. Its petals are pink. May to October..... S. MARINA has five stamens or less. Its leaves are succulent and its petals white or rose. June to October.

SPURREY (or SPURRY), SPERGULA ARVENSIS, stands a foot or so tall and carries circles of 2-inch threadlike leaves 2 or 3 inches apart. The flowers have five white petals ⅛ inch long, ten (or five) stamens and five styles. It is a season-long bloomer.

THE WHITLOW-WORTS (PARONYCHIA) are matted, spreading, variable plants with narrow leaves and minute yellow flowers of five sepals but seldom any petals. A magnifier will reveal almost transparent pairs of appendages where a leaf joins the stem. P. FASTIGIATA, to 10 inches tall, has leafy flower-clusters, the leaf-blades broadest near the tip. Summer.

renaria lateriflora   *Johnson*

Stellaria media   *Rickett*

renaria caroliniana   *Uttal*

Stellaria graminea   *Rickett*

THE SUNDEW FAMILY – DROSERACEAE

Sepals, petals, and stamens all in fives in the one genus (*Drosera*) that occurs in our area. (The Venus'-fly-trap, *Dionaea*, is native in the southeast; two other genera are known in Europe.) Styles three in *Drosera*, so cleft as to appear as six. A distinguishing feature of the family: the ability to trap insects that alight on the leaves and to absorb nourishment from the insects' bodies.

THE SUNDEWS (DROSERA)

The glands on the hairs that cover most of the leaf surfaces are sticky. Any small insect alighting on these is trapped. The surrounding hairs bend towards the captive, completing its entanglement. A digestive material exuded by the glands enables the plant to absorb foods from the insect's body. Such "insectivorous" or "carnivorous" plants are thus more or less independent of the soil for certain elements in their nutrition. The flowers of sundews are borne on a leafless stalk that usually curls downward at the tip. The leaves, no matter what their shape, are in a sort of loose rosette around this stalk. The plants usually grow in bogs, where they flower from June to August.

ROUND-LEAVED SUNDEW, D. ROTUNDIFOLIA, is distinguished by its circular leaf-blades on long stalks. The flowers are white, the petals about ¼ inch long.

DEW-THREAD, D. FILIFORMIS, has leaves shaped like pieces of string, without any distinction between stalk and blade; the purple glandular hairs are borne over their whole surface. They may be 10 inches long. Some stand erect; others assume various curves. The flowers are purplish, on a stem up to 9 inches tall.

D. INTERMEDIA has leaf-blades up to an inch long, round at the tip and tapering into the stalk, which may be 2 inches long. The white flowers have petals nearly ½ inch long.

THE LIVE-FOREVER FAMILY – CRASSULACEAE

Plants mostly succulent; their leaves so protected against loss of water that they remain fresh long after being detached from the stem. Leaves not divided. Flowers small, numerous, symmetric, their parts, including the pistils, in either fours or fives in different species, the stamens generally twice as many as the sepals or petals, the pistils developing into four or five pods (follicles), except in *Penthorum*.

LIVE-FOREVER (SEDUM)

Sepals and petals on *Sedum* species in the New York area number five each.

S. TELEPHIUM, sometimes known in gardens as ORPINE, has escaped from cultivation to the wild. The nearly 2-foot stem bears fleshy, ovate, toothed leaves, generally in pairs. A dense cluster of purplish-red flowers surmounts the stem. August and September..... A taller plant with redder flowers and with leaves borne either singly or in threes is sometimes distinguished as S. PURPUREUM..... Another, with few or no teeth on the leaf margins and with pink flowers, is called S. TELEPHIOIDES.

Sedum sarmentosum *Rickett*

enthorum sedoides *Rickett*

Saxifraga pensylvanica *Scribner*

axifraga virginiensis *Rickett*

SEDUM (*continued*)

WALLPEPPER or LOVE-ENTANGLE, SEDUM SARMENTOSUM, has long been miscalled *Sedum acre*. Where it is too dry or rocky for anything else, this familiar *Sedum* that comes from Europe will grow. The short, pointed, succulent leaves arise close together along the creeping stem. They have a pungent taste. The flowering stems grow up to 4 inches tall and bear their small yellow flowers on spreading branches. June and July..... S. TERNATUM is another creeping species, this one with roundish flat leaves of pale green and short, erect branches of white flowers. Each leafy branch ends in a rosette-like cluster of about six leaves. From the center of many of these the flowering branches rise. This species, a native American, grows in damper areas. April to June.

PENTHORUM

There is but one species, and this, unlike other members of the *Crassulaceae*, is not succulent.

DITCH-STONECROP, P. SEDOIDES, grows 2 or 3 feet tall. It bears finely toothed, lance-shaped or elliptic leaves with prominent veins. The flowers, borne along spreading branches at the summit of the stem, have five sepals, generally no petals, ten stamens, and five pistils united below and developing into a five-horned pod. July to October.

THE SAXIFRAGE FAMILY – SAXIFRAGACEAE

Sepals five, petals five, and stamens either ten or five in all except one genus treated here; the pistil in most genera appearing to be composed of two pistils joined by their basal parts, the two styles projecting as two beaks. Genera with ten stamens: *Saxifraga*, *Mitella*, and *Tiarella*, the last with no leaves on the flowering stem. Genera with five stamens: *Heuchera* and *Parnassia*, the first with small flowers in a tall, branched inflorescence, the second with a single green-veined white flower on a tall stem, usually with a single leaf below it. In *Chrysosplenium*, which floats on water, sepals four or five, petals none, and stamens from four to ten.

THE SAXIFRAGES (SAXIFRAGA)

Since saxifrages mostly grow on rocks, their name (which comes from two Latin words meaning "rock" and "break") is thought by some to be derived from their natural home. By others, however, it is presumed to apply to the early use of certain European species as a cure for the disease called "the stone".

EARLY SAXIFRAGE, S. VIRGINIENSIS, has a basal rosette of toothed leaves that are ovate or elliptic and from ⅜ inch to 3 inches long. From this rises a leafless flowering stem from 12 to 18 inches tall. Its white flowers open in a many-branched inflorescence. The plant is somewhat downy. April to June.

SWAMP SAXIFRAGE, S. PENSYLVANICA, may send up its flowering stems 4 or 5 feet high from within a basal clump of erect leathery leaves to a foot long. On the upper half of the stem many small flowers will appear in a leafy panicle that may develop 8-inch branches after at first being very compact. The sepals of the flowers are bent sharply downwards. The petals are greenish-yellow, whitish, or purple. April to June.

Drosera intermedia   *Horne*

Drosera rotundifolia   *Justice*

Drosera filformis   *Ryker*

Sedum telephium   *Horne*

MITELLA

The plants of the genus *Mitella* are at first glance scrawny, unattractive little specimens with minute flowers – but a hand magnifier reveals unexpected delights. The white or yellowish petals are deeply cleft pinnately so that the flower resembles a bit of lace. The two halves of the pistil form a two-beaked pod – the bishop's cap or mitre. It splits open between the beaks, revealing the black seeds held in a sort of basket.

BISHOP'S-CAP or MITREWORT, M. DIPHYLLA, has a group of long-stalked leaves rising from the ground, their pointed blades indented at the base and slightly lobed; and halfway up the stem two (occasionally three) similar blades with no stalks. The stem grows up to 18 inches tall. The flowers are scattered in a spike-like raceme. Each is only ¼ inch across. April to June. (Other species can be found farther north and west.)

TIARELLA

Only one species of *Tiarella* is at all common in the northeastern states. The name means "little tiara," from the odd form of the fruit. A tiara was the head-dress of the classical Persians – a kind of turban.

FOAMFLOWER, T. CORDIFOLIA, is a delicate plant rarely more than a foot tall. From the underground stem (rhizome) at the base of the flowering stem spring long-stalked leaves with somewhat heart-shaped blades 2 to 4 inches long, variously lobed and toothed. The flowers appear in a slender raceme on the upper half of a scape that may rise 12 inches above the soil. They are less than half an inch across and have five narrow white petals. The two halves of the pistil are curiously different in size, thus giving the resulting fruit one large lobe and one small one. April to July.

HEUCHERA

This genus, known as ALUMROOT, bears a fairly close resemblance to *Tiarella*. The leaf-blades of H. AMERICANA, the only species likely to be found in the vicinity of New York, are quite similar to those of *Tiarella cordifolia*, illustrated here. Both have flowers about ¼ inch long (perhaps slightly larger in the *Heuchera*) with a five-parted calyx and five small petals. The flowers of *H. americana* are generally reddish or somewhat purplish. They are in a cylindric structure on an erect but lax flower-stalk up to 3 feet high. The species exhibits considerable variation. April to June.

GRASS-OF-PARNASSUS (PARNASSIA)

Plants of the attractive group known as grass-of-Parnassus bear no relationship to grasses and no resemblance to them. Only one of the several American species reaches this vicinity.

P. GLAUCA has a basal tuft of smooth, stalked leaves with blades an average of 2 inches long. The leaves have unbranched veins extending from the base of the blade to the apex. Flowering-stems, mostly a foot tall or taller, rise from among these leaves, each one bearing a single flower at the tip and perhaps a single stalkless leaf-blade part way up the stem. The five white petals, each about ½ inch long, are spread outward, only slightly upturned. They have conspicuous parallel veins in green. Five stamens are carried between the petals. Between these, at the base of each petal, are five somewhat ornamental yellow bodies designated as sterile stamens or stamen-substitutes, each cleft into three prongs. The plant grows mainly in wet, limy soils. July to October.

Mitella diphylla — *Johnson*

Tiarella cordifolia — *Johnson*

Mitella diphylla — *Rickett*

Mitella diphylla — *Rickett*

Parnassia glauca
Johnson

THE GOLDEN-SAXIFRAGES
(CHRYSOSPLENIUM)

This is the genus that breaks most of the rules of the saxifrage family. It has four or five sepals, no petals, and from four to ten stamens.

WATER-MAT, C. AMERICANUM, is found in running water or on mud. The creeping stems bear roundish leaves mostly in pairs. They send up occasional very short stalks with a single inconspicuous flower on each. The sepals (four in this species) are wider than they are long. They are essentially green with a reddish or purplish ring around the center. The stamens, up to ten, seem to rise from out this colored area. March to June.

THE FLAX FAMILY – LINACEAE

Only one genus, that of flax itself, concerns us here.

FLAX (LINUM)

Since before history began, flax has been cultivated for the fibers in its stems and the oil in its seeds. The botanical name reflects this antiquity, being the classical Latin name for the fiber; almost the same name existed in Greek and in Old Teutonic. We see it in the words line (still used in parts of England for the fiber), linen, linseed, and even lingerie. Associated with this plant, which is often seen in this country growing wild, are a number of native species, with no English names unless we call them all wild flax. They are all slender plants (often a single unbranched stem), with small, narrow leaves. The flowers have five sepals, five petals, five stamens, and a pistil with five styles. The petals may be blue, white, or yellow (or red in a cultivated species). The fruit is a roundish capsule.

FLAX, L. USITATISSIMUM, the original fiber plant, is our one species with blue flowers. It is sometimes grown in flower gardens and has here and there escaped from cultivation. It sends a single slenderly branching stem up to 3 feet tall. The leaves are extremely narrow and carry three veins lengthwise. The petals are nearly sky-blue, about $\frac{1}{2}$ inch long, and rather broad across the tip. June to September.

L. VIRGINIANUM has yellow flowers of about the same size as the blue-flowered flax, on thin, wiry stalks on a plant approaching 2 feet in height. This is mostly found in open woods. June to August.

L. MEDIUM is rarely more than 2 feet tall and often shorter, with a single main stem topped by a stiff, branching inflorescence. The leaves are very narrow, less than an inch long, with no visible veins. The yellow petals may be $\frac{1}{3}$ inch long, or less. June to August in dry woodlands..... L. STRIATUM, up to 3 feet tall, is distinguished by the narrow flanges ("wings") which extend down the stem from the base of each leaf. The yellow petals are about $\frac{1}{4}$ inch long, the sepals about $\frac{1}{16}$ inch. June to August in damp woods, swamps, and bogs..... L. SULCATUM is rarely seen, but may be distinguished by the fringe of glandular hairs or teeth around the sepals and by the lengthwise grooving of the stem. It is a plant of dry places, growing up to 30 inches high. The petals are yellow and they grow to $\frac{1}{2}$ inch long. June to September.

rysosplenium americanum *Rickett*

Chrysosplenium americanum *Rickett*

um virginianum *Johnson*

Linum usitatissimum *Rickett*

THE WOOD-SORREL FAMILY – OXALIDACEAE

Sepals, petals, stamens all in fives; also five distinct styles on the ovary. Local species all fragile plants.

THE WOOD-SORRELS (OXALIS)

These are recognized by the three heart-shaped segments in the leaf-blades, each one notched at the outer tip and appearing to be folded down the center. The names both refer to the sour taste of the foliage.

YELLOW WOOD-SORREL, O. STRICTA, is the most abundant and most variable species here. There are from five to ten half-inch flowers in a cluster. In fruit their stalks all extend outwards and upwards. May to October..... O. DILLENII, another of the several yellow wood-sorrels, has 2-foot stems that lean and usually bear three flowers each. In fruit the stalks bend down but the pods stand erect. May to October..... CREEPING LADY'S-SORREL, O. REPENS, takes root at the nodes. The flowers, about ¼ inch across, are yellow. Their stalks also bend down in fruiting. April to November..... VIOLET WOOD-SORREL, O. VIOLACEA, has leaves colored on the under surface and flowers with purple or violet petals; a breath of wind across a field of these plants turns it suddenly from green to crimson or violet. April to July.

THE GINSENG FAMILY – ARALIACEAE

Flowers in umbels; sepals mostly indistinct – merely a sort of rim; petals five, stamens five, styles two, three, or five; ovary inferior, fruit a berry or berry-like stone-fruit. Leaves divided.

ARALIA

This genus is distinguished by the way the leaf is divided two or more times into three or more segments, giving the effect of a leafy branch. The very small flowers of greenish-white are in numerous umbels.

WILD SARSAPARILLA, A. NUDICAULIS, has a single, much-divided leaf on an 8-16-inch stalk, and a shorter flowering stem growing from a rhizome. The flowers usually bear five styles, which are still present on the young fruits. The berries are nearly black. The aromatic roots yield a substitute for the pharmaceutical sarsaparilla. May to July..... BRISTLY SARSAPARILLA, A. HISPIDA, has bristles on the lower stem (thus made "hispid"). The leaf-segments are ovate; the umbels of flowers rise above them. June to August..... A. RACEMOSA has a branching stem 2–10 feet tall with the compact flower-clusters slightly taller. June to August.

THE GINSENGS (PANAX)

The ginsengs are easily distinguished from the species of *Aralia* by their leaves, which are on the stem in one circle, usually of three, each leaf palmately divided. White or greenish flowers are in a single simple umbel at the summit of the stem.

DWARF GINSENG or GROUND-NUT, P. TRIFOLIUS, is not more than 8 inches tall. The leaves, near the top of the stem, are divided into three or five stalkless segments. There are usually three styles. The berry is yellow. April to June..... GINSENG, P. QUINQUEFOLIUS, grows from root-tubers and stands to 2 feet high. Its five leaf-segments are stalked; its berry is bright red, and the flower usually has two styles. June and July.

xalis stricta *Johnson* Panax trifolius *Horne*

Aralia nudicaulis
Johnson

THE PARSLEY FAMILY – UMBELLIFERAE

Flowers mostly in umbels (*umbella:* "umbrella"), mostly compound (the flower-stalks, or rays, of the umbels bearing not single flowers but smaller umbels). Bracts (special leaves, in these genera smaller than the foliage leaves) forming an involucre in a circle just below the point where the flower-stalks join the stem. Flowers small, inconspicuous, but in most species numerous. Sepals likely five but sometimes so minute as to be apparently lacking. Petals five; stamens five. Ovary inferior, embedded in the stem below the sepals; styles two, rising in the center of the flower, at the base of each a sort of bulb which may be mistaken for an ovary. Fruit small and dry, in two halves attached to a central stalk, each half bearing lengthwise ribs or projecting flanges called wings. Leaves generally divided and often redivided to give a feathery effect. A conspicuous sheath at the base of the leaf-stalk, which embraces the stem where it is attached.

TAENIDIA

YELLOW PIMPERNEL, T. INTEGERRIMA, which grows in dry, open woods and on rocky hillsides, is easily recognized by the lack of teeth around the margins of the leaf-segments. It is a graceful plant usually between 2 and 3 feet tall. The flowers are in an umbel with no bracts. The fruit bears four lengthwise ribs on each side. May to July.

ZIZIA

While basal leaves on some species of *Zizia* may be divided or not, those on the stem are divided and redivided by threes (five segments very occasionally). The flowers, all yellow, are in umbels which lack bracts. The central flower of each cluster is without a stalk. The fruits are ribbed, not winged.

GOLDEN ALEXANDERS, Z. AUREA, has basal leaves divided like those on the stem. The rays of the umbel are mostly of the same length, and there may be up to twenty of them. April to June.

PASTINACA

Only one species occurs in the United States, and that one was brought from Europe as a food plant. It has now "escaped" to become a common weed.

PARSNIP, P. SATIVA, is a tall plant, up to 5 or 6 feet, spreading out many arms bearing numerous branches of yellow-flowered umbels, usually without bracts. The fruit is flat, its margins extending into thin wings. The leaves are pinnately divided into coarsely toothed and lobed segments. May to October.

MEADOW-PARSNIP (THASPIUM)

Stem-leaves on plants of *Thaspium* are divided into three or five segments, while in some species basal leaves are undivided.

T. TRIFOLIATUM closely resembles *Zizia*, but the basal leaves have ovate blades, usually indented at the base, on long stalks. Besides the usual yellow-flowered plant, there is a variety with purple-brown flowers. May to July.

Taenidia integerrima — *McDowell*

stinaca sativa — *Rhein*

Zizia aurea
Scribner

WATER-PENNYWORTS (HYDROCOTYLE)

The small roundish leaf-blades which rise a few inches above the mud or to the top of shallow water are the "pennies" which give these inconspicuous aquatic plants their name. The flowers, which have white or greenish petals, are minute. Their different forms of growth distinguish them. Both species shown here flower all summer.

H. UMBELLATA, as its name suggests, bears its flowers in umbels, generally just above the mat of foliage. At a central point each leaf is attached to its stalk, which grows about 6 inches upward from the plant's creeping stem. The leaf-blades vary from $\frac{1}{2}$ to 3 inches broad (averaging about an inch) and their margins are scalloped. The species is widespread in wet places.

H. AMERICANA has, if possible, even smaller flowers, almost stalkless, clustered in the axils of the leaves. The fruit, little more than $\frac{1}{16}$ inch broad, has wings on alternating ribs, which are enlarged. While the leaves are roundish in appearance, the stalk is attached at the end of a deep indentation. The plant is found in damp woods and meadows.

CRYPTOTAENIA

HONEWORT or WILD-CHERVIL, C. CANADENSIS, merits inclusion among wild flowers not because it is conspicuously attractive, but because it is so commonly seen in northern woodlands. The plant stands from 1 to 3 feet high bearing dark, thin leaves with blades consisting of three toothed, ovate segments. The tiny white flowers are in small umbels, the stalks of which are of different lengths. A compound umbel may contain no more than three stalks. The fruit, about $\frac{1}{4}$ inch long, is sometimes slightly curved. June to September.

THE SANICLES or BLACK SNAKEROOTS (SANICULA)

The species of *Sanicula* have leaves that distinguish them from most other umbellifers, being palmately divided into three or five more or less elliptic, sharply toothed segments. The flowers are inconspicuous, greenish, in umbels whose main stems (rays) are of different lengths. Some flowers are staminate only, some have both stamens and pistil; the staminate generally have longer stalks. The fruit bears hooked bristles. The species are widespread and the differences between them are minute.

S. GREGARIA and S. MARILANDICA have two styles, curving outward, to be seen on the fruit. In the former the leaves are divided into three or five segments. In the latter there are five segments but the two outer ones are generally so deeply cleft that there appear to be seven..... In S. TRIFOLIATA the fruits have a distinct beak formed by the five erect, pointed sepals..... In S. CANADENSIS neither sepals nor styles appear above the bristles. In general all our species flower in woods from May to July.

The name *Sanicula* is connected with the Latin *sanus*, "healthy," from a supposed power of healing wounds.

LILAEOPSIS

LILAEOPSIS CHINENSIS is a curious (though insignificant) plant that grows in mud along the coast of the New York area. It has no real leaves, only leaf-stalks. These are hollow cylinders with cross-partitions at intervals, making them somewhat resemble horsetails, a green plant below the rank of a flower-producer. The sections, however, are mostly only 1 or 2 inches long, the stalk itself rising vertically to $2\frac{1}{2}$ inches from the horizontal stem which takes root at the nodes. The umbels are all carried to about the same height, and bear just a few minute flowers. June to September.

Sanicula gregaria   *Johnson*

Hydrocotyle americana   *Rickett*

ptotaenia canadensis   *Rickett*

Hydrocotyle umbellata   *Uttal*

Members of the carrot family are so abundant and are all so very much alike, that it is difficult to distinguish them without the use of technical terminology. Little is done here, therefore, beyond the pointing out of a significant characteristic for each species named.

HERACLEUM

COW-PARSNIP or MASTERWORT, H. LANA-TUM, is a tall weed, up to 10 feet, with enormous leaves. June to August.

SWEET-CICELY (OSMORHIZA)

O. LONGISTYLIS grows up to 4 feet tall from a slender carrot-like root that smells of anise..... O. CLAYTONI has styles that do not exceed $\frac{1}{16}$ inch, even on the fruit. This plant grows from 1 to 3 feet tall and is more or less hairy all over.

WILD CARROT (DAUCUS)

QUEEN-ANNE'S-LACE or WILD CARROT, DAUCUS CAROTA, is an annoying weed that has beauty as a wild flower. The many delicate umbels of fine white flowers are set off by bracts which are divided into fine segments. Leaves, too, are lacelike. Distinctive is the flower of dark brownish-red in the center of many umbels. May to October.

CONIUM

POISON-HEMLOCK, C. MACULATUM, is supposedly the plant used for the execution of criminals in ancient Greece; it is deadly poisonous. June to August.

SIUM and OXYPOLIS

WATER-PARSNIP, SIUM SUAVE, has leaf-segments that are narrow and sharply toothed.

HOG-FENNEL, OXYPOLIS RIGIDIOR, is extremely variable in the character of its leaves, the segments ranging from $\frac{1}{3}$ inch to $1\frac{1}{2}$ inches wide and from being without teeth to being sharply and coarsely toothed.

PTILIMNIUM

MOCK BISHOP'S-WEED, PTILIMNIUM CAPIL-LACEUM, is a marshland plant that grows from 4 inches to 6 feet tall. The leaves are divided pinnately into hairlike ("capillaceous") segments. June to October.

ANGELICA

The large leaves are divided either in threes or pinnately, generally several times. The leaf-sheath may be as large as the blade.

A. VENENOSA has fine down on the stem..... A. LUCIDA is the one species whose fruits have thick, corky marginal extensions. Its leaf-segments are irregular in shape. The plant grows to 5 feet...... ALEXANDERS, A. ATROPURPUREA, is the tall, stout plant (to 10 feet) of which the stems and leaf-stalks were once used in place of celery. It is dangerous, however, because of its resemblance to the deadly *Cicuta maculata* (see below). In *Angelica* the veins run to the tips of the teeth of the leaf-segments.

CICUTA

SPOTTED COWBANE, CICUTA MACULATA, one of the water-hemlocks, is among the most poisonous plants of this country, roots and leaves alike being deadly. The segments of its pinnately divided leaves are narrow, widely spaced, and mostly marked by a few distinct, sharp, marginal teeth. *The veins run to the notches between the teeth.*

TORILIS

HEDGE-PARSLEY, TORILIS JAPONICA, has leaves mostly pinnately divided, the segments sharply toothed. The fruit is nearly egg-shaped and covered with hooked bristles.

CONIOSELINUM

HEMLOCK-PARSLEY, C. CHINENSE, grows from 4 inches to 5 feet tall, mostly in wet places and woods. The leaves are pinnately divided two or more times, the ultimate segments being mostly ovate and deeply pinnately cleft. July to September.

Osmorhiza longistylis   *Rickett*

Conium maculatum   *Rickett*

Heracleum lanatum   *Rickett*

Daucus carota   *Rickett*

Daucus carota   *Rickett*

THE PURSLANE FAMILY – PORTULACACEAE

Plants somewhat succulent. Sepals two, petals generally five, stamens five, ten, or more.

SPRING BEAUTIES (CLAYTONIA)

These delicate pink flowers are ornaments of open areas throughout spring.

C. VIRGINICA grows up to a foot tall, the stem rising from a subterranean corm. There are two narrow, thick leaves halfway up the stem, which ends in a succession of flowers. The five petals are pink with red veins, and the stamens have pink heads. The two sepals enclose the seed-pod. March to May.

PURSLANE (PORTULACA)

The purslanes have branched stems that in some lie on the ground. The one wild species in the east is native to Eurasia.

P. OLERACEA, a weed known as "pussley" to southern countryfolk, who cook it as "greens," is a prostrate plant with narrow, succulent leaves, broadest towards the tip. The small yellow flowers in the axils of leaves have two sepals, about five petals, and numerous stamens. June to November.

THE GERANIUM FAMILY – GERANIACEAE

Sepals five, petals five, stamens ten in two circles of five each (five sterile in *Erodium*); the mature pistil separating into five parts, each holding one seed which (except in *Erodium*) is lifted up by the curving of its part of the style, the "crane's-bill," which remains attached at the tip through its maturity. Leaves palmately lobed or cleft or pinnately divided.

THE WILD GERANIUMS or CRANE'S-BILLS (GERANIUM)

In America all have palmate leaves. There are some fifteen species here, nearly half of them around New York, but half of these introduced. (The house-plants known as geranium belong to the genus *Pelargonium* in this family, mostly from South Africa.)

G. MACULATUM is a familiar flower of spring and early summer with rose-purple petals from ½ to 1 inch long. It appears in both woods and meadows, the stem growing from a rhizome to a height of about 2 feet. Several long-stalked leaves rise from the base and a pair of short-stalked leaves from the stem itself, all the blades cleft palmately into five or seven generally straight-sided lobes. April to June.

G. BICKNELLII carries its rose-pink flowers on long stalks, mostly in pairs. Petals are less than half an inch long, only a trifle longer than the sepals. Stem and branches are hairy, with stalked glands among the hairs. Leaves, which are roundish in outline and 1–3 inches across, are deeply cleft and each part is lobed at least once again. The plants grow up to 20 inches tall, mostly in open woods and clearings, where they flower from May to September.

eranium molle   *McDowell*

Portulaca oleracea   *Horne*

laytonia virginica   *Elbert*

Geranium maculatum   *Gottscho*

GERANIUM (*continued*)

GERANIUM CAROLINIANUM, a plant of waste places and other dry areas, carries its pale pink flowers in a dense cluster at the top. The petals are less than $\frac{1}{2}$ inch long. It is a small bushy plant about 2 feet tall, with leaves palmately cleft into from five to nine narrow lobes, each lobe pinnately lobed or cleft. May to August.

HERB-ROBERT, G. ROBERTIANUM, was linked with many legends where it grew originally in England. Brought some time ago from that country to this, it is now well established in the wild throughout the northeastern quarter of the United States. Both plant and flower are slightly smaller than G. *maculatum*, and the flower-petals are more pink. The leaves appear to be divided palmately, but the end-segment is stalked and all the segments are themselves pinnately cleft. The flowers frequently appear in pairs. May to October.

Numerous other geraniums, both native and introduced, can be found in the wild, though not conspicuously. G. PUSILLUM, an Old-World species now established as a weed in fields, is a wide-spreading plant with branches up to 2 feet long and with leaves that are deeply cleft into from five to nine lobes which are themselves lobed at the end. The petals are red-violet and only $\frac{1}{8}$ inch long. The stamens number five instead of the usual ten. June to October..... G. DISSECTUM, an Old-World species, is a loosely branching plant somewhat resembling G. *bicknellii*. April to August..... G. SIBIRICUM is a widely branching plant with a weak stem to 40 inches long. The flowers, of lilac or white with violet markings, are scattered singly over the plant, the petals and sepals both about $\frac{1}{4}$ inch long. August, September..... G. PYRENAICUM grows to $2\frac{1}{2}$ feet tall and is bushy above. It has large rose-colored petals deeply notched. The leaves have a roundish outline but are cleft two-thirds of the way towards the base into from five to seven oblong lobes. Coming from Europe, the plant has established itself in waste places over here..... G. MOLLE is a downy plant called the dove's-foot crane's-bill. Its leaves are cleft to the middle and each segment has three lobes at its tip. The plant somewhat resembles G. *pyrenaicum*, but the petals of G. *molle*, $\frac{1}{4}$ inch long, are barely half the size..... G. PRATENSE, the common roadside or meadow crane's-bill of Europe, is occasionally seen here. It has woolly flower-stalks and deep blue-purple flowers.

STORK'S-BILL (ERODIUM)

As with the related genus *Geranium*, the names attached to this genus, both common and botanical, refer to the long bird's-beak which appears to be on the fruit. *Erodium*, however, is distinguished by the corkscrewlike twisting of the five "beaks."

ALFILARIA or FILAREE, E. CICUTARIUM, is the species best established from across the ocean. It grows largely in waste places, and its foliage often winters over as a rosette on the ground. The leaves are pinnately cleft and their segments pinnately divided. The flowers, which rise from the midst of these rosettes, at first only a few inches high, are rose-red or purple, $\frac{1}{2}$ inch across. Only five of their stamens bear pollen. March to November.

Geranium robertianum   *Gottscho*

Erodium cicutarium   *D. Richards*

Geranium carolinianum   *Allen*

THE LOOSESTRIFE FAMILY – LYTHRACEAE

Sepals and petals variable in number, from four to seven; stamens of the same number or twice as many (with some irregularity). The sepals and petals growing around a tubular or cup-shaped flower-base (receptacle), the stamens on its inner surface. Petals generally crimson or purple. Leaves usually narrow, mostly in pairs.

THE PURPLE LOOSESTRIFES (LYTHRUM)

Flowers of *Lythrum* have from four to seven sepals and petals, the stamens corresponding in number. In certain species there may be two or three types of flowers, differing in relative heights of stamens and pistil.

PURPLE LOOSESTRIFE, L. SALICARIA, is a beautiful weed of wet places, an immigrant from the Old World, up to 6 feet tall. The leaves, in pairs or threes or fours, are lanceolate and stalkless. The flowers are clustered in the upper axils, forming a spike at the top. June to September..... L. LINEARE grows up to 4 feet tall, principally in salt marshes. Its very narrow (linear) leaves come in pairs. The flowers, of white or pale purple, in the axils of the upper leaves, are of two types: with long stamens and short style or *vice versa*. July to September..... L. HYSSOPIFOLIA also grows in wet places, chiefly near the coast. It is a narrow-leaved plant about 2 feet tall. The pale purple flowers come singly or in pairs. June to September.

DECODON

WATER-WILLOW, DECODON VERTICILLATUS, has willow-like leaves and is found in water. The stems, up to 3 feet long, arch and often root at the tips. The leaves have short stalks and lanceolate blades, with flowers clustered in the upper axils. The base of the flower is bell-shaped. The petals are narrow and purplish-pink. July to September.

CUPHEA

CLAMMY WAXWEED, CUPHEA PETIOLATA, is covered with sticky hairs. Its paired leaves are lanceolate and have long stalks. The flowers grow singly or in pairs in the leaf-axils. The base of the flower is a diagonal tube with a saclike expansion on the upper side. On its rim are six reddish-purple petals of unequal size. The sepals are six triangular teeth. The plant stands generally less than 2 feet high. July to October.

MELASTOME FAMILY – MELASTOMATACEAE

One small genus of herbaceous plants reaches us from the tropics.

MEADOW-BEAUTIES (RHEXIA)

The parts of the flower are in fours, the sepals and petals seated on the rim of the tubular base of the flower. The pollen-bearing heads of the eight stamens are long, narrow, and of an upturned crescent shape. The pistil becomes enclosed in the enlarged flower-base. The leaves, in pairs, are toothed and generally have three main veins.

R. VIRGINICA shows its vivid pink flowers in wet sandy or peaty places. It has tubers on its roots. The stem, up to 2 feet tall, has four thin lengthwise "wings." The leaves are ovate, without stalks. July to September.

caea lutetiana *Scribner*

Lythrum salicaria *Gottscho*

Rhexia virginica *Miller*

Decodon verticillatus *Elbert*

EVENING-PRIMROSE FAMILY – ONAGRACEAE

Petals generally four and stamens eight (with variations); sepals generally four, united into a tube which surmounts the inferior ovary. The fruit a dry pod which splits into four parts.

CIRCAEA

This genus is unique in having only two sepals, two cleft petals which give the impression of four, and two stamens. The fruit is covered with bristles.

ENCHANTER'S NIGHTSHADE, C. LUTETIANA, is a woodland plant growing from 8 inches to 3 feet tall. The leaf-blades, 1–6 inches long, have wavy margins and a tapering point. The numerous small white flowers are widely spaced in an erect raceme. June to August..... C. ALPINA grows not over a foot tall and has coarsely toothed leaves about 2 inches long with an abrupt point. The flowers are closely clustered but few in number. June to September.

EVENING-PRIMROSES and SUNDROPS (OENOTHERA)

Much variation, even within species, exists in this large genus. The general pattern shows an inferior ovary carrying a long tube above it. Four sepals and four petals (yellow on the species in the New York City area) are borne on the rim of this tube, the narrow sepals folding back against it as the flower opens, the wide petals spreading out fairly flat. There are eight stamens and, in our local species, four stigmas, cross-like, at the tip of the style. The fruit-pod is often useful in identifying species. The leaves, borne singly, are mostly narrow. The fragrant flowers of the evening-primroses themselves attract night-flying insects for pollination. The sundrops are day-bloomers.

COMMON EVENING-PRIMROSE, O. BIENNIS, is the most frequently seen. The petals are not more than an inch long; the stem, 3–6 feet tall, is often red; leaves and flowers are often crowded in the raceme, gland-tipped hairs among them. June to October.

O. PARVIFLORA is similar to O. *biennis* but slightly smaller. Stem, leaves, and flower-buds may be either smooth or hairy. Small projections behind the tips of the sepals are spread apart in the bud. July to October.

O. LACINIATA has distinctive leaves that are mostly pinnately lobed and cleft, with small flowers growing from the upper axils. The petals, which turn reddish as they age, are $\frac{1}{4}$–$\frac{3}{4}$ inch long. The seed-pod is narrow and usually slightly curved. The plant is generally low with wide-spreading branches, but may reach 2 feet. May to October.

SUNDROPS, O. FRUTICOSA, may be erect and over 3 feet tall or branched and spreading, forming bushes of less than 1 foot. The plant usually has short white hairs lying flat or longer hairs extending outward. The leaves are narrow and lanceolate. The petals are wide and $\frac{1}{2}$–1 inch long. The pod is widest near the summit, tapering down to a sort of stalk, with four sharp angles. May to August..... O. TETRAGONA is similar but variable, and with gland-tipped hairs on the tube of the flower. The seed-pod is oblong and four-angled and it tapers sharply to its stalk. Plant often seen in cultivation. June to August..... O. PERENNIS, growing to 2 feet tall, droops the tip of its flower-cluster before all the buds are open. The petals are about $\frac{1}{3}$ inch long. The seed-pod tapers downward and has four narrow wings. The leaves are either elliptic or wider towards the tip. Open areas, May to August.

Oenothera parviflora   *Johnson*

Oenothera fruticosa   *Gottscho*

Oenothera biennis   *Gottscho*

Oenothera perennis   *Scribner*

Oenothera laciniata   *Murray*

THE PRIMROSE-WILLOWS (LUDWIGIA)

The plants of *Ludwigia* grow in water or wet places. Most have leaves borne singly and without teeth. The mainly yellow flowers rise alone in the leaf-axils or at the tip of the stem. A number of species lack petals; others have four or five. The number of stamens varies from four to ten – as many as the petals or twice as many.

L. ALTERNIFOLIA has sepals and petals about $\frac{1}{3}$ inch long, the petals yellow. The fruit is almost a cube, with four sharp angles. The plant grows erect, from 1 to 4 feet tall, and it is smooth or nearly so. June to August..... Few other species can be found in the New York City area..... L. PALUSTRIS has a floating or creeping stem bearing paired, stalked leaves with lanceolate or elliptic blades and minute flowers. The fruit is nearly cylindric and marked with four lengthwise green stripes. June to September..... L. SPHAERO-CARPA has smooth stems up to 3 feet tall with narrow lance-shaped leaves borne singly. Minute petals may be present. The fruit (*-carpa*) is nearly spherical (*sphaero-*) and very finely downy. July to September.

WILLOW-HERBS and FIREWEEDS (EPILOBIUM)

This essentially northern genus contains flowers that vary greatly in size, but their pattern changes little. The four petals of pink, purplish, or white are notched in all but the plant called fireweed. They are seated on a long receptacle within which is the inferior ovary – the whole simulating a flower-stalk. There is no appreciable floral tube above the ovary. The fruit is a slender pod, its seeds each fitted with a tuft of hairs. All the species flower from June or July until September.

FIREWEED, E. ANGUSTIFOLIUM, was so named because of its appearance in burned-over land, not excepting the bombed parts of London after World War II. It is a tall plant (to 6 feet or more) bearing vivid spires of rose-magenta flowers. Unopened buds at the tip point downward, but rise as they expand. The stamens emerge first, the style with its four stigmas projecting after pollen has been shed. The petals are about $\frac{1}{2}$ inch long. This is a circumpolar plant.

HAIRY WILLOW-HERB, E. HIRSUTUM, an immigrant from the Old World, is a much-branched, bushy plant from 2 to 7 feet tall. The stem and leaves are hairy, and toothed along the edges. The flowers are in several racemes. They are purplish-red and smaller than those of fireweed, the petals rarely exceeding $\frac{2}{3}$ inch.

E. LEPTOPHYLLUM grows from 8 inches to 4 feet tall. Its stem and leaves are hoary with dense, short, curved hairs. The leaves are very narrow – not more than $\frac{1}{8}$ inch wide. The flowers are pink or white, the petals $\frac{1}{8}$–$\frac{1}{4}$ inch long.

E. COLORATUM, so called from the red tone of the mature stem, is a very bushy plant up to 3 feet tall, very finely downy all over. Even the seeds are covered with white hairs. The leaves are very narrow. The pink or white flowers have petals only $\frac{1}{8}$ inch long. The receptacle below the petals forms a slim pod up to 2 inches long. There are so many of these that the plant seems full of branches that have no leaves..... E. PALUSTRE, a resident of bogs, has very narrow leaves on a stem 4–16 inches tall, which bears curved hairs. There is often only one flower, at the tip of the stem; but there may be several. The petals, $\frac{1}{4}$–$\frac{1}{2}$ inch long, vary greatly in color from violet through pink to white..... E. STRICTUM, also a bog-dweller, has a stem 1–2 feet tall covered with a grayish down; it is not much branched. The leaves are narrowly lanceolate. The pink petals are $\frac{1}{4}$–$\frac{2}{3}$ inch long.

pilobium hirsutum   *J. Smith*

Epilobium angustifolium   *Myrick*

Ludwigia alternifolia   *Scribner*

Epilobium coloratum   *Gottscho*

Epilobium leptophyllum   *Elbert*

THE SHINLEAF FAMILY – PYROLACEAE

Sepals generally five, petals five, stamens ten, discharging their pollen through tubes in the end, five chambers in the ovary. Plants small, mostly woodland dwellers, some evergreen, some without green coloring. Leaves undivided. Family often merged with the heath family (*Ericaceae*).

PIPSISSEWA (CHIMAPHILA)

Plants of *Chimaphila* grow from underground stems (rhizomes) and bear leaves which last all winter. At all seasons they are refreshing to chew. The flowers are pink or white. The style on the pistil is very short and bears a round stigma.

"SPOTTED" PIPSISSEWA, C. MACULATA, has no spots. The leaves are irregularly striped with white; they are lanceolate and sharp-pointed, with teeth at wide intervals on the margin. The flower is nearly an inch across, white and fragrant; several hang face down at the ends of their stalks, which spread from the tip of the stem, about 5 inches tall. June to August.

PRINCE'S-PINE or PIPSISSEWA, C. UMBELLATA, has white or pale pink flowers about ¾ inch across. The leaves have no white marks and tend to be broader than those of C. *maculata* and wider in their outer half; they are sharply toothed all around. June to August.

SHINLEAF (PYROLA)

The name is said to be derived from an early use of the leaves in making plasters for injured shins! The leaves, generally rather dark green and lasting through the winter, are all at or near the base of the stem. The flowers are in the long cluster called a raceme.

P. ELLIPTICA is probably our commonest shinleaf. The leaf-blades are dull green, broadly elliptic, on short stalks. The stem rises from 6 to 12 inches above the leaves. The ivory-white petals are more than four times as long as the small teeth of the calyx. June to August.

P. ROTUNDIFOLIA is so similar to *P. elliptica* that one species is perhaps a form of the other. The supposedly round leaf-blades for which *P. rotundifolia* has been named may be elliptic. The flowers are smaller, but any other difference is scarcely noticeable. June to August..... ONE-SIDED PYROLA, P. SECUNDA, has greenish-yellow petals, drawn together at their tips rather than expanded, the flowers pendent and all directed to one side of the stem, which is about 8 inches tall. The shining leaf-blades, on short stalks at the base of the plant, are elliptic or ovate, toothed or scalloped. June to August..... P. VIRENS may have thick, broad leaf-blades with round ends, on long stalks, or it may lack leaves, then depending on matter in the soil for its nutrition or being parasitic on the roots of other plants. The stem, which bears greenish flowers, is from 3 to 12 inches tall. The style is directed downward, with its tip curved upward. It thrives best in coniferous woods, flowering from June to August.

imaphila umbellata *Ryker* Pyrola elliptica *Elbert*

imaphila maculata *Gottscho*

Pyrola rotundifolia *Johnson*

INDIAN-PIPE and PINESAP (MONOTROPA)

Certain genera of the shinleaf family develop no green leaves, but are instead dependent for their nourishment and growth upon organic matter that has been built up by other plants in the soil or in forest litter. Their fleshy stems may be white, tawny, or red. Their leaves are merely scales of similar color. Their flowers, too, have much the same coloring and texture. The number of sepals, petals, and stamens varies. The flower hangs head down, but as the fruit develops the stem straightens so that the tip eventually points upward.

INDIAN-PIPE or CORPSE-PLANT, M. UNIFLORA, is generally white, turning black as the fruit ripens. The stem is from 2 to 12 inches tall, and bears one white flower. June to September. A pink form flowers a little later.

PINESAP or FALSE BEECH-DROPS, M. HYPOPITHYS, is tawny, yellow, or red. The stem stands from 4 to 16 inches tall and bears several flowers at its tip. June to October.

THE CASSIA FAMILY – CAESALPINIACEAE

Closely related to the bean family (pages 152–166) through the structure of the seed-pod, and by some botanists united with it, though quite different in the flower's appearance. Largely a family of woody plants – including the redbud and the honey-locust tree – and, except for these, inhabiting mainly tropical regions. *Cassia* is the only genus of concern to us here.

SENNA (CASSIA)

Five sepals, scarcely joined at the base; five petals, always yellow in our species, generally slightly dissimilar in shape but all spread outwards, not assembled like a bean-flower; five or ten stamens, commonly unequal in length and some at times forming no pollen; the ovary like a many-seeded pea- or bean-pod, in some species with cross-partitions: these are the marks of *Cassia* flowers. The leaves are all evenly pinnate – that is, with no terminal segment – and in some species they fold together at night.

PARTRIDGE-PEA, C. FASCICULATA, which grows up to 3 feet tall, bears flowers an inch or more across, many with a purple spot at the base of two or three of its petals. Four of the ten stamens have yellow heads, the others purple. The leaf-segments, less than 1 inch long, number from ten to fifteen pairs; under certain conditions they fold at night. Dry, sandy soil, July to September. .... WILD SENSITIVE-PLANT, C. NICTITANS, is similar but with flowers only $\frac{1}{4}$ inch across, five stamens, and ten to twenty pairs of leaf-segments, closing at night..... WILD SENNA, C. MARILANDICA, is a roadside plant with small yellow flowers emerging from the axils of the leaves. The foliage consists of from three to six pairs of leaf-segments up to 3 inches long. The seed-pods are $2–3\frac{1}{2}$ inches long, slightly curved, and divided into sections much shorter than they are broad. The seeds inside are twice as long as they are thick. July and August.

Monotropa uniflora *Rickett*

notropa hypopithys *Horne*

notropa hypopithys *Rickett*

Pyrola secunda *Scribner*

THE BEAN FAMILY – FABACEAE

Flowers like those of the sweet-pea, with five joined sepals, five petals; one petal, the "standard," more or less erect, two "wings" at the side, a "keel" formed of two petals joined. Ten stamens and pistil in the keel. Fruit a pod splitting into two halves. Leaves generally divided, with a pair of stipules at the base of the stalk.

THE VETCHES (VICIA)

Flowers of vetches are mainly some shade of purple, commonly in a raceme. Their leaves are pinnately divided, with the terminal segments replaced by tendrils.

COMMON VETCH, V. ANGUSTIFOLIA, is one of our few native species. It has up to five pairs of leaf-segments, besides the tendrils, with single, purple, half-inch flowers in the leaf-axils, blooming from midsummer through October.

HAIRY WINTER VETCH, V. VILLOSA, is covered with soft hairs (it is "villous"). The leaves have from five to ten pairs of segments, fairly widely spaced. The flowers, each one nearly an inch long, in a raceme, are violet and white. The flower-stalk is not attached at the end of the calyx, as in other species, but instead, with the flower facing sideways, it is attached under the bulge of the calyx. This Old-World species has spread throughout most of the United States. May to October.

COW VETCH or CANADA-PEA, V. CRACCA, appears with dense, one-sided racemes of flowers, usually purple (otherwise blue or white). Each flower, up to $\frac{1}{2}$ inch long, points slightly downward. The leaves at the base of these racemes, and about two-thirds as long, have from eight to twelve pairs of leaf-segments, besides tendrils at the tip. The pod becomes about an inch long. The stem is sometimes smooth, sometimes

clothed with short, silky hairs that may lie flat. May to August..... V. HIRSUTA and V. TETRASPERMA are other Old-World species that have become naturalized. V. hirsuta has flowers about $\frac{3}{16}$ inch long, three to six growing together; each pod bears two seeds. V. tetrasperma has flowers measuring about $\frac{5}{16}$ inch, not more than two together and the pods four-seeded.

MILK-PEAS (GALACTIA)

This genus is confusingly named because none of the species has milky juice. They are all low, trailing plants with three segments to the leaves.

G. REGULARIS has purplish flowers slightly under 1 inch long in a small, dense raceme. June to August..... G. VOLUBILIS has hairy stems much intertwined. The small pinkish flowers (under $\frac{1}{2}$ inch) are in a long, loose raceme. The pods may measure 2 inches. July and August.

CLITORIA

BUTTERFLY-PEA, C. MARIANA, has handsome large flowers which vary from pinkish-lavender to blue. They are commonly upside down and have a standard nearly 2 inches long. The three ovate leaf-segments, also to 2 inches long, are pinnately arranged. The plant is low and generally twining. June to August.

Galactia regularis   *Uttal*

Vicia villosa   *Johnson*

Vicia angustifolia   *Elbert*

Vicia cracca   *Johnson*

LATHYRUS

The sweet-pea of our gardens comes from *Lathyrus*, but the local wild species are far different. They resemble plants in *Vicia* (page 152), but the stipules, leaf-segments, and flowers are in general larger and the flowers in each raceme are fewer. The hairs on the style are along the upper side.

BEACH-PEA, L. MARITIMUS, highly variable, can be found on coasts around the world. Its flowers, about 1 inch long, are bluish, pinkish, or purple, or a combination with white. From three to ten grow together in a long-stalked cluster. The leaves have from four to twelve segments 1–2 inches long and about half as wide, besides tendrils at the tip. The two basal lobes of the stipules are almost as large as the leaf-segments. June to August..... L. PALUSTRIS is also a variable species growing in damp areas. Its climbing stems, to 4 feet long, often have thin "winged" edges. The leaves have from four to ten narrow segments to 3 inches long. Several reddish-purple flowers, from ½ to 1 inch long, bloom at the end of a long stalk. June to September.

AMPHICARPAEA

There is but one species outside of Asia.

HOG-PEANUT, A. BRACTEATA, has stems up to a yard long which twine around the stems of other plants. Downward-pointing hairs, often reddish, cover stems, leaf-stalks, and the midrib of each of the three leaf-segments. (Two of these pointed, ovate segments, from two different leaves, may be seen in the illustration.) Up to fifteen slender, pale purple flowers, ½ inch long or more, are in a raceme. The calyx has only four teeth. The two halves of the flat seed-pods coil after opening. At the base of the plant, at ground level, are succulent, round, one-seeded pods which do not open. These are the "peanuts." They are developed at the base of the plant from flowers that lack petals. August and September.

APIOS

Except for one little-known southern vine, *Apios* has but one species in North America.

GROUND-NUT, A. AMERICANA, has an underground stem (rhizome) which is thickened at intervals to form small, edible tubers. Above-ground the slender stem twines and climbs. The leaves are pinnately divided, usually into seven or nine narrow segments. The half-inch flowers, a rich purplish-brown, highly scented, are in a dense, round-topped raceme. July to September.

STROPHOSTYLES

These so-called wild-beans are not true beans (*Phaseolus*), though they resemble them. The leaves are similar but smaller, and the two halves of the seed-pod twist when ripe. Two or more pale purplish-pink flowers about ½ inch broad and long, are close together at the tip of a long stalk.

S. HELVOLA may have three lobes on some of its leaf-segments, the largest of which may be 2½ inches long. June to October..... S. UMBELLATA has narrower, unlobed leaf-segments, not more than 2 inches long. It takes to sandy areas. July to October.

PHASEOLUS

The genus *Phaseolus*, which provides the beans that reach our dining tables, also furnishes one wild species in this part of North America.

WILD BEAN, P. POLYSTACHIOS, may twine with its stem or merely trail. Its leaves, up to 4 inches long, are pinnately divided into three ovate or roundish segments. The pale purple flowers, about ½ inch long, are strung out loosely on a long stem. The keel in each (with the style inside) is coiled at the end. The two halves of the pod coil after they separate. July to September.

pios americana   *Johnson*

Amphicarpaea bracteata   *Rickett*

thyrus maritimus   *Johnson*

Strophostyles helvola   *D. Richards*

FALSE INDIGO (BAPTISIA)

Plants tall, widely branched, and bushy-appearing, growing from horizontal underground stems (rhizomes). Leaves divided palmately into three segments, generally turning black as they wither or dry. Flowers in racemes; pods thick and rather woody and marked by both a stalk and a beak.

B. TINCTORIA, known also as WILD-INDIGO and RATTLEWEED, may grow up to 3 feet tall, inhabiting dry soil and bearing an abundance of small leaves and yellow flowers. The wedge-shaped leaf-segments seldom reach an inch in length and the flowers and pods only about ½ inch. The flowers are loosely arranged. The ripe pods, small though they may be, are sometimes used as rattles. May to September.

In colonial days the plants were often cultivated for their dyeing qualities. The dye obtained from them, however, was not as good as true indigo, obtained from Asian and tropical American species of *Indigofera* in the same family.

LUPINE (LUPINUS)

Only one wild species of *Lupinus* reaches this part of the northeast. (The garden lupines are mostly hybrids.) Lupine leaves are palmately divided into narrow segments. The flowers are in a tall raceme.

WILD LUPINE, L. PERENNIS, grows up to 2 feet tall. The leaves each have from seven to eleven somewhat elliptic segments about 2 inches long in a circle at the tip of the leaf-stalk. The flowers, in racemes from 3 to 12 inches tall, are generally purplish-blue, though white and pink forms occur. April to July.

RATTLEBOX (CROTALARIA)

Distinguished in the bean family by leaves that blacken on drying. Yellow flowers are carried in racemes. The pods are large and the seeds inside are loose when dry.

C. SAGITTALIS can be recognized by its stipules, which form an arrowhead pointing downward from the base of each leaf. The plant is bushy, up to 16 inches tall, and hairy. The leaves are mostly lance-shaped but blunt-tipped. June to September.

THE CLOVERS (TRIFOLIUM)

Some kinds of clover are familiar to nearly everyone, for they are seen in lawns, in fields, and along roadsides. Their flowers are in heads, mostly roundish, sometimes cylindric. The uppermost petal, the standard, does not stand erect like that of a sweet-pea, but is folded over the wings and keel. The petals of many species remain attached even as they wither. The pods are very short, mostly hidden by the calyx and whatever remains of the corolla. Their leaves are divided, generally palmately, into three segments more or less toothed on their edges.

We will first consider two species whose flower-heads are cylindric. The remainder in our area have their flowers in the more familiar roundish heads.

RABBIT-FOOT CLOVER, T. ARVENSE, is a softly hairy plant generally about a foot tall. The leaf-segments are narrow, and toothed only near their tips. The heads are cylindric, up to nearly 2 inches long. The sepals are beset with long hairs which conceal the small petals, giving a furry effect to the whole cluster. May to October.

CRIMSON CLOVER, T. INCARNATUM, is readily distinguished by the vivid color of its flowers. The plant is softly downy. The flower-heads, which are bright red, are ovate in outline or cylindric. The flowers are about ½ inch long. May to July. This species comes from Europe, is planted here, and escapes from gardens.

aptisia tinctoria *Rickett*   Lupinus perennis *Johnson*

Trifolium incarnatum *Phelps*

rifolium arvense *Gottscho*

TRIFOLIUM (*continued*)

TRIFOLIUM PRATENSE is the familiar "red" clover of fields and roadsides, originally from Europe, extensively planted for hay and forage, and widely escaped. The plants may grow up to nearly 3 feet tall, the lower leaves with long stalks. The three leaf-segments, generally at least an inch long and covered with short, soft hairs, are each marked with a light-colored V, pointing toward the tip. The purplish-pink flowers, in ovoid heads an inch or more long, are pleasantly fragrant. May to September.

WHITE CLOVER, T. REPENS, is the common clover that creeps through lawns, blooming steadily all summer. Its main stem lies flat on the ground, sending up long-stalked, erect leaves. Branches in the axils of some of these are each tipped by a head of flowers. The leaf-segments are broadly elliptic and toothed. The flowers, less than ½ inch long, turn from white to pinkish-brown as they turn downward with age.

ALSIKE, T. HYBRIDUM (which is not really a hybrid), has similar-appearing heads, averaging ¾ inch in diameter, except that the flowers are pink or pink-and-white, soon turning brown. They may grow 2 or 3 feet tall, rising well above the leaves. The leaf-segments, usually broadly elliptic and toothed, may be 2 inches long. This clover also has escaped to fields and roadsides after having been introduced from Europe and planted here for forage. May to October.

YELLOW CLOVER, YELLOW TREFOIL, or HOP CLOVER, T. AUREUM, has small yellow flowers in somewhat elongate heads, three-eighths to three-quarters inch long. The petals are marked with fine lines; they turn brown as they age. The plants are erect and branching and grow up to 18 inches tall. The leaves have very short stalks; their three segments, each about ½ inch long, have none. May to September. By some botanists this naturalized European plant is called *T. agrarium*..... LESSER YELLOW TREFOIL, T. DUBIUM, is a somewhat similar yellow-flowered, branching, but trailing plant. The individual flowers and flower-heads are both about half the size as those in the erect species (*T. aureum*). In the leaves, the terminal segment has a short stalk, which distinguishes the species. This plant too comes from Europe and has become widespread in waste places in the United States. April to October.

Trifolium repens   *Scribner*

Trifolium aureum   *Johnson*

Trifolium hybridum   *Gottscho*

Trifolium pratense   *Gottscho*

THE SWEET-CLOVERS
(MELILOTUS)

The sweet-clovers can be identified by their fragrance alone. Even the uninjured masses of foliage along roadsides give off, in hot sunlight, the odor of very sweet new-mown hay; this is still more intense when the plants are crushed or dried. The plants have scant resemblance to the true clovers (*Trifolium*). They are tall and very bushy. The leaves are pinnately divided into three. The small flowers are in numerous spikes which grow from the leaf-axils. These plants are naturalized from the Old World. Both species continue in flower all summer and last until October.

WHITE SWEET-CLOVER, M. ALBUS, is a tall plant, sometimes up to 10 feet, with small leaves and flowers. Leaf-segments, toothed only in the outer half, are about an inch long; the white flowers, in long, slender spikes, barely ¼ inch. These are plants of roadsides and waste areas.

YELLOW SWEET-CLOVER, M. OFFICINALIS, is similar to the white, but about half as tall and with bright-yellow flowers. This too is widely distributed in waste lands. Originally, in Europe, it was used medicinally and for flavoring.

PENCIL-FLOWER
(STYLOSANTHES)

One species of *Stylosanthes* occurs in our range; one grows farther south and several more are in tropical regions.

S. BIFLORA, like others in the group, has a tube which carries yellow or orange petals at its tip and the pistil within it. This tube is the "pencil" of the name. The plant stands from 6 inches to nearly 2 feet high. The three leaf-segments, to 1½ inches long, are pinnately arranged, the terminal one having a longer stalk than the other two. They are generally lance-shaped with a minute spine at the tip. The stalks of the uppermost leaves, which are crowded around the flowers, are surrounded at their base by small bristly tubes. It flowers from June to September.

MEDICAGO

The genus *Medicago* includes alfalfa, a bushy plant with bluish-purple flowers, and other species which have yellow flowers.

BLACK MEDICK or NONESUCH, M. LUPULINA, has tiny yellow flowers crowded in almost round heads, borne on stems that lie flat on the ground, more than a foot in length. The broad leaf-segments are widest near their tips, which are blunt. The flower's five calyx-teeth are all alike. Its seed-pods coil and turn black when they ripen. This is a weed which seems to flower whenever snow is not on the ground..... ALFALFA or LUCERNE, M. SATIVA, has stems which branch and form a bush up to 3 feet tall. The leaf-segments are narrow, toothed mostly at the end, which is blunt. The flowers are blue-purple, in short racemes or heads, less than ½ inch long. May to October. A valuable crop-plant, naturalized along roadsides.

Melilotus albus   *Scribner*   Stylosanthes biflora   *Horst*

Medicago lupulina   *Rickett*

Melilotus officinalis   *Johnson*

THE TICK-TREFOILS
(DESMODIUM)

The weedy plants that cover one's clothing with small, flat, bristly triangles or ovals in late summer and fall are the tick-trefoils (*Desmodium*). Each "tick" is a joint of the seed-pod. The leaves are in three segments (trefoil), the terminal one with a noticeable stalk. The small flowers, characteristic of the bean family, are all so much alike that many different species can be distinguished most easily by the shape of the pods' joints. Most species flower in July and August.

D. CANADENSE is a decorative species with from one to several stems up to 4 feet tall and many rose-purple flowers branching out widely at the summit. The leaf-segments are relatively narrow and are densely downy on the lower side. The joints of the pod are curved below, less sharply so above, and have a relatively wide connection..... D. RIGIDUM has an erect and finely downy stem. The leaves are short-stalked, with thick, ovate segments, softly hairy especially on the lower surface. The flowers are pale pink or almost white. The pods' joints are almost semicircular below, barely arched across the top..... D. VIRIDIFLORUM has flowers which are pink at first, then turn green. The plant is rather velvety. The leaf-segments are broadly ovate. Lower points of pod-joints are rounded.

D. NUDIFLORUM has flowers on a leafless stem growing directly from the ground. Leaves on most plants branch out on separate stems below them. The seed-pods are triangular, connected only at the top.

D. PANICULATUM has leaf-segments barely ½ inch wide – the narrowest of all. Plants are about 2 feet tall with flowers sparsely arranged. The pod-joints are slightly curved below, even less so above.

D. MARILANDICUM is a rather smooth plant, about 3 feet tall, the leaves slightly downy on the lower surface, the segments nearly round. The pod-joints are round on the lower edge, slightly arched across the top. .... D. CILIARE has small, blunt, ovate leaf-segments, the leaf on a stalk less than ½ inch long. The pod-joints are curved on both edges, but the divisions are not deeply indented from the top..... D. SESSILIFOLIUM has a leaf with almost no stalk and extremely narrow segments, whitish on the lower surface. The plant, hairy in all its parts, may grow to more than 40 inches, bearing panicles of lavender or pinkish flowers. The pod-joints are round on both edges.

D. ROTUNDIFOLIUM has almost round leaf-segments. Both stem and leaves are downy and the stem lies on the ground. The pods have from four to six joints averaging ¼ inch long and slightly less in width. These plants bear purple flowers into September.

D. CANESCENS has seed-pods with up to six joints which are joined about half their width and more deeply curved below. The stems are hairy. The terminal leaf-segment is from 2 to 5 inches long and ovate. The flowers are at first pinkish, then green..... D. CUSPIDATUM stands up to 3 feet tall but its flowers are rather sparse. The leaf-segments are generally ovate, tapering to a sharp point. The joints of the seed-pod tend to be angled below and slightly curved above.

D. GLABELLUM and D. DILLENII are difficult to tell apart: Both have ovate or elliptic leaf-segments and somewhat triangular joints to the pods, a sharper angle in the pods of *D. glabellum*. Their stems may sprawl or may grow up to more than 4 feet tall. Leaves and stems on both are slightly downy.

D. LAEVIGATUM grows up to 4 feet tall, with deep rose to purple flowers. Most stems are smooth, the leaf-segments ovate. The pods have joints which are slightly angled on the upper margin, sharply so below.

Desmodium canadense *Gottscho*

smodium nudiflorum *Rickett*

Desmodium nudiflorum *Johnson*

THE BUSH-CLOVERS
(LESPEDEZA)

The bush-clovers bear little resemblance to the true clovers, beyond details of individual flowers. Though a few species creep, most are rather tall, bushy-appearing plants. The three leaf-segments are essentially blunt-tipped and relatively narrow. The stalk on the middle segment is generally short, but on the leaf itself (the three segments together) in nearly all species it is long. The plants are mostly found in dry open places or in light woods, flowering over a long season. The flowers may be pink, lavender, yellow, ivory, or a combination of colors, and they occur in heads, spikes, or racemes or singly in leaf-axils. The roundish pods contain but a single seed. Some species form additional pods in flowers that never open.

L. VIRGINICA. The lavender flowers of *L. virginica* are crowded on very short branches in the upper leaf-axils of this 1–4-foot plant. The leaves are also crowded, with long stalks to bear the three narrow segments. July to September..... L. SIMULATA, which closely resembles this species, is undoubtedly a hybrid between this and another, perhaps L. INTERMEDIA, which is also similar, but has longer and broader leaf-segments and longer flowering branches. Like *L. virginica*, this has very short calyx-lobes (barely ⅛ inch)..... L. NUTTALLII grows from 2 to 4 feet tall, with a hairy stem. The leaf-stalk is fairly long; the leaf-segments are elliptic. The flowers (pink or purple) are crowded in a cluster on a stalk longer than the adjacent leaf. August to October. This species is known to hybridize with several others, creating considerable variation within the genus..... L. VIOLACEA has a stem from 8 inches to nearly 3 feet tall, with spreading branches. The leaves are distinctive: the three leaf-segments are elliptic, scarcely 2 inches long and half as broad; on the branches they are often much smaller than on the main stem. The flowers are purple, in small, rather loose clusters on long stalks.

July to September..... L. STUEVEI is from 1 to 4 feet tall, downy all over. The leaves are crowded, with three elliptic segments on a short leaf-stalk. The purple flowers are in dense heads seated in the leaf-axils. August and September.

L. PROCUMBENS is a softly hairy creeping plant with upright branches bearing clusters of purple flowers on long stalks. The leaf-segments, scarcely 1 inch long, are about ⅛ inch wide – one variety narrower. August to October..... L. REPENS is much like *L. procumbens* but has rounder leaf-segments, usually smooth, only a bit of silkiness sometimes on the lower surface. May to September.

L. CAPITATA, from 2 to 4 feet tall, carries dense heads of ivory-colored flowers, each with a purple spot at the base of the standard, in the axils of the upper leaves. The hairy calyx, up to ½ inch long, conceals the seed-pod after the petals fall. Flowers that never open are hidden among the others. The leaves are on short stalks; the leaf-segments narrow and rather thick. This species also hybridizes widely, creating numerous varieties. July to September.

L. HIRTA, up to 5 feet tall, has dense heads of yellowish-white flowers on long stalks in the upper leaf-axils. The standard of the flower is purple at the base. The leaf-segments are typically broad and the leaf-stalk is short. The seed-pod is about the length of the calyx, which surrounds it. July to October..... L. ANGUSTIFOLIA is similar but its leaf-segments are only about ¼ inch wide. It grows mainly in sandy coastal areas. August and September.

AMORPHA

FALSE INDIGO, A. FRUTICOSA, is a very tall shrubby plant. The leaves have up to 35 inch-long segments. Its purple flowers, in long, dense, tapering spikes, have only one petal, the standard. May and June.

spedeza virginica *Ryker*

Lespedeza procumbens *Clewell*

pedeza hirta *Rhein*

Lespedeza capitata *Gottscho*

CORONILLA

CROWN-VETCH, C. VARIA, is a tall bushy plant with leaves divided pinnately into many segments, and long-stalked clusters (umbels) of small pink pea-flowers. May to September.

LOTUS

BIRD'S-FOOT TREFOIL, L. CORNICULATUS, has five rather than three segments to its leaves, as its name ("trefoil") implies. The flowers are deep yellow, sometimes reddish. June to September.

TOUCH-ME-NOT FAMILY (BALSAMINACEAE)

The *Balsaminaceae* are represented in our area by only two species.

IMPATIENS

ORANGE TOUCH-ME-NOT or JEWELWEED, I. CAPENSIS, has a flower hanging from a slender stalk and consisting mostly of a large, saclike, orange sepal, besides three orange petals. This showy sepal ends in a small spur which bends sharply forward. June to September. YELLOW TOUCH-ME-NOT, I. PALLIDA, differs in its yellow color, and its spur bends down at a right angle.

THE VIOLET FAMILY – VIOLACEAE

Except for one green-flowered genus (*Hybanthus*), the only members of the violet family in America are the violets themselves.

THE VIOLETS (VIOLA)

The flowers of the violets have a flat lower petal which provides a landing-place for insects, two side petals or "wings," and two upper petals. The lower petal is generally prolonged backwards into a hollow sac or tube, a "spur." The five stamens closely surround the pistil, generally leaving only the short style and stigma visible. The two lower stamens bear nectaries that extend into the spur and that exude nectar. The arrangement favors cross-fertilization. Many violets also form flowers that fertilize themselves without opening. The fruit is a capsule which splits into three parts, each bearing a row of seeds.

All the violets are spring-flowering. If, however, frosts are long delayed in the autumn until the days are short again, flowers may be seen in this season also.

It is easy to place the violets in two groups according to the type of stem from which leaves and flowers grow.

I.   *The so-called stemless violets have a short, horizontal, underground stem (rhizome), from the tip of which leaves and flowers grow. The leaves of the first group of species described may be toothed but they are not lobed or cleft. For the violets with above-ground stems and branches* (II), *see page 172.*

VIOLA PAPILIONACEA, the common blue violet, is the most familiar of all. The flowers are mostly violet-blue with dark veins and small white center; sometimes grayish-white with purple veins. The side petals wear tufts of short white or yellowish hairs towards the center. The leaves are broadly heart-shaped and toothed.

tus corniculatus *Ryker*

Coronilla varia *Rickett*

Viola papilionacea *Rickett*

patiens capensis *Rickett*

Viola papilionacea *Rickett*

MARSH BLUE VIOLET, VIOLA CUCULLATA, has long flower-stalks which carry the flowers well above the heart-shaped leaves. In color the flowers range from pale violet to white, with darker veins. The hairs on the side petals end in knobs (seen only through a magnifier). The plants grow in wet places.

V. HIRSUTULA is a resident of dry woods. It is a small plant with leaf-blades not more than 2 inches wide, the under surface purplish and smooth, the upper silvery with a fine down and usually marked with purple veins. The light violet-colored flowers are relatively large and, on stalks about 2 inches long, rise considerably above the leaves. The seed capsules are purplish.

WOOLLY BLUE VIOLET, V. SORORIA, is much like *V. papilionacea* except for its hairy leaf-stalks, leaf-blades, and flower-stalks. The petals are likely to be white at the base..... V. AFFINIS also resembles *V. papilionacea*. The leaf-blades, however, are somewhat narrower and more tapering, and the lower petal wears a "beard" like that of the side petals..... V. SEPTENTRIONALIS is somewhat like a small version of *V. papilionacea*, except that it is downy. The leaves are pale green and toothed, the flowers deep violet to pale lilac, or occasionally white..... V. LATIUSCULA is a smooth plant, the leaves of which are tinged with purple on the under surface. The leaf-margins are inwardly curved just below the tip. The flowers are rich violet in color. The lowest petal is slightly hairy and its spur is rather large.

This concludes the descriptions of the blue and violet-colored stemless violets which have heart-shaped leaves. For white and yellow flowers in this group see page 170.

Stemless blue violets with leaves that are deeply cleft palmately.

BIRD'S-FOOT VIOLET, V. PEDATA, is a much-prized wild flower, existing in two forms. In one, more familiar in the New York area, all petals, which are fairly large (the flower often an inch or more broad), are of uniform deep lilac color. In the other form the two upper petals are of a deep velvety purple, the three lower petals lilac. The upper petals flare backward and the orange tips of the stamens are conspicuous in the middle. The deeply cut leaf-blades give this violet its common name..... The WOOD VIOLET, V. PALMATA, is a hairy plant with from five to eleven deeply cleft lobes in its leaves, the middle one somewhat broader than the others. Plants with few lobes to the leaves closely resemble forms of *V. triloba*. The lowest petal of both species has a tuft of hairs at the base..... V. TRILOBA is also hairy, with leaves at flowering time lobed or cleft into from three to seven parts, the middle one wider than the others and the basal ones usually somewhat wider than those just above. The specific name "triloba" is a bit misleading. Leaves that appear in early spring before flowering, and afterward, in late spring and summer, are apt to be unlobed..... V. STONEANA can be distinguished from *V. triloba* chiefly by its smoothness and by its lowest petal having no "beard."

V. BRITTONIANA, found mainly in moist sandy or peaty soil, has a fan-shaped leaf with narrow, slightly toothed lobes indented nearly to the base. The plant's lack of hairiness distinguishes it from *V. palmata* and *V. triloba*. The flower has a conspicuous white center.

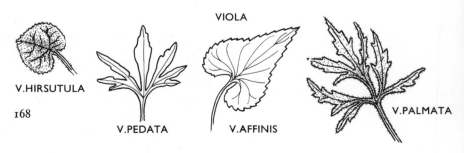

VIOLA

V.HIRSUTULA

V.PEDATA

V.AFFINIS

V.PALMATA

Viola hirsutula   *Elbert*

iola cucullata   *Rickett*

iola brittoniana   *Elbert*

Viola pedata   *Rickett*

Stemless blue violets with somewhat lance-shaped leaves, often with prominent teeth or lobes near the base.

ARROW-LEAVED VIOLET, VIOLA SAGITTATA, has some leaves with stalks that are longer than the blades, and the blades on some leaves longer than on others. The purple flowers, which have relatively narrow petals, a broad white center, and dark veins on the lower petals, are also long-stalked..... V. EMARGINATA is quite similar, but the leaves are more nearly triangular. They vary greatly, sometimes closely resembling those of *V. fimbriatula*. They are sometimes deeply lobed at the base and are often prominently toothed. The leaf-stalk is much longer than the blade. The petals are likely to be broader than those of *V. sagittata*, but are otherwise similar..... V. FIMBRIATULA is a small plant with elongate leaves, often with a small lobe on each side at the base.

Stemless violets with white flowers.

SWEET WHITE VIOLET, V. BLANDA, is a tiny white-flowered plant with exceptional fragrance. The flowers are barely ½ inch across, the heart-shaped leaves about an inch wide, on stalks not much longer. The flower-petals have no hairs. The upper ones are narrow and apt to be bent back and twisted. The lower petals have brownish veins. The plants are found in cool, moist woods..... PRIMROSE-LEAVED VIOLET, V. PRIMULI-FOLIA, also an inhabitant of moist places, has oblong to ovate leaf-blades which taper at the base into the broad, thin stalk. The small white flowers have brownish-purple veins on the three lower petals.

LANCE-LEAVED VIOLET, V. LANCEOLATA, has truly narrow leaves which stand erect on margined stalks that are often red at the base. Their blades, from 2 to 5 inches long, have obscurely rounded teeth. The white flowers, which have somewhat twisted petals and long stalks, open at about the same height as the leaves. The three lower petals are marked with brownish-purple veins. They all lack hairs.

Stemless violet with yellow flowers.

ROUND-LEAVED or EARLY YELLOW VIOLET, V. ROTUNDIFOLIA, does not really have round (*rotundi-*) leaves, but rather ovate or heart-shaped ones, often minutely hairy. The flowers are bright yellow, the three lowest petals with brown veins, the two at the sides with "beards" also.

iola lanceolata   *Rickett*   Viola sagittata   *Johnson*

Viola blanda   *Johnson*

ola rotundifolia   *Johnson*

II. *Violets in this group have both leaves and flowers on the stem that rises above ground, the flowers being borne singly in the axils of the leaves. (Caution: Young plants of some species have scarcely any erect stem.) The leaves of most of these are more or less heart-shaped.*

CANADA VIOLET, VIOLA CANADENSIS, may grow more than a foot tall, its violet-tinted white flowers often rising above the leaves, though at times on rather short stalks. The lowest petal, which is likely to be longer than the others, is yellowish at the base and marked with brownish-purple lines. The two side petals carry tufts of hairs.

PALE or CREAM VIOLET, V. STRIATA, has toothed stipules at the base of the leaves. The stem is up to a foot tall at flowering time, with leaves from 1 to 3 inches long. The cream-colored flowers, which are rounder in outline than the somewhat elongate ones of *V. canadensis*, all bear brownish-purple lines toward the center and tufts of hairs on the two side petals.

AMERICAN DOG VIOLET, V. CONSPERSA, at flowering time may have a stem only an inch tall, its leafy stem later growing to 6 or 8 inches. The stipules are deeply toothed. The small flowers are usually pale violet; a white-petaled form is occasionally found. The side-petals bear tufts of hairs..... THE LONG-SPURRED VIOLET, V. ROSTRATA, is similar to *V. conspersa*, except that the lowest petal has a half-inch spur extending backward and curving upward. Also the flowers are likely to be very pale in color at the edges of the petals and of deeper lilac marked with dark veins toward the center. The side petals have no hairs..... JOHNNY-JUMP-UP, V. RAFINESQUII, has distinctive leaves – most of them slender, hairy blades that taper into the stalk, and relatively large stipules cleft into narrow lobes like a cock's-comb. The lower leaves are somewhat more rounded. The small flowers, with two erect upper petals turned sideways, vary in color from cream to blue-violet, often marked with yellow..... V. TRICOLOR, one of the ancestors of the pansies, sometimes appears in cultivated ground as an escape. The two upper petals on its relatively small flowers are purple; the three lower ones show a variation in coloring.

SMOOTH YELLOW VIOLET, V. PENSYLVANICA, has up to three large, long-stalked leaves rising from the base in addition to the several leaves on the stem. The blades are broad and generally heart-shaped, but the base is sometimes not indented. The flowers are bright yellow with purplish veins. Tufts of hairs are borne on the side petals. One variety has pods covered with white wool.

DOWNY YELLOW VIOLET, V. PUBESCENS, has softly hairy stems and not more than one – if any – long-stalked leaf rising from the base. The expanding stem-leaves, the stipules, and the capsules are all downy.

HYBANTHUS

One species of this generally warm-climate genus may be found in the rich woodlands and moist ravines of the region around New York.

GREEN-VIOLET, H. CONCOLOR, is an erect plant from 1 to 3 feet tall. More or less oblong leaves grow out at intervals directly from the stem, with little or no stalk. The all-green flowers hang singly or in very small clusters from their axils. The sepals and petals are about equal in length and they expand very little. The resemblance to a violet comes in the lowest petal being sac-like and in the pistil and stamens having much the same structure as in the genus *Viola*. April to June.

ola striata   *Johnson*   Viola canadensis   *Johnson*

ola conspersa   *Rickett*

Viola pensylvanica   *Johnson*

THE HEATH FAMILY – ERICACEAE

Woody plants, but some so small as to merit treatment here. Leaves simple (not divided into segments) and mostly evergreen (lasting through the winter). In some of the species mentioned here, the sepals mere points beneath the five (or four) united petals. Stamens five or ten (or eight), discharging their pollen through tubes or pores, not splitting lengthwise.

EPIGAEA

Of the two species of *Epigaea*, only one is known in the New World.

TRAILING ARBUTUS or MAYFLOWER, E. REPENS, is a much-prized flower of early spring. Its clusters of waxy pink or white flowers are exquisitely fragrant. They bloom close to the ground among oval, leathery, veiny leaves. The petals are five, the stamens ten, sometimes in a separate flower from the pistil, which develops into a five-lobed, many-seeded capsule. March to May. The plant is protected by law in many states because of its near-extermination. It is extremely difficult to cultivate.

ARCTOSTAPHYLOS

Only one species is familiar in this vicinity. One other appears farther north and many shrubs known as manzanita occur in the west.

BEARBERRY or KINNIKINICK, A. UVA-URSI, crawls on the ground and dangles small, waxy, narrow-mouthed, white, pink, or pink-tipped bells from branches that stand about 2 inches high. On these branches the small, narrow, thick, evergreen leaves are likely to rise above the flowers. Tasteless red berries follow the flowers, which appear from May to July. The Indians used the leaves as a substitute for tobacco – which is the meaning of the name kinnikinick.

GAULTHERIA

Two species are native in the northeastern United States, the more familiar one with five petals, the second with four. Both have creeping, slightly woody stems and somewhat leathery oval leaves with short-stalked flowers nodding from their axils. The flowers are waxy-white and bell-shaped with a narrow mouth. The fruit, which is round and red, has the appearance of a berry.

WINTERGREEN or CHECKERBERRY, G. PROCUMBENS, is the true aromatic wintergreen, with the pleasantly familiar odor and taste. The species shown opposite has five joined petals in its corolla and five stamens. Its leaves average an inch and a quarter in length. The leafy flowering stem stands erect, from 2 to 6 inches high. While the flowers appear in July and August, the red fruit matures slowly over winter and is at its best for nibbling in the spring.

CREEPING SNOWBERRY, G. HISPIDULA, forms mats with leaves barely ½ inch long. The corolla is deeply cleft to make four petals; it encloses eight stamens. The fruit is white and juicy and has much the same flavor as *G. procumbens*. April and May.

Epigaea repens   V. Richard

ctostaphylos uva-ursi   V. Richard   Gaultheria procumbens   D. Richards

KALMIA

The well-known mountain-laurel and its sister shrub, sheep-laurel, belong in this genus. Swamp-laurel, the third member of the group, is the only one to be considered here, because it scarcely resembles a woody plant. The flowers of all three are closely similar, the saucer-shaped corolla of five joined petals having ten small pouches in which the heads of the ten stamens are caught. At the touch of an insect these heads (the anthers) are released, scattering pollen over the intruder – who, presumably, will drop some of it on the stigma of another flower, thus promoting seed production. The fruit is a rounded capsule, its five compartments holding many seeds when mature.

SWAMP-LAUREL, K. POLIFOLIA, grows not more than 3 feet tall. Its narrow leaves, about 1 inch long, are mostly paired. They are poisonous for animals to eat. The flowers, in a small cluster at the tip of each stem, are pink or crimson and about ¾ inch across. May to July.

THE DIAPENSIA FAMILY – DIAPENSIACEAE

A small family of low plants bearing flowers with their parts in fives; the leaves small, crowded, and evergreen.

PYXIDANTHERA

The one species grows largely in the pine-barrens of New Jersey. It may reach the southern limit of our range.

PYXIE or FLOWERING-MOSS, PYXIDANTHERA BARBULATA, creeps on sandy ground, its branching stems crowded with sharp-pointed leaves not more than ⅓ inch long. The white or pink flowers which cover these mats in spring are ¼ inch across. March to May.

THE LEADWORT FAMILY – PLUMBAGINACEAE

Limonium is the only northern genus in this warm–climate family.

SEA-LAVENDERS (LIMONIUM)

Salt marshes are the home of our two northern species of sea-lavender – which are in no way related to true lavender (*Lavandula*) of Europe in the mint family. In our native species a widely branching stem rises up to 2 feet above a basal cluster of thick leaves. Many small flowers of light purple are borne along one side of each of the numerous branches. The five petals are more or less joined at the base, a stamen attached to each one. There are five styles on the ovary. Both species flower from July to October.

L. CAROLINIANUM has a bristly point at the tip of each leaf. Its calyx-tube is completely smooth..... L. NASHII has hairs on its calyx, especially on the ribs. The leaves are blunt, occasionally notched at the tip; the branches are somewhat zigzag.

Limonium carolinianum   *Uttal*

almia polifolia   *Scribner*   Pyxidanthera barbulata   *Elbert*

THE PRIMROSE FAMILY – PRIMULACEAE

Petals and stamens usually five, the petals joined at the base, a stamen opposite the center of each one. Calyx free from the ovary. Style and stigma one. Ovules borne on a central column that rises from the base of the ovary but is not attached at the tip. Either the style or the stamens (not both) projecting from the corolla. In all except the aquatic genus *Hottonia*, the leaves neither lobed nor divided; borne either at the base of the plant or in pairs or circles on the stem.

HOTTONIA

One species of this aquatic genus occurs in America, one other in the Old World.

FEATHER FOIL or WATER-VIOLET, H. INFLATA, inhabits ditches and shallow pools. The leaves, which extend horizontally from the base, are finely divided feather-fashion. The stems are extremely thick, hollow, and jointed, and have circles of small flowers growing out from the joints. The white corolla is shorter than the calyx, which is less than ½ inch long. April to August.

TRIENTALIS

There is but one species of this genus in North America.

STAR-FLOWER, T. BOREALIS, has a stem from 2 to 10 inches tall, bearing at its summit a circle of lanceolate leaves about 4 inches long. Directly above these, one or several star-shaped white flowers rise on delicate stalks. The slender petals most often number seven, but may be from five to nine. The plant is sometimes called chickweed-wintergreen, but without reason, for it bears

neither resemblance nor relationship to either of these plants. May to July or later.

THE LOOSESTRIFES
(LYSIMACHIA and STEIRONEMA)

These two genera are so closely similar that they are treated here together. Both calyx and corolla are either five- or six-parted, and the stamens are of the same number. In *Lysimachia* the stalks of the stamens are joined at the base to make a sleeve around the ovary; in *Steironema* the stamens are quite separate. The flowers are yellow in all the species. These loosestrifes are not to be confused with the purple ones of the genus *Lythrum* in the loosestrife family (page 142). (For species of *Steironema* see page 182).

GARDEN LOOSESTRIFE, L. VULGARIS, which grows to 4 feet tall, has inch-wide yellow flowers circling the stem in the leaf-axils. The lance-ovate leaves, 3 to 5 inches long, may be in circles or in pairs. Originally a garden plant introduced from Europe, *L. vulgaris* now can be seen on roadsides and in wet places the entire summer – June to September. (For another garden loosestrife, see *L. punctata* on page 180).

Hottonia inflata   *Phelps*

simachia vulgaris   *Mayer*   Trientalis borealis   *Rickett*

SWAMP-CANDLES, LYSIMACHIA TERRESTRIS, which inhabits wet places, bears its yellow flowers, ½ inch across, in a slender raceme. The petals may have dark markings. Leaves and petals both tend to be narrow, and the leaves are mostly paired. The plant grows up to 3 feet tall. June to August.

MONEYWORT or CREEPING-JENNY, L. NUM-MULARIA, crawls along the ground displaying pairs of nearly round leaves (the "money") and yellow flowers an inch across in the leaf-axils. The petals, which are broad across the center, may show dark dots. The plant comes from Europe and is now widely naturalized in the United States, particularly in damp places. June to August.

WHORLED LOOSESTRIFE, L. QUADRIFOLIA, carries its slender leaves, averaging 2½ inches long, in circles (whorls) often of four (*quadri-*), but quite as often of other numbers. In the axil of each leaf there is usually a delicate yellow flower on a fragile-appearing stalk about half the length of the leaf. The petals have dark dots or streaks. The stamens are of unequal lengths. This species crosses with *L. terrestris*. May to August.

GARDEN LOOSESTRIFE, L. PUNCTATA, carries its leaves chiefly in whorls of three or four, with flowers half an inch or so across in their axils. At any level the flowers are more numerous than the leaves. The plant may grow 3 feet tall. It comes from Europe and has escaped from gardens into waste places in the northeastern states. June to September.

simachia quadrifolia   *Gottscho*

Lysimachia punctata   *Scribner*

simachia terrestris   *Johnson*

Lysimachia nummularia   *D. Richards*

STEIRONEMA

In the loosestrifes that are placed in the genus *Steironema*, the flowers are mostly clustered at the ends of leafy branches. The petals are broad their entire length (half an inch, more or less), then they have a sharp-pointed tip. Their distinguishing characteristic, as noted in the introduction to the loosestrifes (page 178), is stamens that are entirely free from each other. In the bud each lobe of the corolla is wrapped around a stamen.

S. HYBRIDUM (which is *not* a hybrid but a native species) often has a long reclining stem, though it sometimes stands erect. The narrowly lanceolate leaves are green on both sides and short-stalked. A basal rosette is formed in autumn. The plant inhabits wet places. July and August..... FRINGED LOOSESTRIFE, S. CILIATUM, gets its name from the large hairs with which the long leaf-stalks are fringed. It is a widely and loosely branched plant that stands from 1 to 4 feet tall and usually grows in damp areas. The leaf-blades are from ovate-lanceolate to ovate and 1–6 inches long. The clear yellow flowers on long slender stalks are usually whorled and they mostly face outward. The petals are toothed on their outer margins. June to August.

NAUMBURGIA

This is a genus of only one species, by some botanists placed in *Lysimachia*.

TUFTED-LOOSESTRIFE, N. THYRSIFLORA, bears dense tufts of narrow-petaled yellow flowers in the leaf-axils around the middle part of the stem. The leaves, which are in pairs, are stalkless and narrowly lanceolate to elliptic. The plants stand from 8 to 30 inches tall and commonly grow in swamps and bogs, flowering from May to July.

ANAGALLIS

An Old-World genus, one species of which has migrated to America.

PIMPERNEL, A. ARVENSIS, is a small, branched plant, often spreading horizontally. The small, paired, stalkless leaves bear in their axils single flowers on fairly long stalks. The flowers, usually scarlet but occasionally white or blue, have five flaring corolla-lobes and five protruding stamens with bearded stalks. May to August.

SAMOLUS

WATER-PIMPERNEL or BROOKWEED, SAMO LUS PARVIFLORUS, grows up to 2 feet tall in shallow water, mud, or wet sand. Its white flowers, with a five-lobed corolla about ⅛ inch across, are in small racemes at the ends of branches. The leaf-blades are widest toward their tips; they taper downward into their stalks. May to September.

GLAUX

SEA-MILKWORT, GLAUX MARITIMA, is a small succulent plant of salty places. It bears small narrow leaves in pairs. The five-parted calyx, about ¼ inch long, takes the place of the corolla and is variously colored from white to crimson. The stamens alternate with the lobes of the calyx. June and July.

nolus parviflorus   *D. Richards*   Steironema hybridum   *V. Richard*

Anagallis arvensis   *D. Richards*

umburgia thyrsiflora   *Houseknecht*

THE GENTIAN FAMILY – GENTIANACEAE

Petals united; mostly four or five in the plants of our region, but up to twelve in one species. Stamens of the same number and inserted on the tube of the corolla. Leaves in pairs or circles – except on the plants of two genera that dwell in water.

THE GENTIANS (GENTIANA)

The species of gentian are of two distinct types: either with the four or five corolla lobes separate from each other or with five lobes all connected with additional lobes or plaits between them. The first two species below have four large and beautifully fringed lobes on the corolla. The first three species all favor damp dwelling-places.

FRINGED GENTIAN, G. CRINITA, one of our most beautiful wild flowers, bears a fringe up to ¼ inch long around its four violet-blue corolla-lobes. The corolla may be 2 inches long, twisted at first, its lobes flaring in sunshine to make a flower nearly 2 inches across. The calyx-teeth are unequal, two of them being narrow, two wider. The plant will grow from 4 to 40 inches tall, bearing paired leaves and carrying its flowers on long stalks at the tips of the stem and its branches. August to November.

NARROW-LEAVED FRINGED GENTIAN, G. PROCERA, resembles G. crinita but it has a much shorter fringe and very slender leaves. August to October.

AGUEWEED, G. QUINQUEFOLIA, has a sharply angled stem from 1 to 3 feet tall, with pairs of mostly ovate leaves clasping the stem by their rounded bases. The flowers, with a corolla up to ¾ inch long, are pale violet or greenish white. There are five lobes but they do not open out flat. Each is tipped with a bristle. August to November.

The remaining species of Gentiana within the New York City region have extra lobes or plaits between the five lobes of the corolla. The calyx sends up slender teeth from a cup-shaped base. The leaves are in pairs or fours.

CLOSED or BOTTLE GENTIAN, G. ANDREWSII, has a corolla that never opens; the teeth, or lobes, connected by plaits, never separate; fertilization takes place within the one flower. In color the "bottle" may be purple, violet, pinkish or white. Two to six flowers about 1½ inches long are closely clustered at the summit of a stem from 1 to nearly 3 feet tall. A few additional flowers sometimes spring from the upper leaf-axils. The leaves are mostly lanceolate and up to 4 inches long. August to October..... Another closed gentian, G. CLAUSA, can be distinguished from its sister species only by opening the corolla. In G. andrewsii the plaits are longer than the lobes; in G. clausa, they are shorter..... SOAPWORT GENTIAN, G. SAPONARIA, was so named because of the resemblance of its foliage to that of bouncing-Bet (*Saponaria*) in the pink family (page 118). The flowers, of intense blue or purplish, open very slightly; the toothed plaits are approximately the same length as the lobes. September and October.

Gentiana crinita
Gottscho

Gentiana andrewsii
Johnson

SABATIA

The species of *Sabatia* are found chiefly in wet places near the coast. Most have five petals and five stamens but one in our area has up to twelve of each. The petals seem scarcely joined. They are largely rose-color varying to white or yellow, often with a yellow "eye." They flower mainly from July to September.

MARSH-PINK or SEA-PINK, S. STELLARIS, has attractive pink (occasionally white) flowers with a yellow or green "eye" bordered with reddish-brown, the petals from ¼ to ¾ inch long. The flowers are on leafless stalks; the leafy stems, bearing pairs of small elliptic leaves, are from 12 to 20 inches tall.

ROSE-PINK or BITTER-BLOOM, S. ANGULARIS, has a sharply four-angled stem up to 3 feet tall, usually much-branched and bushy, with a rosette of broad-tipped leaves at the base. Lobes at the lower end of the stem-leaves appear to clasp the stem. The five-petaled pink (occasionally white) flowers are fragrant. Each petal, from ½ to ¾ inch long, has a yellow spot at the base. The plant grows in fields and open woodlands.

LARGE MARSH-PINK or SEA-PINK, S. DODE-CANDRA, may reach a height of 2 feet, bearing pairs of narrow, stalkless leaves along its stem. The flowers have up to twelve petals and stamens surrounding the pistil, the petals of pink, lavender, or white, each about ⅝ inch long, with a reddish-brown-bordered yellow spot at the base. The calyx-lobes are narrow but tend to increase in width above the middle. The plant inhabits salt and brackish marshes on the eastern coast.

MENYANTHES

BUCKBEAN or BOGBEAN, MENYANTHES TRI-FOLIATA, is the only species in this genus, and it is found only in mud or shallow water. The plant rises from a horizontal under-ground stem (a rhizome). The leaves, which consist of three broad segments, have stalks which expand at the base into sheaths that surround the rhizome. The flowering stem rises 4–12 inches above the water surface, bearing a long cluster (a raceme) of white (sometimes pink-tinged) flowers each about an inch across. The petals, which are joined nearly half-way up, are covered with long hairs. April to July.

NYMPHOIDES is a genus of aquatic plants suggesting miniature water-lilies. But the floating leaves have almost no stalks; they are borne directly on the long stem that also bears the flowers. The corolla has five petals that are joined only at the very base. There are five stamens; the pistil has a very short style or none and a two-lobed stigma..... YELLOW FLOATING-HEART, N. PELTATA, has pairs of somewhat heart-shaped leaves. They vary greatly in size, the largest reaching 6 inches in width. The yellow flowers are about an inch across and slightly fringed. July to September. Introduced from Europe; now spreading in the wild.

BARTONIA is the most insignificant of all the genera in the gentian family. The leaves are mere scales. The tiny flowers are on branches at the summit of the stem. The plants are seldom seen because they are so inconspicuous. Both species inhabit principally wet soil..... B. VIRGINICA does not exceed a foot in height. The entire plant, including the fifth-inch flowers, is yellowish. The leaves (scales) are mostly paired. July to September..... B. PANICULATA, a less common species, called screw-stem because of the tendency of the stem to twist, has leaves that are mostly borne singly. The flowers, up to a quarter-inch long, may be white, cream-colored, or purplish. The whole plant is yellowish or purplish. August to October.

batia dodecandra   *Phelps*

Sabatia angularis   *Horne*

batia stellaris   *V. Richard*

Menyanthes trifoliata   *Gottscho*

THE DOGBANE FAMILY – APOCYNACEAE

Milky juice (possibly poisonous) in evidence when stem or leaf is broken. Leaves generally paired, undivided and unlobed, with short stalks or none. Petals five, united to form a tube or bell. Stamens five, inserted on the corolla. Two ovaries, developing into two seed-pods (follicles) but only one style (or none) and one stigma.

THE DOGBANES (APOCYNUM)

The dogbanes are tall, widely branching plants with numerous small flowers in clusters at the ends of branches. The petals form a bell or funnel. A large stigma sits directly on the two ovaries; there is no style. The fruit is a long, thin follicle from each ovary, the seeds inside each provided with a tuft of silky hairs, as on milkweed.

SPREADING DOGBANE, A. ANDROSAEMI-FOLIUM, grows from a few inches up to nearly 2 feet tall, its branching habit sometimes obscuring any main stem. The ovate leaf-blades are on short stalks. The small fragrant flowers are bells of pale pink with stripes of deeper pink inside. The five corolla-lobes curve outward. The pods become from 3 to 8 inches long. June to August.

INDIAN-HEMP, A. CANNABINUM, has an erect stem from 3 to 5 feet tall, with branches sprouting from the leaf-axils. The leaf-blades are ovate or lanceolate, those on the main stem with short stalks, those on the branches often without stalks. The flowers are greenish-white, narrow, and more or less erect on straight stalks. The pods are from 5 to 8 inches long. June to September.

PERIWINKLE (VINCA)

The familiar ground-cover, *Vinca minor*, brought to our gardens from Europe, has spread into the wild. Its trailing stems bear short-stalked, glossy leaves about an inch long in pairs. From their axils spring stalks bearing single flowers of violet-blue (occasionally white), about an inch across. The corolla is a funnel-shaped tube that flares into five broad, flat lobes. March to June.

Vinca minor   *Johnson*

ocynum cannabinum   *Johnson*

Apocynum androsaemifolium   *Johnson*

THE MILKWEED FAMILY – ASCLEPIADACEAE

A thick white sap oozing from any cut or broken surface on plants in all except one species of milkweed (*Asclepias tuberosa*). Flower structure extraordinary, the tips of the five stamens being more or less joined with each other and also with the broad stigma, which is supported by two styles, one for each of the two ovaries. The pollen of each stamen in two waxy masses, each one connected with the mass of the adjacent stamen (further details given under *Asclepias*). The fruit a pod (follicle), two obtainable from each flower but not formed by many of the flowers in a cluster. Seeds tipped with long silky hairs.

THE MILKWEEDS (ASCLEPIAS)

Flowers in *Asclepias* have a deeply cleft corolla, the five lobes of which are turned back and downward so as to conceal the calyx. A crown or *corona* is formed of five cups just above the junction of the corolla-lobes, each on a short tube. From within each cup rises a curved horn, its point directed toward the stigma.

The adjoining masses of pollen are tightly attached to a triangular gland that comes between them. Insects alighting on the stigma may get their feet in this. If they are large enough they can pull it out and fly away with the two masses of pollen – the grains of which can be rubbed off on the next stigma visited. The flowers are borne in sizable clusters on stalks that all radiate from a central point, at the tip of a branch or stem, or in the axil of a leaf.

COMMON MILKWEED, A: SYRIACA, is seen everywhere along roadsides and in fields. Its flowers of dull crimson-purple, sometimes greenish, come in several clusters from the axils of the leaves. The fruits, which are thick, warty follicles, stand erect on stalks which are bent downward. The leaves are large (4–10 inches long), oblong, broad, and blunt, and on the under surface they are coated with a grayish down. They are borne in pairs and have very short stalks. While the stem most frequently ranges from 1 to 4 feet tall, it sometimes reaches 7 feet. June to August.

Two kinds of milkweed in our range have at least some leaves in circles, or whorls.

FOUR-LEAVED MILKWEED, A. QUADRIFOLIA, has ovate or lanceolate leaves in both pairs and fours on a slender stem 1–2½ feet high. The flowers are in loose clusters at and near the summit of the plant. The petals are normally pale pink, the corona white, but the color varies to all-lilac. May to July.

A. VERTICILLATA has from three to six leaves in circles on a generally unbranched stem from 1 to 4 feet tall. The leaves are very narrow and their margins are rolled underneath. The flowers, which crop out in clusters at the summit and along the stem, are small and greenish-white. June to September..... SWAMP MILKWEED, A. INCARNATA, carries its slender, pointed, short-stalked leaves in pairs on a stem from 1 to 5 feet tall. Flattish clusters of rose-crimson flowers with whitish coronas top the stem. The pods are slender, tapering to both ends. The plant inhabits swamps and shores. June to August.

clepias syriaca   *Johnson*   Asclepias verticillata   *Johnson*

clepias syriaca   *Rickett*   Asclepias quadrifolia   *Johnson*

BUTTERFLY-WEED or PLEURISY-ROOT, A. TUBEROSA, is the one species of milkweed that has no milky juice. The flowers are bright orange. The leaves are roughly hairy, long, narrow, pointed, and the only ones in the genus to be borne singly. The long, deep, tough rhizome ("root") was once reputed to furnish a cure for pleurisy. A highly variable species. June to September.

The remaining species of Asclepias *all carry their leaves in pairs.*

A. EXALTATA has pairs of ovate or lanceolate leaves with irregular margins on a stem from 2 to 5 feet tall. The greenish flowers with a white corona are in dangling clusters from the summit and the upper axils. The slender, tapering pods stand erect on stalks that are bent down. This is a woodland plant blooming in June and July.

PURPLE MILKWEED, A. PURPURASCENS, customarily has dark purple flowers, but the color varies to a distinctly reddish tone. The cups of the corona are so tall that they hide the horns. The plant grows to 3 feet tall. The paired leaves taper to the point and are finely downy on the under surface. The pods too are finely woolly but not warty. May to July..... A. RUBRA, which has purplish-red flowers, barely touches wet coastlands near New York. The flowers are closely packed in from one to a few clusters on a plant that grows up to 4 feet tall. The leaves, which have slightly wavy margins, taper to the tip from a rounded or heart-shaped base. The pods are smooth, tapering at both ends and up to 3½ inches long. June and July..... A. VARIEGATA has white or pinkish flowers, generally with purplish coronas, the cups of which are round rather than toothed. The pods are slender. The leaves are blunt and oblong. The entire plant is smooth; it stands from 1 to 3 feet high. May to July.

GREEN-MILKWEED (ACERATES)
One of the four eastern American species of *Acerates* can be found in dry woodlands within the New York area. Its principal distinction from the true milkweeds is that the five cups of the corona have no horns.

A. VIRIDIFLORA, which grows from 1 to 3 feet tall, has leaves much like those of common milkweed (*Asclepias syriaca*), thick and blunt, with nearly parallel sides, and veins running out approximately at right angles from the midrib. The flowers, small and green, are in dense clusters. June to August.

lepias exaltata   *Gottscho*

Asclepias purpurascens   *Johnson*

rates viridiflora   *Johnson*

Asclepias tuberosa   *Johnson*

THE PHLOX FAMILY – POLEMONIACEAE

Five corolla-lobes flaring outward from a tubular or bell-shaped base, the stamens attached inside. Three-chambered ovary developing into a pod (a capsule), the style having three branches – a distinguishing trait. Close resemblance between phlox and pink families (pages 114–121), the petals separate in the latter.

PHLOX

In our gardens we have many kinds of phlox besides the one called moss-pink (*Phlox subulata*), and they have all originally come from the American wild. Relatively few, however, are native in the northeastern states. Some, such as moss-pink, have returned to the wild.

MOSS-PINK, P. SUBULATA, has a creeping stem with needle-like leaves nearly an inch long closely surrounding it. Stalks bearing numerous flowers of rose, rose-purple, or white rise up several inches. Other colors can be seen in gardens. April to July. The plant is native on Long Island besides elsewhere in the east.

P. PILOSA stands from 8 to 30 inches tall.

The leaves are mostly very narrow and sharp-pointed, but plants may occasionally be seen with ovate leaves. The stem is often downy. The flowers, in close clusters, are from roseate through violet to a light reddish purple. April to July.

WILD-SWEET-WILLIAM, P. MACULATA, bears no relationship to *Dianthus barbatus* in the pink family, the sweet-William of our gardens. It is a wild phlox that grows from 1 to 3 feet tall bearing reddish-purple flowers. The stem is usually marked with reddish spots. May to September..... PERENNIAL PHLOX, P. PANICULATA, is a tall plant, up to 7 feet. The numerous leaves, mostly in pairs, are either elliptic or ovate. The flowers are of varying colors (particularly in gardens) but typically purplish-pink. July to October.

FORGET-ME-NOT FAMILY – BORAGINACEAE

Flowers alternating to right and left on one side of the stem (a false raceme), the lower ones opening first, the stem usually coiled at first, eventually straightening. Bracts, if present, opposite instead of beneath the flower stalks. Flower-parts in fives except for the ovary, which has four chambers, each becoming a small nutlike body containing one seed. Many species covered with stiff hairs.

ECHIUM

An Old-World genus, one species of which has reached the United States.

VIPER'S-BUGLOSS, BLUEWEED, or BLUE-DEVIL, E. VULGARE, has bristly stems from 1 to 3 feet tall. In axils of upper leaves are numerous short, curved false racemes of

bright blue flowers (very rarely pink or white), their red-stalked stamens projecting from the corolla. The upper lobes of the corolla are much longer than the lower – an unusual design in the forget-me-not family. June to October. The chief common name is not "bug-loss" but "bu-gloss," from two Greek words meaning "ox-tongue."

Phlox subulata   *Johnson*

Echium vulgare   *Rickett*

Echium vulgare   *Horne*

Phlox pilosa   *Johnson*

MERTENSIA

A genus of mostly smooth plants, in some species known as lungwort. The blue flowers (which are pink before they open) hang from false racemes. The petals form a funnel with only slight lobing on the margin.

VIRGINIA-BLUEBELLS or VIRGINIA-COWSLIP, M. VIRGINICA, bears many flowers from ¾ to 1 inch long. Growing on plants to 2 feet tall or more, they can brighten meadows and light woods with their color. March to June.

FORGET-ME-NOTS (MYOSOTIS)

Most forget-me-nots have come to us from Europe, particularly those that have reached the American wild from gardens. The plants are relatively small, often lax, and smooth. The stem usually ends in two false racemes, each coiled at first, uncoiling from the base as the fruits ripen. The flowers in most species are blue; in a few white, and in one temporarily yellow. Many have a yellow center. At the mouth of the corolla-tube there are five small scales. Most species of *Myosotis* grow naturally in wet places.

TRUE FORGET-ME-NOT, M. SCORPIOIDES (the garden plant), has branched, angled stems up to 2 feet long and clear blue flowers up to ⅓ inch across with a yellow center. The five scales on the corolla appear to be ten. The calyx, of five sharp points, bears straight hairs which lie against the surface. The leaves are mostly oblong-lanceolate. May to October.

M. LAXA is a native species similar to *M. scorpioides* but with smaller flowers and usually some leaves in the inflorescence. May to September..... M. VERNA, another native, has minute white flowers on erect stems up to 16 inches tall. Dry soil. April to July..... M. ARVENSIS comes from Europe. The blue corolla lobes form a cup less than ¼ inch across. The plant grows largely in waste places. June to August..... M. VERSICOLOR,

also from Europe, has pale yellow flowers that change to blue, then violet. The plant grows from a basal rosette of leaves. April to July.

LYCOPSIS ARVENSIS is another invader from Europe that is called bugloss. (See also *Echium vulgare*, page 194.) The corolla-tube is bristly and short; the five round lobes are blue and make flowers about ⅛ inch across in dense clusters at the summit of the stem. The plant grows to 2 feet high, mostly in fields. June to September.

STICKSEEDS (LAPPULA and HACKELIA, the latter formerly called *Lappula*). BEGGAR'S-LICE, L. ECHINATA, an immigrant from the Old World, has barbed prickles covering each of the four small nutlike sections of the ovary. These cling to the coats of animals and the clothing of man. The entire plant is rough-hairy. It grows from 8 to 30 inches tall, bearing narrow leaves to 2 inches long and several inflorescences of small blue flowers scarcely ⅛ inch across. May to September..... H. VIRGINIANA resembles *Lappula*, but the plants are taller (to 4 feet), more extensively branched, and the flowers, white or pale blue, are about ⅛ inch across. June to September.

THE GROMWELLS (LITHOSPERMUM)

Most local gromwells come from Europe.

L. OFFICINALE has lanceolate leaves about 2 inches long so numerous as to seem to be overlapping. The flowers, borne singly in the leaf-axils, are minute, the white corolla scarcely emerging from the calyx. The plant is hairy all over. May to September..... L. ARVENSE, called CORN GROMWELL or BASTARD ALKANET, has whitish flowers about ⅛ inch across borne singly in the axils of the narrow leaves. The entire plant is hoary and grows up to 2 feet tall, mostly in waste places. April to July.

Myosotis scorpioides   *Williamson*

osotis scorpioides   *Rickett*

Myosotis laxa   *Becker*

Mertensia virginica   *Mayer*

THE COMFREYS (SYMPHYTUM and CYNOGLOSSUM)

The name "comfrey," which is derived remotely from the early medicinal uses of the plants in these two related genera, applies to species of both *Symphytum* and *Cynoglossum* in the forget-me-not family.

SYMPHYTUM OFFICINALE is the one best known by the common name of comfrey. It is a coarse plant that stands from 20 to 40 inches tall. The leaves are rough and lanceolate or ovate, the lower ones up to 8 inches long, the upper ones appearing to run down onto the stem with projecting flanges or "wings" on the stem. The branching of the veins shows prominently on the under surface. The flowers, which hang from false racemes, may appear in a dull tone of almost any color, from white through yellow to red or blue. May to September. In the past the plant has had numerous uses, and until recent years, at least, a decoction from its mucilaginous root has been an ingredient of cough mixtures.

CYNOGLOSSUM

The comfreys of this genus are coarse plants with large, usually oblong, rough leaves

(which account for the name of hound's-tongue – *cyno-glossum*). The small flowers are borne in false racemes, and they have five scales at the "throat" of the corolla, like the forget-me-nots.

WILD COMFREY, C. VIRGINIANUM, is a native plant of open woodland, growing from 1 to nearly 3 feet high. Its relatively few leaves clasp the stem with their heart-shaped base. Bristly hairs cover the entire plant, and the four sections of the ovary (the "nutlets") are prickly. The flowers are pale blue, violet, or white, less than ½ inch across. April to June.

HOUND'S-TONGUE, C. OFFICINALE, comes to us as a weed from Europe. It is a hairy plant from 2 to 3 feet tall or taller. The lower leaves have stalks; the upper are stalkless lanceolate blades. The flowers are dull reddish-purple, about ⅓ inch across. The "nutlets" that develop from the ovary are beset with hooked bristles which cause them to stick to animals and man. The plant has an unpleasant mousey odor. It is found mostly in waste places. May to August.

THE WATERLEAF FAMILY – HYDROPHYLLACEAE

A North American family, more common in the west, with only one species to concern us in the New York City area.

WATERLEAF (HYDROPHYLLUM)

Plants of the several species of *Hydrophyllum* may have leaves either palmately or pinnately lobed, cleft, or divided. As a whole the plants are hairy. The clusters of flowers are at first dense and coiled in several directions, later unrolling and revealing themselves as false racemes. The corolla is a small funnel cleft into five lobes which do not

flare outward. The stamens project beyond.

JOHN'S-CABBAGE or VIRGINIA WATERLEAF, H. VIRGINIANUM, has pinnately cleft or divided leaves, with usually five sharply toothed lobes or segments tapering to sharp points. The clusters of pale bluish-purple or white flowers are carried on long stalks well above the leaves. The long slender calyx-lobes are bristly. May to August.

noglossum virginianum *Johnson*

Symphytum officinale *Phelps*

noglossum officinale *D. Richards*

Hydrophyllum virginianum *Johnson*

THE POTATO FAMILY – SOLANACEAE

Sepals, petals and stamens in fives; the ovary generally with two chambers, becoming a berry or a pod (a capsule). Leaves mostly coarsely and irregularly toothed, in some species pinnately lobed or divided. The family noted for the number of medicines and poisons (including nicotine) that it provides, as well as for the food and garden plants it furnishes: potatoes, tomatoes, peppers, eggplant, petunias, *Salpiglossis*, *Nierembergia*, and *Schizanthus*.

SOLANUM

Out of some 2,000 species of *Solanum* growing over most of the world, a few can be counted as wild flowers in eastern North America. (More can be found in the west.) The flower-clusters mostly arise from the stem *between* the points at which the leaves are attached, instead of in the leaf-axils. The fruit is a berry with many seeds in its two chambers.

BITTERSWEET or NIGHTSHADE, S. DULCAMARA, is a twining plant, but of no relationship to the woody vine called bittersweet. On some leaves the blade has two distinct lobes at the base. The flowers, about ½ inch across, are purple, the corolla-lobes slender and pointed. A cone of yellow stamens stands up in the center. The poisonous berries, about ½ inch long, turn red. Late spring to early fall..... BLACK NIGHTSHADE, S. AMERICANUM, is a slender branched plant up to 3 feet tall, with undivided and unlobed leaves 1–4 inches long. The flowers, white or purple-tinged, are in small clusters. The black berries are dangerous to eat unless completely ripe. June to November. .... HORSE-NETTLE, S. CAROLINENSE, carries prickles on the lower side of the leaves along the midrib. The leaves are more or less oval and coarsely toothed or even lobed. The plant, to 3 feet tall, is covered with straw-colored hairs. The flowers, which are white or pale violet, are followed by yellow berries. May to October..... BUFFALO-BUR, S. ROSTRATUM, about 2 feet tall, is beset on stem and leaves with yellowish prickles and also starlike hairs. The calyx forms a bur around the berry. Flowers are bright yellow. One stamen protrudes beyond the others. July to October.

GROUND-CHERRIES (PHYSALIS)

The ground-cherries are mostly about 2 feet tall with branched stems. The flowers are borne singly. The upper leaves are generally paired, and a flower-stalk is likely to arise between them. The lower leaves are carried singly. The corolla forms a hanging bell. The calyx enlarges to enclose the fruit.

P. HETEROPHYLLA has yellow flowers up to an inch across with five dark spots at the base of the corolla. The berry is yellow. The leaves are ovate, heart-shaped at the base, and 2–4½ inches long. Both stem and leaves are covered with short, sticky and longer, soft hairs. April to September..... P. VIRGINIANA has similar flowers and ovate, often toothed leaves. The berry is red. April to July.

DATURA

JIMSONWEED or THORN-APPLE, D. STRAMONIUM, is a smooth plant up to 5 feet tall with coarsely toothed leaves and a green or purple stem. The flowers are borne singly, each accompanied by a single leaf. The corolla forms a flaring funnel of white or pale violet, up to 4 inches long, the lower half enclosed in a tubular, angled calyx. The fruit is a spiny capsule containing deadly poisonous black seeds. July to October.

Datura stramonium   *D. Richards*

Physalis heterophylla   *Johnson*

lanum dulcamara   *Johnson*

THE MORNING-GLORY FAMILY –
CONVOLVULACEAE

In temperate regions, mostly twining or trailing plants. Petals joined to form a funnel, with or without five lobes or teeth. Sepals almost separate from each other; some species with bracts below the calyx. Ovary with either two or three chambers, two seeds in each. The style or stigma distinctive: in *Convolvulus*, two stigmas; in *Ipomoea*, one stigma of either two or three lobes; in *Quamoclit*, one unlobed stigma; in dodder (*Cuscuta*), two styles.

BINDWEEDS (CONVOLVULUS)

These familiar twining or trailing plants have handsome funnel-shaped flowers in white or pink, only a small point marking the tip of each of the five corolla-lobes. Below the calyx there are two bracts. The leaves are arrow-shaped or heart-shaped. There are two stigmas; the ovary's two chambers may give the appearance of four.

HEDGE BINDWEED, C. SEPIUM, has a white or pink corolla 2 or 3 inches long. The two broad bracts at the flower's base enclose the calyx. This is a variable species sometimes placed in the genus *Calystegia*. A weedy climber in evidence from May to September.

FIELD BINDWEED, C. ARVENSIS, is a smaller plant than *C. sepium* but a more troublesome pest. The twining, trailing stems form tangled mats. The leaves, of triangular outline, are smaller, shorter-stalked, and more bluntly tipped than those of *C. sepium*. The flowers are barely an inch long. The narrow bracts are ½ inch below the calyx. May to September..... LOW BINDWEED, C. SPITHAMAEUS, grows from 3 to 20 inches tall. The plants are generally downy. The leaves, on short stalks, have oblong blades that are either indented or tapering at the base. The few flowers grow from the lower axils, the white corolla from 2 to 3 inches long. The calyx is concealed by the two bracts much as in *C. sepium*. In sandy or rocky places. May to July.

MORNING-GLORIES (IPOMOEA)

The corolla of a morning-glory flares into more or less of a flat disk at the end of a trumpet, the tips of the petals barely indicated by a point. The single stigma may have two or three lobes. There are no bracts beneath the calyx. In our local species the leaf-blades are mainly heart-shaped.

COMMON MORNING-GLORY, I. PURPUREA, is a tropical species that has been grown for its showy blue, purple, red, white, or variegated flowers, and then escaped from cultivation. The corolla is 2 or more inches long. The stigma has three lobes and the ovary three chambers. July to October..... MAN-OF-THE-EARTH, I. PANDURATA, has white flowers up to 3 inches long, sometimes with a purple center. The stigma is two-lobed, the capsule two-chambered. Otherwise it closely resembles *I. purpurea*. The plant's remarkable feature is its tuberous root, which may weigh up to 20 pounds and, like that of the sweet-potato (*I. batatas*), is edible. June to September..... I. HEDERACEA has leaves resembling those of English ivy (*Hedera helix*) though the blades are usually cleft into three. The flowers are blue (sometimes white), turning reddish as they age. The corolla is less than 2 inches long. The stigma is three-lobed and the ovary three-chambered. July to October..... I. LACUNOSA is a smaller morning-glory with generally white flowers less than 2 inches long. The stigma is two-lobed, the ovary two-chambered. Moist areas. August to October.

Convolvulus arvensis   *Johnson*

omea purpurea   *Johnson*   Convolvulus sepium   *Johnson*

QUAMOCLIT

Tropical America is the home of these red-flowered, cultivated vines that have spread into the wild. "Quamoclit" is their Mexican name.

RED MORNING-GLORY, Q. COCCINEA, has a slender, twining stem with leaf-blades somewhat heart-shaped, often angled on their basal lobes, sometimes cleft into three or more rounded or pointed lobes. From two to several flowers appear on a single branch. The tube of the corolla is about an inch in length, the expanded portion approximately ¾ inch across. Both stamens and style protrude from the throat of the flower. The single stigma is unlobed. July to October. (By some botanists placed in the genus *Ipomoea*.)

DODDER (CUSCUTA)

This is a genus of diminutive parasitic plants without leaves. Though their seeds germinate in the ground, the plants soon lose this contact with the soil and their yellow or orange stems are in a tangled mass around the plants that they attack. Sending suckers into the tissues of the "host" plant, the parasite thus absorbs the nourishment by which it lives. The flowers are white and more or less rotund, the divisions of calyx and corolla being little more than points. There are many species but probably only one that approaches the City of New York.

C. GRONOVII attacks mainly herbs and low shrubs. The five teeth of its corolla extend outward at right angles. Scales below the calyx are fringed. July to October.

THE BLUEBELL FAMILY – CAMPANULACEAE

Petals five, joined into a bell or spreading into a five-lobed disk, generally blue, occasionally white. Calyx five-cleft. Stamens five. Stigmas three atop a single style. Ovary inferior; the fruit a three-chambered capsule shedding its seeds through pores on the sides or at the top or base.

BLUEBELLS (CAMPANULA)

The corolla in all except one species is bell-shaped; in color it may be blue, violet, or almost white.

HAREBELL or BLUEBELLS-OF-SCOTLAND, C. ROTUNDIFOLIA, is the species upon which the genus and the family are both based. It is of worldwide distribution. The name *rotundifolia*, meaning "round-leaved," comes from the short-lived, round basal leaves that are seldom seen. The majority of the leaves are very narrow and they are numerous. The plant grows from 4 to 20 inches high. The stem is slender and much branched; the bells hang from the tips of the branches. The purplish-blue corolla is from ⅝ to 1⅛ inches long, the calyx about half that length. In all its characteristics the plant is highly variable. It is called "harebell" chiefly in England to distinguish it from the English bluebells, which are in the lily family. June to September.

Campanula rotundifolia   *J. Smith*

Cuscuta gronovii   *Rickett*

amoclit coccinea   *Johnson*

CAMPANULA (*continued*)

C. RAPUNCULOIDES is a handsome immigrant from Europe often 3 feet tall. Its purplish-blue flowers dangle from racemes that terminate the stems. The corolla is about an inch long. The seeds are ejected through pores at the base of the capsule. The leaves are essentially ovate, the lower ones broad and long-stalked, the upper ones narrower and short-stalked or stalkless. July to September.

MARSH BLUEBELLS, C. APARINOIDES, grow in low, moist areas. The half-inch flowers are nearly white instead of blue. The stem, up to 2 feet tall, is weak. The leaves are narrow and pointed, mostly 2 or 3 inches long. June to August.

TALL BELLFLOWER, C. AMERICANA, growing up to 6 feet in height, is the one species that does not have bell-like flowers. Its five light blue and fairly narrow corolla-lobes open out flat, making a flower an inch across. The style projects from the corolla and bends downward with its tip bent upward. A tall plant may bear a 2-foot terminal raceme of flowers, with additional flowers below in the leaf-axils. The leaves are toothed and range in shape from lanceolate to ovate. The pores through which the seeds are shed are at the summit of the capsule. A woodland plant. June to September.

JASIONE

Unlike the bluebells in the bluebell family, *Jasione* has the heads of its stamens united at their base into a ring around the style. The flowers are minute and they grow close together in heads.

SHEEP'S-BIT, J. MONTANA, is an Old-World plant that has extremely narrow flowers condensed into a tight head of bloom about ½ inch across. The leaves too are very narrow; the plant may reach 2 feet in height. June to September.

VENUS'-LOOKING-GLASS (TRIODANIS)

This genus is called *Specularia* (from *speculum*, "mirror") in many books, the name referring to the flattish, polished seeds, which suggest small mirrors.

T. PERFOLIATA is the common species. It has nearly round leaves which partly encircle the stem. Flowers are borne in their axils. The lower leaves hold flowers that do not open; they pollinate themselves. Flowers that do open have five clear blue petals nearly ½ inch long, joined only at the base. The three stigmas are prominent; the five stamens also project from the corolla. The capsule has three chambers; each has a lateral valve above the middle through which it sheds its seeds. May to August.

Jasione montana — *Phelps*

Campanula aparinoides — *Elbert*

Campanula rapunculoides — *Rickett*

Triodanis perfoliata — *Johnson*

THE BLUET FAMILY – RUBIACEAE

Sepals, petals, and stamens mostly in fours; the flowers small. Leaves paired or in circles. Ovary inferior.

BLUETS (HOUSTONIA)

Paired leaves, a four-lobed corolla, and a style bearing two narrow stigmas distinguish these small plants, most of which appear in early spring.

QUAKER-LADIES or INNOCENCE, H. CAERULEA, grows in tufts. Leafy, branching stems from 2 to 8 inches tall arise from the basal rosettes. Each branch is tipped with a single flower about ½ inch across. The corolla is pale blue or lavender with a yellow center. Its four lobes expand at a sharp right angle from the tube. White-flowered plants are occasionally seen. April to June..... H. LONGIFOLIA, a less common species that inhabits gravelly soil, has only one main leaf-vein. The flowers open all summer from pink buds.

MITCHELLA

PARTRIDGE-BERRY or RUNNING-BOX, M. REPENS, is a low, creeping plant with small, roundish, evergreen, sometimes variegated leaves in pairs. The fragrant white flowers, barely ½ inch long, also come in pairs at the ends of the branches. The four petals are hairy on the inside. The style bears four narrow stigmas. In some flowers the stigmas show while the stamens are concealed within the corolla-tube. In others the four stamens are revealed while the stigmas are held below. A single scarlet berry is developed from the fused lower parts of the two adjacent flowers. May to July.

BUTTONWEEDS (DIODIA)

These are small plants with weak stems and small, stalkless leaves connected around the stem in pairs with long bristles projecting from the joint. From one to three stalkless flowers are borne in each leaf-axil.

D. TERES, which grows most often along sandy roadsides, has stiff, narrow leaves and white, pink, or purplish flowers about ¼ inch long. The flowers have four sepals, petals, and stamens and a single style and stigma. June to October..... D. VIRGINIANA has elliptic leaves and white or pink flowers nearly ½ inch long. There are four petals but only two sepals. The style is branched, each branch ending in a narrow stigma.

HEDYOTIS

H. UNIFLORA is a rather straggling plant with elliptic or ovate leaves and small white flowers in their axils. The corolla has a short tube and four lobes that are shorter than the sepals. Long Island. July to October.

THE BEDSTRAWS (GALIUM)

The flowers of *Galium* are minute, but in many species so numerous that they make a handsome show. The foliage of some is fragrant when it is dried. Both foliage and fruits of certain species cling, or "cleave," to the hair of passing animals by means of bristles or backward-pointing hooks.

LADY'S or YELLOW BEDSTRAW, G. VERUM, is easily recognized by its numerous minute and fragrant yellow flowers. The plant grows stiffly 2 or 3 feet tall and carries its very narrow leaves in circles of six or eight. Its roots are the source of a red dye. In Europe this plant has had countless practical uses for many centuries, including that of stuffing mattresses; the dried leaves are very fragrant. It is now accessible in the northeastern quarter of the United States and beyond. June to September.

tchella repens   *Johnson*

Houstonia caerulea   *Gottscho*

dia teres   *Allen*

Galium verum   *Gottscho*

GALIUM (*continued*)

NORTHERN or WHITE BEDSTRAW, GALIUM SEPTENTRIONALE, is fragrant in both flowers and foliage. The narrow leaves encircle the 1- to 3-foot stem in fours. The plant is highly variable – it may or may not be hairy and the small fruits may or may not be bristly. As in *G. verum*, its roots yield a red dye. June to August.

CLEAVERS or GOOSEGRASS, G. APARINE, is a tall but straggling weedy plant of worldwide distribution in the northern hemisphere. The stem and narrow leaves (mostly in eights) are furnished with backward-pointing hooks, and the fruit has bristles by which it too cleaves. The relatively few minute white flowers grow on branches from the leaf-axils. The plants are sometimes used in feeding geese. The seeds, roasted, have been used as a substitute for coffee. May to July.

ROUGH BEDSTRAW, G. ASPRELLUM, has hooked prickles on stem and leaves; the fruits, however, are smooth. The leaves are in fours, fives, or sixes. The white flowers are in many clusters at the ends of branches and from upper axils. July to September.

G. MULLUGO, of European origin, is widely naturalized in the eastern United States. The small white flowers are very numerous. The narrow leaves tend to be wider near the tip. They occur in circles of eight on the main stem; on the branches they may be in sixes. May to August..... WILD-LICORICE, G. CIRCAEZANS, has greenish flowers, bristly fruits, and rather broad, elliptic, three-veined leaves in fours. The flowers, which are without stalks, are often on zigzag branches that rise from the axils. Found in woods and thickets. June to July..... G. LANCEOLATUM, also called wild-licorice, has narrower leaves. It is a plant of dry woods. Its yellowish flowers turn purple. June and July..... SWEET-SCENTED BEDSTRAW, G. TRIFLORUM, bears its greenish flowers and its burs in threes on stalks at the ends of branches from the axils. The leaves are narrowly elliptic or lanceolate, mostly in sixes, the upper ones with a minute spine at their tip. May to September..... G. PILOSUM has elliptic leaves in fours, each about an inch long and with only one conspicuous vein. The plants are generally softly hairy. The flowers are greenish or purplish, stalked, and on forking branches from the axils. June to August..... G. CONCINNUM, a slender, erect plant up to 2 feet tall, bears its narrow leaves in sixes. The whitish flowers are numerous on many forked branches from the axils. June and July..... G. TINCTORIUM, an inhabitant of wet places, has prickles on the angles of its stem by which it clambers over other plants. The narrow leaves are mostly in fives and sixes. The whitish flowers are generally in threes at the ends of forking branches. Mostly they have three petals. June to September. The plant has been used for dyeing.

ium asprellum   *Gottscho*

Galium septentrionale   *Johnson*

um aparine   *Rickett*

Galium mollugo   *Murray*

THE VALERIAN FAMILY – VALERIANACEAE

Corolla five-lobed; calyx-lobes insignificant, the calyx-tube surrounding the inferior ovary. Only one chamber of the ovary functioning, this one in fruit holding only one seed. Stamens three, attached to the tube of the corolla. Of the two species found in the New York City area, both have escaped from cultivation.

VALERIAN (VALERIANA)

In place of sepals the valerians have feathery bristles of white or pink. The corollas are also of these colors. The small flowers are clustered at the tips of stems, on which the pinnately divided leaves are opposite.

GARDEN-HELIOTROPE, V. OFFICINALIS, is a stout plant from 2 to 5 feet tall. The leaves are divided into segments – from eleven to twenty-one. The pinkish flowers, with corollas less than ¼ inch long, are in a broad, dense, terminal cluster. They have a spicy fragrance. May to August.

VALERIANELLA

Plants of this genus have no visible calyx. They differ from *Valeriana* also in having undivided leaves.

CORN-SALAD or LAMB'S-LETTUCE, V. OLITORIA, was long raised as a salad plant. It grows up to 20 inches tall. The paired leaves, which are oblong, blunt, and stalkless, are attached to angular stems. They are toothed in their lower half. The minute flowers, clustered at the tips of stem and branches, are pale bluish. The fruits are yellowish. April to June, also October.

HONEYSUCKLE FAMILY – CAPRIFOLIACEAE

Most species woody; only one herbaceous genus within our range. One other, the twinflower (*Linnaea*), found a bit farther north.

TINKERWEEDS (TRIOSTEUM)

The tinkerweeds are also called feverwort, horse-gentian, and wild-coffee, among other names. They are coarse, strong plants with stalkless flowers seated in the axils of their pairs of more or less oblong leaves. The corolla is irregularly funnelform (slightly swollen on one side) with five erect lobes. There are five stamens. The fruit, developed from an inferior ovary, is crowned by the five long sepals.

T. PERFOLIATUM is so named (*per*, "through" and *folia*, "leaves") because the stem seems to grow right through the paired leaves, which are joined around it at their base. The stem is downy with gland-tipped hairs. The flowers, mostly six to eight in a pair of axils, are greenish, yellowish, or dull purple; the fruits dull orange. The leaves are thickish and dark green, the larger ones from 2 to 6 inches broad and from 4 to 12 inches long. May to July..... T. ANGUSTIFOLIUM has pairs of leaves that taper to narrow bases. The larger blades are from ¾ to 2¼ inches broad and from about 3 to 7 inches long. The stem, from 12 to 32 inches tall, is covered with long, stiff, glandless hairs. The flowers are greenish or yellowish and usually only one appears in each axil. The berry-like fruit is orange-red. April to June..... T. AURANTIACUM has opposite leaves that taper to their bases so that their blades are not joined. There is, however, generally a ridge connecting them across the stem. From one to three reddish-purple flowers develop in each axil. The fruits are orange-red. May to July.

Triosteum aurantiacum   *Johnson*

steum perfoliatum   *Elbert*

Valerianella olitoria   *Johnson*

THE CUCUMBER FAMILY – CUCURBITACEAE

Tendril-bearing vines, the tendrils all three-forked. The flowers either staminate or pistillate. Sepals and petals five or six, stamens three, the fruits in our regional species covered with prickles.

ECHINOCYSTIS

BALSAM-APPLE or WILD-CUCUMBER, E. LO-BATA, is a fast-growing, high-climbing vine with palmately lobed leaves, the lobes sharply pointed. From the axil of a leaf a branch of greenish-white staminate flowers arises, with a pistillate flower at its base. The six petals are as thin as threads and barely ⅓ inch long. Stamens are joined. The ovary develops into an oval fruit up to 2 inches long with soft prickles. Four flat seeds are set off from each other in pairs by

netlike walls. Ripe fruit opens at the top.

SICYOS

BUR-CUCUMBER, S. ANGULATUS, has large heart-shaped leaves, often with sharp-pointed lobes. The flowers are greenish, about ½ inch across, the staminate ones on clustered stalks, pistillate clustered on a single stalk. The five triangular corolla-lobes open out flat. The three stamens are united. The ovary, covered with barbed bristles, develops a single seed.

THE VERVAIN FAMILY – VERBENACEAE

Petals five in a bilaterally symmetric corolla. Stamens four, in pairs of different lengths. Ovary with four lobes.

THE VERVAINS (VERBENA)

The leaves are sharply toothed or lobed or cleft, often rather jaggedly. Flowers occur in long spikes, individual flowers with a narrow tube with five flaring lobes, the three lower ones slightly larger than the upper two. The calyx is five-toothed. The slender style carries a two-lobed stigma. The upper pair of stamens sometimes lacks anthers. All the species bloom all summer.

BLUE VERVAIN, V. HASTATA, has a slightly thicker spike than others. Though the flowers are only about ⅛ inch across, their violet-blue is so intense that half a dozen on a spike makes a vivid showing when the plant fills a meadow. The leaves are pointed, narrowly lanceolate, and stalked..... V. SIMPLEX is a smaller plant (to 2 feet) with flowers of lighter violet, ¼ inch across, and more in evidence at one time. The plant grows in dry, open places. The leaves, narrow and lanceolate, 1¼–4 inches long, are not stalked.

.... V. URTICIFOLIA has a long spike scarcely thicker than the stem, bearing at one time a few white flowers of $\frac{1}{12}$ inch diameter. The plant closely resembles a nettle (*Urtica*, "nettle"; *folia*, "leaf") but does not prick. It grows up to 5 feet tall and bears coarsely toothed, ovate leaves with short stalks..... V. OFFICINALIS comes from Europe, where it was formerly used medicinally. The flowers, in a slender spike, are violet or purple, about ⅛ inch across. The lower leaves are pinnately cleft, the upper ones lobed or merely toothed.

LIPPIA

FOG-FRUIT, L. LANCEOLATA, is a sprawling plant of bottom lands. The leaves are lanceolate, toothed, tapering to each end, generally without distinct stalks. The flowers, pale blue, pink, or white, are mixed with broad, sharp bracts in dense heads of bloom, with little more than a ring open at one time. May to October.

Sicyos angulatus   *Johnson*

rbena hastata   *Rickett*

Echinocystis lobata   *Johnson*

THE MINT FAMILY – LABIATAE

The corolla composed of two "lips" (*labia*) in most genera, two petals forming the upper lip, three petals the lower, all united at the base into a tube or funnel; in certain genera, however, the corolla almost radially symmetric, with four or five equal lobes. Stamens four, but two of them in some genera not bearing pollen or even lacking. Ovary four-lobed, generally forming four small "nuts"; a forked stigma on the style. Stem square; leaves paired. A pronounced odor in the plants of many species. Because flowers are small, a magnifier may be necessary for separating the genera.

I. *Genera with only two of the four stamens fully developed.*

CUNILA

DITTANY, C. ORIGANOIDES, has a wiry, branching stem about a foot tall. The leaves are ovate, toothed, and nearly stalkless. The small purplish or white flowers are in little tufts in leaf-axils and at tips of branches. The five lobes of the corolla are almost equal. July to November.

BUGLEWEEDS (LYCOPUS)

The bugleweeds, which are also known as water-horehounds, have the general aspect of mints without the odor. They are mostly 2 or 3 feet tall and generally grow in moist ground. Most of the leaves are toothed, otherwise lobed or pinnately cleft, and in all but one species, stalkless or nearly so. The tiny flowers, generally white, encircle the stem in a mass at each pair of leaves.

L. VIRGINICUS has blunt calyx-lobes. The leaves are ovate, tapering to both ends, and stalked. July to October..... L. UNIFLORUS has sharp-pointed calyx lobes. The leaves are lanceolate, tapering gradually to both ends. The plant bears edible tubers. June to September..... The remaining species of *Lycopus* have spine-tipped calyx-lobes. L. AMPLECTENS is hairy or smooth and has leaves from elliptic to ovate, but usually with a few broad teeth. This species also has edible tubers. August and September. ..... L. AMERICANUS is mostly smooth, and the leaves are generally lanceolate. June to September..... L. EUROPAEUS has purple spots on its corolla. Leaves tend to be ovate. August to October..... L. RUBELLUS may grow up to 4 feet, with toothed leaves varying from elliptic to lanceolate or ovate, and either smooth or downy. July to October. ..... L. ASPER has a hairy stem and rough, sharply toothed, lanceolate leaves. The calyx-lobes are triangular, tapering to sharp points. July and August.

COLLINSONIA

HORSE-BALM, RICHWEED, or STONE-ROOT, C. CANADENSIS, is a somewhat bushy plant from 2 to 5 feet tall, with large, ovate, toothed leaves. The widely branched inflorescence bears many yellow flowers ½ inch long. The lower lip, consisting of one petal, is long and delicately fringed. The two stamens protrude far beyond the mouth of the corolla. Leaves and flowers alike have a pleasant lemony odor. July to September.

AMERICAN PENNYROYAL (HEDEOMA)

Clusters of a few small, blue, two-lipped flowers appear in the leaf-axils of *Hedeoma*.

H. PULEGIOIDES is strongly aromatic, often perfuming an entire field or woodlot. It stands about a foot tall. Leaves are lanceolate or ovate and stalked. July to September.

Collinsonia canadensis *Rickett*

copus virginicus *Rickett*

Hedeoma pulegioides *Rickett*

llinsonia canadensis *Rickett*

Cunila origanoides *Uttal*

SALVIA

The large genus that gives us the sage we use in cooking and also the house-plant known as scarlet sage contributes only one species to the wild in the region around New York.

CANCER-WEED, S. LYRATA, has circles of blue or violet flowers about an inch long on its stem at intervals, in the axils of bracts. The stem grows from 1 to 2 feet high. The flowers are two-lipped, the lower lip long and conspicuous. Two stamens develop inside. The calyx also is two-lipped, with three short teeth above and two longer ones below. The leaves appear mostly in a rosette at the base of the flowering stem. A sandy woodland plant. April to June.

THE HORSE-MINTS (MONARDA)

The word "horse" here, as in many other plants, signifies "coarse" – and these are large plants, also very handsome ones. Showy heads of flowers open at the summits of the stems and in some species in leaf-axils also. The flower-heads are surrounded by broad, pointed, often colored bracts. The individual flowers are slender, curved, and markedly two-lipped. The upper lip continues the tube; the long, thread-like style and the two stamens lie close under it. The lower lip arches downward and is slightly broader.

BEE-BALM or OSWEGO-TEA, M. DIDYMA, has handsome scarlet heads of flowers subtended by red bracts, the inner ones bristle-like. The leaves are sometimes bronze in hue, the larger ones 2½–5½ inches long. The plants grow up to 5 feet tall. Widely culti-vated as well as growing wild, this species has spread even farther into the wild from gardens. Despite its name, bees are said not to be attracted to it, but its nectar is often sipped by humming-birds. June to September..... M. MEDIA resembles *M. didyma* but the flowers are of a dark rose-purple color. The bracts are also purplish and they have bristly margins. July to September.

WILD BERGAMOT, M. FISTULOSA, is the common and much admired species of eastern roadsides and woods. The flowers are generally lilac, sometimes pinkish. The upper lip of the corolla has a tuft of fine hairs at its tip. The plant stands from 1 to 5 feet tall. The leaves are on short stalks and they have toothed, lanceolate blades, which may be smooth or softly hairy. This species customarily grows in large colonies, which give a minty fragrance to the atmosphere. June to September..... M. CLINOPODIA is similar to *M. fistulosa*, but seldom more than 3 feet tall, and the bracts beneath the flower-cluster are somewhat whitish. The lower lip of the corolla has purplish spots. A woodland plant. June to September..... DOTTED MONARDA or HORSE-MINT, M. PUNCTATA, gets most of its show of color from the numerous bracts, which are lilac or sometimes whitish. The flowers are pale yellow with purple spots. The upper lip of the corolla is arched and is longer than the stamens. Several clusters appear below the one at the summit of the stem. The stem, from 1 to 3 feet tall, may be either hairy or nearly smooth. The lanceolate leaves, 1–3 inches long, are narrowed toward the base. The plant grows in open, sandy places. July to October.

Monarda fistulosa   *Johnson*

via lyrata   *Johnson*   Monarda didyma   *Scribner*

II. *Genera with four stamens developed.*

THE MINTS (MENTHA)

While the plants in many genera of the mint family contain essential oils that give them more or less of a minty odor, the true mints – those that are used commercially for this flavor – belong to the genus *Mentha*. Curiously, few other genera are so little characteristic of the family. The flowers are almost radially symmetric. The corolla is four-lobed, the upper lobe usually broader than the other three and often notched. There are four stamens. All except our one native species have come to us from Europe, most of them having escaped from cultivation. For commercial plantings so many different races have been developed that the resulting plants, when escaped into the wild, are mostly difficult to assign to a species.

FIELD MINT, M. ARVENSIS, is our native species; even this is highly variable. The stem, for instance, may be hairy, downy, or smooth. The leaves, which are paired and stalked, range from ovate to lanceolate. The pinkish-lilac flowers encircle the stem, being clustered in the axils of the leaves, but there are often none in the upper axils. July to September.

PEPPERMINT, M. PIPERITA, has most of its flowers in a dense spike at the summit of the stem, which may be up to 3 feet tall. The corolla is pale purplish, the calyx rather large. The leaves are somewhat lanceolate, smooth, sharply toothed, and stalked. The plant is found most often in wet places. June to October.

SPEARMINT, M. SPICATA, also grows to 3 feet, and the stem and leaves are usually smooth. The leaves are lanceolate, toothed, and nearly stalkless. The flowers, which are pinkish or pale violet, sometimes almost white, are in long slender spikes, with additional clusters below. The bracts beneath the clusters are narrow. Like peppermint, this grows in wet places. June to October. ..... M. LONGIFOLIA resembles *M. spicata* but has narrower leaves.

ISANTHUS

The single species of *Isanthus* is a small plant of dry soil areas.

FALSE PENNYROYAL, I. BRACHIATUS, scarcely grows beyond 8 inches tall. It is a clammy plant with pale blue flowers about ⅛ inch long and nearly radially symmetric, the corolla not much longer than the calyx. There are four stamens. The paired leaves are narrow and almost stalkless. They have one or three lengthwise veins and few or no teeth. July to September.

Mentha piperita   *Donahue*

Mentha spicata   *Rickett*

Mentha arvensis
Elbert

nthus brachiatus   *D. Richards*

THE MOUNTAIN-MINTS
(PYCNANTHEMUM)

The rather stiff plants called mountain-mints do not necessarily grow in mountains, but they do have a strong minty odor. The flowers, which are crowded in heads at the many branch-tips, often in leaf-axils also, are white or purplish, strongly two-lipped, and mixed with conspicuous bracts. The first three species described below have narrow leaves – at least five times as long as wide – with parallel sides. The remaining three have ovate leaves. All the species flower from June or July to September.

P. VIRGINIANUM is 1–3 feet tall. Its square stems carry hairs only on the angles. The leaves are lanceolate and smooth, commonly with plain margins but occasionally with a few small teeth. They vary greatly in width. The plant grows beside water, also in wet meadows and thickets..... P. VERTICILLATUM has a minutely downy stem bearing leaves much like those of *P. virginianum* but more uniformly toothed. It grows in either dry or moist thickets.

P. TENUIFOLIUM is a much-branched plant up to 3 feet tall. The leaves are very narrow and they have no teeth. The entire plant is smooth (or nearly so). It grows in dry open ground and thickets.

P. INCANUM has a covering of white hairs on most of its ovate leaves and bracts and on its stem. The lower leaves, however, are likely to be smooth and green above. The larger leaves are up to 4½ inches long, half as broad, and somewhat rounded toward the stalk. The flowers are spotted with purple. ..... P. MUTICUM has leaf-blades that are rounded or even indented where they meet the short stalk. They are smooth on top and toothed around the edge. The bracts beneath the flower-heads are broad across the base. The stem and bracts are hoary with minute white hairs. This is a woodland plant..... P. SETOSUM is distinguished by the stiff, sharp points (bristles, *setae*) on its bracts and by the loose disposition of its flower-heads. The plant grows up to nearly 3 feet tall and is minutely downy. The leaves, on very short stalks, are about 2 inches long and narrowly ovate. This is a plant of the coastal plain, growing in sandy woods and marshes.

SATUREIA

Satureia is the genus from which savory and other culinary herbs are derived. Several species can be found in the wild in different parts of the country, but except for two in the central United States, all are European or Eurasian in origin; they have escaped from gardens. Only one is likely to be found in the New York City area.

WILD-BASIL, S. VULGARIS, has creeping stems from which hairy branches rise from 1 to 2 feet bearing terminal heads of pink or pale purple flowers. A pair of leaves expands directly below each flower-head. The leaves are ovate or elliptic, stalked, hairy, and usually without teeth. The veining is prominent on the lower surface. Dogmint is the name of a less hairy native American variety of this European species.

nanthemum tenuifolium   *Johnson*

Satureia vulgaris   *Rickett*

nanthemum virginianum   *D. Richards*

Pycnanthemum incanum   *D. Richards*

ORIGANUM

This is an Old-World genus, one species of which has found its way to this country.

WILD-MARJORAM, O. VULGARE, is a hairy plant 1–3 feet tall, with dense heads of vivid flowers crowning stem and branches. Both the flowers and the bracts beneath them are bright crimson. The leaf-blades are ovate, tapering into fairly long stalks, and generally without teeth. Often prominent along roadsides, June to October. It was much used as a medicinal tea by the early American colonists. It is not, however, related to marjoram, the culinary herb.

PRUNELLA

Close-set, generally purple flowers in heads or blunt spikes terminate each stem and branch of *Prunella*. The plant may be 2 inches or 2 feet high, but it seldom stands erect. The flowers are conspicuously two-lipped, the upper lip of the corolla forming a long hood, the lower lip bent down and its middle lobe so toothed as to appear almost fringed. Broad bracts, toothed at the tip and often colored, are mixed with the flowers.

SELF-HEAL or HEAL-ALL, P. VULGARIS, is the species commonly seen here. It is highly variable in flower-color (from white through pink and blue to purple), calyx-color (green or purple), leaf-shape (lanceolate or ovate, sharp or blunt at tip, round or tapering at the base), and other features. Its typical form, however, is as illustrated. May to October.

GERMANDER (TEUCRIUM)

One native eastern species of this genus appears within our range.

AMERICAN GERMANDER or WOOD-SAGE, T. CANADENSE, has a corolla unlike that of any other of our mints. The upper lip is cleft and has a small horn rising on either side. The four stamens, later the style, project through here. The lower lobe is broad, almost diamond-shaped, and wavy-edged. The flowers are in a spike, about six open at a time. The corollas are $\frac{3}{8}$–$\frac{3}{4}$ inch long and are purplish, pink, or creamy. June to September.

HEMP-NETTLES (GALEOPSIS)

The calyx in the hemp-nettles has triangular teeth which end in five sharp spines. The corolla has a hoodlike upper lip and a three-lobed lower lip, at the base of which a hand magnifier will reveal two projections. The flowers are in dense masses in the axils of leaves.

G. TETRAHIT has white or tinted bristles on the outside of the upper lip of the corolla. The lower lip has three distinct, widely spreading lobes, the middle one marked with purple. The corolla is otherwise essentially white, and about $\frac{3}{4}$ inch long. The stem is bristly. The leaves are ovate and sharply toothed. June to September.

Prunella vulgaris *Gottscho*

Origanum vulgare *Elbert*

Galeopsis tetrahit *Gottscho*

Teucrium canadense *Rickett*

NEPETA

This Old-World genus is the one which gives us the well-known plant called catnip.

CATNIP or CATMINT, N. CATARIA, is recognized at once by its odor, beloved of cats. It was once cultivated for its supposed medicinal value. The stem, 1–3 feet tall, bears fairly long-stalked leaves with ovate or heart-shaped, round-toothed blades covered with a white down. The flowers, in dense spikes at the tip of stem and branches, are whitish with purple spots. The upper lip of the corolla is two-cleft or notched and slightly hooded. The lower lip has three lobes, the broad middle lobe extending outward and downward and often being sharply toothed. June to October.

THYME (THYMUS)

The herb thyme that is commonly used for seasoning is *Thymus vulgaris*. A different aromatic species has escaped from gardens, where many varieties have been cultivated, and run wild over the eastern United States.

CREEPING THYME or WILD THYME, T. SERPYLLUM, bears many pairs of leaves about ½ inch long, often with bunches of smaller leaves in their axils. The flowers are in erect but not sharp-pointed spikes at the ends of branches. The pinkish or purplish corolla has a flat, notched upper lip and a lower lip of three spreading lobes. The calyx has three triangular teeth in its upper lip and two longer, narrower teeth below. June to September.

THE HEDGE-NETTLES (STACHYS)

The leaf-shape of certain species is what puts "nettle" in the common name of these plants. They do not have the stinging propensity of true nettles (*Urtica*), in the nettle family. The flowers surround the stem at intervals, in an "interrupted spike." The individual flower has a hooded upper lip and a longer, three-lobed, downward-pointing lower lip. The first two species described here have hairy leaves and a downy or hairy calyx. The two remaining species have a generally smooth calyx. The stem also may be smooth or it may be bristly on the angles.

WOUNDWORT, S. PALUSTRIS, may grow to 7 feet tall; it may also not go beyond 8 inches. Its square stem is downy or hairy on the flat sides as well as on the four angles. The leaves, which are lanceolate to narrowly ovate with rounded teeth, have very short stalks or none. The flowers are rose mottled with purple. July to September, in meadows and waste land..... S. ARVENSIS has long, stiff hairs on stem, leaves, and calyx. June to October.

S. TENUIFOLIA, which bears a rather tall interrupted spike of pink flowers, is a highly variable creeping plant. The stem may be quite hairless or it may be bristly along the angles. The leaves, too, may be either smooth or bristly and may range from very narrow to ovate. The calyx may be smooth or may bear conspicuous bristles on the veins. June to September, in bottomlands, meadows, and low woods..... S. HYSSOPIFOLIA grows in bogs and sandy places on the coastal plain. It is a small plant, 4–30 inches tall, with a stem which is smooth except sometimes on the angles. The leaves may be very narrow, even-edged, smooth, and stalkless. June to October.

:hys palustris *Scribner*

Nepeta cataria *Johnson*

:hys tenuifolia *Rickett*

Thymus serpyllum *Gottscho*

BUGLE or BUGLEWEED (AJUGA)

Three species of this Old-World genus are used horticulturally, largely as ground-covers, and any one may be found growing wild, two of them in this area. They flower from April to July or later.

A. REPTANS has creeping stems bearing pairs of short, broad leaves with wavy margins, sometimes toothed. The flowers, which are bluish-purple, are on upright stems to a foot high, the lower ones in the axils of leaves, the upper ones in a sort of spike. The lower lip of the corolla, with three diverging lobes, is much larger than the upper..... A. GENEVENSIS is similar, but does not creep, and the stem and leaves are downy.

HYSSOP (HYSSOPUS)

There is only one species of this Old-World genus that has found its way into the wild in the United States.

H. OFFICINALIS, long cultivated as a medicinal herb, is a plant 1–2 feet tall, with narrowly lanceolate, stalkless leaves without teeth on the margins. The flowers, with purplish corollas about ½ inch long, are in dense spikes at the ends of stem and branches, with clusters also in the axils of the leaves. July to October.

THE GIANT-HYSSOPS (AGASTACHE)

These plants bear scant resemblance to hyssop, beyond the spike or "interrupted spike" in which the flowers are arranged. The flowers themselves have two pairs of long protruding stamens, the upper pair curving downward, the lower pair upward, so that they often cross. The leaves are ovate, toothed, and stalked. The plants appear mostly in woods and thickets, flowering from July to September.

PURPLE GIANT-HYSSOP, A. SCROPHULARIAE-FOLIA, grows 2–5 feet tall and is slightly downy or hairy on the stem and the lower surface of the leaves. The flowers are purplish, the spikes 2–20 inches long..... YELLOW GIANT-HYSSOP, A. NEPETOIDES, is similar but has a greenish-yellow corolla, very little longer than the calyx. The stem and leaves are essentially smooth.

FALSE DRAGONHEAD (PHYSOSTEGIA)

Obedience or obedient-plant is another name applied to this genus, for if a flower is bent up or down or sideways, it will stay in that position. The flowers are borne in spikes at the summit of the stem. The upper lip forms a hood over the four stamens; the lower lip has three diverging lobes. The leaves are narrow, toothed, stalkless, and smooth.

P. FORMOSIOR grows 1–5 feet tall. The several spikes, which sprout from the uppermost leaf-axils and also from the summit of the stem, bear flowers with purplish-pink corollas about an inch long. The sharp teeth on the leaves curve forward. The plant is found in wet woods and swampy thickets. June to September.

stache scrophulariaefolia   *D. Richards*

Physostegia formosior   *Johnson*

ia reptans   *Rickett*

Hyssopus officinalis   *Rhein*

THE SKULLCAPS
(SCUTELLARIA)

The skullcaps form a large and widespread genus with distinctive flowers. The calyx wears a hump on the upper side; this is the "skullcap." The corolla (mostly of blue or violet but occasionally pink, white, or variegated) has a rather long tube which curves upward, then opens into two lips. The upper lip is hoodlike, the lower more or less flat; the two side lobes seem connected with the upper rather than the lower lip. Instead of being aromatic like most other mints, plants are bitter; some of them were once recommended for fevers. The species may be separated into three groups.

I. *Species whose flowers are in spikes or racemes at summit of stems.* (Additional flowering stems may be in axils of upper leaves.)

S. INCANA (1–4 feet) has blue flowers about an inch long, in spikes at summit of stem and also in the upper axils. The leaf-blades are ovate (occasionally heart-shaped), white on the under side with minute hairs, scalloped, and long-stalked. The stem and corolla are also covered with fine white hairs. June to September..... S. SERRATA (8–28 inches) also has blue flowers at least an inch long, generally in a short raceme only at the stem-tip. The leaves are ovate or nearly elliptic, scalloped, and on short stalks. The entire plant is smooth or nearly so. May and June..... S. ELLIPTICA (6–24 inches) has a softly hairy stem bearing, at wide intervals, short-stalked, scalloped leaves with ovate, *not* elliptic blades. The corolla is violet, less than an inch long. May to August.

S. INTEGRIFOLIA (1–2 feet) has densely hairy, slender stems bearing narrowly lanceolate leaves without stalks and without scalloped edges. The inch-long corolla is purplish-and-whitish (sometimes pink). May to July.

II. *Species with flowers in one-sided racemes in axils of leaves from middle of stem upward.*

MAD-DOG SKULLCAP, S. LATERIFLORA (4–40 inches) has a small violet (or pink or white) corolla about ¼ inch long. Besides the axillary racemes there is usually either a raceme or a solitary flower at the tip of the stem. The leaf-blades may be lanceolate or ovate or triangular, with toothed margins, on stalks an inch long. June to September. Once believed to be a remedy for rabies.

III. *Species whose flowers are borne singly in the axils of leaves.*

S. PARVULA (3–12 inches) forms slim horizontal stems which are swollen at intervals into tubers. From these rise branches bearing bluish flowers about ¼ inch long in the axils of leaves. The leaf-blades are usually ovate, toothless, stalkless, and less than 1 inch long, with veins running lengthwise. May to July..... S. NERVOSA (8–20 inches) has a weak, slender, smooth stem bearing short, broad, stalkless leaves, the margins with a few notches. The corolla is pale blue, about ⅜ inch long. May to July..... S. GALERICULATA is the name of an Old-World species believed by some to be the same as the native American S. epilobiifolia. This grows 4–40 inches tall and bears violet flowers with a whitish corolla-tube up to an inch in length. The leaves, with little or no stalk, are lanceolate or ovate, their margins indistinctly toothed. June to September.

PERILLA

BEEFSTEAK-PLANT, P. FRUTESCENS, is a rank-smelling plant 1–3 feet tall, with white or reddish (or purplish) flowers about ¼ inch long loosely arranged in a one-sided raceme. The corolla has five lobes, the lowest one the largest. The calyx is two-lipped and becomes enlarged and papery after the corolla has fallen. The leaves are ovate, tapering, toothed, often bronzy. August to October.

Scutellaria parvula   *Johnson*

ellaria incana   *Johnson*

Scutellaria integrifolia   *Rhein*

ellaria serrata   *Elbert*

GLECOMA

GROUND-IVY or GILL-OVER-THE-GROUND, GLECOMA HEDERACEA, from the Old World, forms mats on the ground. The leaf-blades, about an inch across, are roundish with scalloped edges. Branches in the leaf-axils bear bright violet flowers. April to July.

DEAD-NETTLES (LAMIUM)

The corolla is erect, the upper lip a hood; the three-lobed lower lip extends forward. The leaves are stalked except just beneath the flowers, their blades broad and either toothed or scalloped. They have no sting.

HENBIT, L. AMPLEXICAULE, has several stems spreading out at various angles. The lower leaves, long-stalked, are round and scalloped; the upper ones may be coarsely toothed. The flowers are purplish and dark-spotted, the upper lip with a tuft of magenta hairs on top. March to November. (Early flowers often do not open.)

RED DEAD-NETTLE, L. PURPUREUM, grows erect to 12 inches high. The leaf-blades are ovate, usually indented at the base, and scalloped. The lower ones are long stalked, the upper ones, which are crimson below and carry half-inch crimson flowers in their axils, are short-stalked. April to October. .... WHITE DEAD-NETTLE, L. ALBUM, has 1-inch cream-colored flowers with two black-and-gold stamens to be seen if the plant is turned upside-down. All the leaves are stalked. Their long-pointed ovate blades are coarsely toothed. April to October.

MOTHERWORT, LEONURUS CARDIACA, has come to us from the Old World. Its leaves are long stalked and the blades generally have three sharply-toothed parts. In their axils are clustered ½-inch pale purple flowers, their upper lips hairy. June to August.

HOREHOUND, MARRUBIUM VULGARE, also from the Old World, is 1–2 feet tall and covered with a white down. The leaves are short-stalked, their blades ovate and edged with blunt teeth. Dense clusters of small white flowers are in the leaf-axils. The upper lip of the corolla is erect and notched, the lower lip three-lobed. The calyx has ten teeth alternating. May to September.

BLACK- or FETID-HOREHOUND, BALLOTA NIGRA, a weed from the Old World, 1–3 feet tall, has purplish flowers in the leaf-axils. The upper lip is hooded, the lower one three-lobed; the calyx has five teeth. The leaves are ovate, coarsely toothed, and stalked; the plant is hairy. June to October.

HEMP-NETTLE, GALEOPSIS TETRAHIT, from the Old World, has a bristly stem and sharply toothed, ovate leaves. The calyx has triangular teeth which end in five sharp spines. The white corolla about ¾ inch long, marked with purple, has a hoodlike upper lip crowned with bristles and a three-lobed lower lip with two projections at its base. The flowers are clustered in the leaf-axils. June to September.

BALM, MELISSA OFFICINALIS, from Asia, long cultivated here as a lemon-scented medicinal tea, is now found in the wild. It grows from 1 to 3 feet tall, bearing ovate and scalloped leaves. The half-inch white flowers are in small clusters in their axils. The corolla curves upward. Four stamens are beneath the upper lip. The calyx has three short, broad teeth in its upper lip, two narrow ones in the lower. June to September.

BLUE-CURLS, TRICHOSTOMA DICHOTOMUM, is a delicate plant up to 30 inches tall, bearing blue flowers singly at the ends of its many branches. The corolla has four point-ed lobes above and a broader, blunter lobe below. The long, *curved*, blue stalks of the two stamens give the plant its name. Bastard pennyroyal is another name for it. The plant is usually sticky. Leaves are narrow, without teeth, and stalkless. August to October.

ecoma hederacea   *Rickett*   Lamium purpureum   *D. Richards*

mium amplexicaule   *Johnson*   Leonurus cardiaca   *Johnson*

SNAPDRAGON FAMILY – SCROPHULARIACEAE

Petals mostly five (or four) joined to form two "lips," the opening between the two closed by an elevated part on the lower lip, called the "palate." In some species the palate lacking and the corolla open, being almost radial in its symmetry. Calyx in most species five-parted. Fertile stamens (those producing pollen) five, four, or two – most commonly four.

THE MULLEINS (VERBASCUM)

Mullein flowers all contain five functional stamens – the only members of the snapdragon family having that number. The corolla consists of five almost equal petals joined at the base, the three lower petals only slightly larger than the upper ones.

COMMON MULLEIN, V. THAPSUS, is a familiar roadside weed, a narrow spike of yellow flowers (very few open at a time) rising up to 6 feet from a broad rosette of downy leaves. Over much of the flowering stem there are additional leaves, their lower edges running down the stem. Flannel-plant and beggar's-blanket are other names, based on the leaves' wooliness. June to September.

V. PHLOMOIDES resembles *V. thapsus*, but the spike is likely to be taller and to show more flowers at a time. Also, the leaves do not run down the stem.

MOTH MULLEIN, V. BLATTARIA, is a slender plant up to 5 feet tall, with leaves on the lower part of the stem, flowers on the upper part. The leaves are lanceolate and toothed. The entire plant is smoothish and green except for some glandular hairs here and there. In the flower, the lower three hairy stamens simulate the tongue and antennae of a moth. The corolla may be either white or yellow. As the flowers open, from below upward, the flowering stem extends in height. June to October..... V. PHOENICEUM is similar, but the flowers are purple.

CULVER'S-ROOT (VERONICASTRUM)

V. VIRGINICUM grows from 2 to 6 feet tall. The leaves, which have lanceolate blades on short stalks, are borne in circles. Several tapering spikes of small, rather close-set white flowers appear at the summit of the stem. Each flower has four corolla-lobes. The style and two stamens which project from the corolla give the spikes a fuzzy appearance. Also called Culver's-physic from early medicinal uses. June to September.

FALSE PIMPERNELS (LINDERNIA)

Wet shores and other muddy places are home for the relatively small branching plants of *Lindernia*. The paired stalkless leaves, mostly elliptic, and seldom more than 1 inch long, bear in their axils pale lavender flowers less than $\frac{1}{2}$ inch long. The upper lip is short and notched, the lower lip longer and three-lobed. L. DUBIA grows from 2 to 14 inches tall. Its leaves may be plain or toothed..... L. ANAGALLIDEA does not rise above 8 inches. June to October.

HEMIANTHUS

The botanical name means "half-a-flower"; there is no upper lip to the corolla. The lower lip is three-lobed, the larger, middle lobe curling upward. H. MICRANTHEMOIDES is a creeping plant with leaves about $\frac{1}{8}$ inch long. The minute white flowers are borne singly in their axils. The plant grows on tidal mud. August to October.

234

Verbascum blattaria   *Johnson*

Verbascum phlomoides   *Rhein*

Verbascum blattaria   *Rickett*

Verbascum thapsus   *Gottscho*

THE SPEEDWELLS (VERONICA)

The flowers of the speedwells are borne either singly in leaf-axils or in racemes. Many of them are bright blue, others purple or white. Their four petals are slightly joined at the base, then open out, the lowest of them narrowest. Several species have dark stripes. There are two stamens. The seed-capsule is heart-shaped. The plants fall into two groups.

I. *Species with flowers in racemes.* (Leaves on non-flowering stems paired.)

GERMANDER SPEEDWELL or BIRD'S-EYE, V. CHAMAEDRYS, has slender branches 4–16 inches tall, rising from a creeping stem. The bright blue flowers, less than ¼ inch across, white-centered and dark-striped, are loosely arranged at the summit. The scalloped leaf-blades, on short stalks, are ovate or heart-shaped. May to July.

GYPSYWEED or COMMON SPEEDWELL, V. OFFICINALIS, forms mats with its creeping stems and rather small, thick, elliptic, and toothed leaves. The erect branches end in loose racemes of pale blue or lavender flowers ¼ inch across. May to July.

AMERICAN BROOKLIME, V. AMERICANA, is a rather succulent plant with creeping stems turning upward at their ends. The leaf-blades are lanceolate or ovate, toothed, and on short stalks. The flowers, about ¼ inch across, in small racemes from the leaf-axils, tend towards violet. May to August, in swamps and shallow water.... BROOK PIMPERNEL or WATER SPEEDWELL, V. ANAGALLIS-AQUATICA, resembles *V. americana*, but the leaf-blade clasps the stem and its edges may be either toothed or plain. The lilac flowers are only ⅛ inch across. May to October, in brooks and on wet shores..... MARSH SPEEDWELL, V. SCUTELLATA, is a weak plant with slim creeping stems bearing very narrow, stalkless leaves, mostly without teeth. The flowers are lilac with a flat corolla. May to September, in wet places.

II. *Species with flowers borne singly in the axils of leaves.* (Leaves borne singly, rather than paired.)

FIELD SPEEDWELL, V. AGRESTIS, has stems that lie on the ground with tips turning up. The leaves are ovate to roundish, coarsely toothed, and bristly-hairy. The flower, about ¼ inch across on a ½-inch stalk, may be white, but is more often blue with a lighter lower lip, dark stripes, and a white center. May to September..... BIRD'S-EYE, V. PERSICA, is similar to *V. agrestis*, but larger, the corolla about ½ inch across. March to September..... CORN SPEEDWELL, V. ARVENSIS, has minute blue flowers on foot-tall plants with ovate, toothed leaves about ½ inch long. March to August..... THYME-LEAVED SPEEDWELL, V. SERPYLLIFOLIA, has creeping stems covered with half-inch ovate or elliptic leaves. The flowers are loosely disposed on erect branches in the axils of smaller leaves, or bracts. The corolla, which is whitish or pale blue with darker stripes, is little more than ⅛ inch broad. April to July..... NECKWEED or PURSLANE SPEEDWELL, V. PEREGRINA, is a smooth, rather succulent plant 2–18 inches tall. Most of its leaves are oblong and blunt. Inconspicuous white flowers open in the upper axils. March to August.. ... IVY-LEAVED SPEEDWELL, V. HEDERAEFOLIA, has leaves broader than long, usually with a few wide teeth or lobes. Minute blue or lavender flowers open on branches which curve upwards. March to June.

CHAENORRHINUM

DWARF-SNAPDRAGON, C. MINUS, is a small, branched, glandular plant 2–16 inches tall. The leaves are short and very narrow, without teeth. The small, snapdragon-like flowers, borne singly on long stalks from their axils, are lilac with a yellow center. June to September.

onica officinalis *Elbert*

Veronica americana *Rhein*

onica anagallis-aquatica *Elbert*

Veronica chamaedrys *Elbert*

HEDGE-HYSSOPS (GRATIOLA)

In America, hedge-hyssops grow in mud or other wet places, not hedges, and they do not resemble hyssop. They are small plants with paired, stalkless leaves, mostly without teeth. Yellow or white (or occasionally pink) flowers appear singly in their axils. The calyx bears unequal teeth, and has a pair of bracts beneath it. The corolla appears to have four lobes at the summit of its tube, but the upper one – the upper lip – is notched; it therefore represents two petals. The lower lip has three lobes.

GOLDEN-PERT, G. AUREA, is the handsomest species in the New York vicinity. Its half-inch yellow (occasionally white) flowers rise from the axils of inch-long leaves on plants that grow about a foot tall. One form grows under water. At the base – or just under ground – plants are likely to have purplish runners that take root. June to September..... G. VIRGINIANA, which rises from 4 to 18 inches out of wet or muddy places, bears leaves $\frac{1}{2}$–$2\frac{1}{4}$ inches long with occasional teeth. The half-inch flowers may be white or pink or honey-colored. March to October, late flowers not opening.

G. NEGLECTA, the most abundant species, is the least conspicuous. The plants seldom rise more than 1 foot out of the wet mud. The narrow leaves, up to 2 inches long, are clammy and softly hairy. The lobes of the corolla vary from yellowish to cream-white, the tube being honey-colored. May to October.

TOADFLAXES (LINARIA)

Linaria has the typical snapdragon flower, with a ridge or "palate" on the lower lip closing the mouth of the corolla, and a hollow "spur" being carried downward. The flowers are in racemes or spikes. The leaves are very narrow, without teeth, and mostly in circles.

BUTTER-AND-EGGS or COMMON TOADFLAX, L. VULGARIS has yellow-and-orange flowers about an inch in total length, growing tightly together at the stem's tip. Long a weed in the European fields of flax (*Linum*), it is now a weed here, spreading readily from underground. May to October.

OLD-FIELD TOADFLAX, L. CANADENSIS, is a native species with numerous flowers of violet-and-white $\frac{1}{4}$–$\frac{1}{2}$ inch long. The short and narrow leaves are sparse. The plants are slender but may grow to nearly 3 feet. They often have runners at the base, also overwintering rosettes. March to September.

LOUSEWORTS (PEDICULARIS)

The flowers of the louseworts are clustered in dense terminal heads or spikes; the leaves are narrow and pinnately lobed or cleft. The upper lip of the corolla arches and forms a sort of beak, while the lower three-lobed one spreads downward.

WOOD-BETONY or COMMON LOUSEWORT, P. CANADENSIS, is 6–16 inches tall. The oblong leaf-blades are rough-surfaced and pinnately cleft into blunt lobes. The flowers are either yellow or red. April to June..... P. LANCEOLATA grows in wetter areas, up to 3 feet tall with several branches near the top bearing spikes of pale yellow flowers. The calyx has distinct, toothed lobes. The pinnately lobed leaves are toothed or scalloped. August to October.

KICKXIA

Flowers in this genus are much like those in *Linaria*, with which they were formerly placed. They have trailing stems bearing small ovate leaves and small purple-and-yellow, snapdragon-like flowers.

CANKER-ROOT, K. ELATINE, has triangular leaf-blades with sharp basal lobes and sometimes a few marginal teeth. The lower leaves are paired, the upper single. June to October..... FLUELLIN, K. SPURIA, has oval leaf-blades with no teeth and no sharp lobes at the base. June to September.

tiola aurea   *Gottscho*

Gratiola neglecta   *D. Richards*

Linaria vulgaris   *Johnson*

aria canadensis   *Schuler*

Pedicularis canadensis   *Gottscho*

PAINTED-CUP (CASTILLEIA)

Only one species of this large western genus occurs in the vicinity of New York.

INDIAN PAINTBRUSH, C. COCCINEA, stands out brilliantly with its mass of red-tipped bracts at the tip of its unbranched stem. In the flowers they obscure, the calyx consists of two rounded lobes, the corolla of a slender tube with two lips. Bracts and stem-leaves are deeply cleft, mostly into three narrow lobes. Occasional yellow or white-bracted forms are seen. The plants stand from 8 inches to 2 feet tall. April to August.

MONKEY-FLOWERS (MIMULUS)

The face-like corolla of the monkey-flowers consists of an erect upper lip of two lobes, a lower lip of three lobes, and (in our local species) a palate closing the tube. The flowers appear on long stalks from the axils of the paired leaves. The plants grow in wet places. Those described here bloom from June to September.

M. ALATUS has a square stem with thin wings (*alae*) along its angles. Its leaves have ½-inch stalks. The corolla, up to an inch long, is blue-violet..... M. RINGENS is similar, but its leaves are stalkless and toothed. The calyx is tubular and angled; the corolla is violet-blue and up to 1½ inches long.

MUSK-FLOWER, M. MOSCHATUS, is a somewhat clammy, woolly plant with yellow flowers about ¾ inch long, often red-striped in the throat. The stems are weak; frequently they take root from their lower nodes, then grow upward. The short-stalked leaves have ovate blades. The plants may give off a musky odor.

GERARDIA (AGALINIS)

These are delicately branching plants with slender leaves and stalked, pink or crimson flowers growing singly from their axils. While the corolla may appear almost radially symmetric, the bell-like portion bulges more on its lower side, and the three lower lobes differ slightly from the upper two.

A. ACUTA, found in sandy soil, has a bell-shaped calyx up to ⅛ inch long, with very small, sharp points. The ½-inch corolla has notched lobes. August and September..... A. TENUIFOLIA, a plant of dry woods and fields, is similar, but has broad spaces between the five minute teeth of its calyx. In the corolla the two upper lobes arch over the three lower ones. The leaves are extremely narrow. August to October..... A. PURPUREA, a resident of damp places, may grow to 4 feet in height. The leaves, about an inch long, are up to ⅛ inch broad. The flowers, which have corollas about an inch long and broad, with five nearly equally rounded lobes, grow in racemes. July to September..... A. SETACEA has threadlike leaves on bushy plants up to 2 feet or more high. It grows in dry sandy woods fairly close to the shore (on Long Island, for example). The calyx-teeth are scarcely visible. The corolla has a tube close to an inch long with broad lobes. August to October..... A. MARITIMA, a salt-marsh plant, is somewhat succulent and either green or purplish. The calyx-teeth are about 1/16 inch long and the corolla from ½ to nearly 1 inch. July to September.

SCHWALBEA

CHAFFSEED, S. AMERICANA, is the only species in the genus. It grows from 1 to 3 feet tall, carrying a spike of purple-and-yellow flowers. The corolla is narrow, two-lipped, nearly 1½ inches long. May to July.

mulus alatus *Scribner*

Castilleia coccinea *Rickett*

galinis acuta *Ryker*

Mimulus moschatus *Scribner*

FIGWORTS (SCROPHULARIA)

Figworts were so named because the European species were once used as a remedy for "fig" (piles) and also for scrofula. The plants are tall and have a widely branching inflorescence of small brownish or greenish flowers. The corolla stands almost erect, with a two-lobed upper lip standing straight up, two small lobes at the sides, and a lower lip bent straight down. There are four fertile stamens and one rudimentary stamen.

S. LANCEOLATA has leaf-blades that run down onto the stalk as two narrow flanges, or "wings." The corolla is greenish-brown; the rudimentary stamen is greenish-yellow, often wider than long. May to July..... CARPENTER'S-SQUARE, S. MARILANDICA, has stalked leaves; the stem may reach 10 feet in height. The corolla is brown, the rudimentary stamen brown or purplish. June to October.

TURTLE-HEAD (CHELONE)

Except in color, there is a true resemblance between the head of a turtle and the flower of a *Chelone*.

C. GLABRA, also known as snakehead or balmony, generally bears off-white flowers, though occasionally they are tipped with purple or yellow. The leaves are lanceolate or ovate, toothed, equipped with short stalks or none, and variable in hairiness. The plants grow from 1 to 7 feet tall. July to October.

MELAMPYRUM

Mainly an Old-World genus, which used to be a common weed in wheatfields, *Melampyrum* has only one native species in North America.

COW-WHEAT, M. LINEARE, is an inconspicuous plant from 2 to 20 inches tall, branched or not, and bearing leaves of various shapes from exceedingly narrow to ovate and partly toothed. The flowers are borne singly in their upper axils. They are white with a yellow "palate," slim, and shaped like a tiny snake's head. Dry or moist woods, bogs, or rocky places. May to September.

LIMOSELLA

MUDWORT, L. SUBULATA, sends a smooth mat of creeping stems through muddy stretches. From them grow tufts of thread-like leaves about 2 inches long, and from among them shorter stalks, each bearing one minute white flower with five radially symmetric lobes. June to October.

THE BEARD-TONGUES (PENSTEMON)

A fifth stamen that often bears a tuft of hairs (a "beard") and no pollen is what gives this genus its common name. It is a large and handsome group of plants, particularly in the west, many of them deserving of cultivation here as well as there. The flowers arise chiefly from the axils of the paired leaves or bracts, often in small clusters. The corolla forms a distinct tube with five spreading lobes at the end; these are two-lipped in some species, almost radially symmetric in others.

P. HIRSUTUS has a flower an inch long, tinted violet outside. The corolla is two-lipped, the upper lip erect and two-lobed, the lower three-lobed and directed forward. The plant stands 8–24 inches tall and its stem is covered with a fine, whitish down, the hairs often tipped with glands. May to July..... P. DIGITALIS has smooth, shining leaves and stem, and it may grow up to 5 feet tall. In the flowering part the stem is glandular. The flowers are white, often with purple lines inside, and an inch or more long. May to July.

Melampyrum lineare *Rickett*

rophularia lanceolata *Horne*

nstemon hirsutus *Rickett*

Chelone glabra *Johnson*

THE FALSE FOXGLOVES (AUREOLARIA)

The narrowly bell-shaped corolla which gives these plants their English name flares into five almost equal yellow lobes. The larger leaves are paired; the smaller upper leaves have flowers in their axils.

A. PEDICULARIA stands 1–4 feet tall. The stem is hairy or downy with some of the hairs gland-tipped. Most of the leaves are pinnately cleft. The calyx-teeth are usually pinnately lobed or bluntly toothed. The flower-stalks range from ⅔ to 1 inch long, the yellow corolla to 1½ inches. August and September..... DOWNY FALSE FOXGLOVE, A. VIRGINICA, is 1–5 feet tall, with both stem and leaves downy. The lower leaves are usually pinnately lobed or cleft – or they have at least a wavy edge. The upper leaves may be not lobed at all. There is generally a short leaf-stalk; the flower-stalks do not exceed ⅛ inch. June to September..... A. FLAVA may reach a height of 8 feet, with a smooth stem. The lower leaves are deeply cleft pinnately, the upper leaves merely lobed or toothed. The corolla is usually 1½ inches long. July to September.

LOPSEED FAMILY – PHRYMACEAE

The lopseed family contains only one genus, *Phryma*, and in America that genus contains but one species.

LOPSEED, PHRYMA LEPTOSTACHYA, is a slender plant, sometimes branched, bearing ovate, coarsely toothed leaves on short stalks. The flowers are in long spikes. The corolla is much like that in the snapdragon family – two-lipped, the lower lip longer and three-lobed. After the corolla has fallen, the "seed" (the achene) lies downward along the stem – it "lops." June to September, in woods.

THE BROOMRAPE FAMILY – OROBANCHACEAE

Parasitic plants, lacking green pigments; instead, attaching selves to roots of other plants. Whitish scales for leaves. Flowers more or less two-lipped; stamens four, in two pairs.

CANCER-ROOT, OROBANCHE UNIFLORA, bears a single flower at the summit of each of several stems up to 10 inches tall. Its tubular corolla, which flares into five nearly equal lobes, is pale lavender or lilac with two yellow bands inside on the lower side. April to June..... O. MINOR bears its two-lipped, purplish flowers in a rather loose spike on a plant from 4 to 18 inches tall. It lives chiefly on the roots of clovers. Introduced from Europe.

BEECH-DROPS, EPIFAGUS VIRGINIANA, which feeds on beech roots, is a brownish plant 6–18 inches tall, bearing small scales for leaves, the flowers in their axils. Only the upper ones open but only the lower ones form fruits, wearing the unopened corollas for a time on their tips. August to October.

SQUAW-ROOT, CONOPHOLIS AMERICANA, appears mostly under oak-trees, many scales (leaves) surrounding its several thick yellowish stems that stand 4–10 inches tall. In the axils of these scales the flowers develop, the corolla of each becoming about ½ inch long, the tube curved, the upper lip forming a narrow hood. April to July.

Aureolaria pedicularia   *Rhein*

banche uniflora   *Rhein*

nophilis americana   *Elbert*

Epifagus virginiana   *Rhein*

BUTTERWORT FAMILY – LENTIBULARIACEAE

Insect-trapping plants, with flowers resembling those of snapdragons, differing mainly in the pistil and in the two stamens.

BUTTERWORT, PINGUICULA VULGARIS, has a small rosette of smooth, even-edged, yellowish-green leaves. When insects alight on them, they are caught and digested by the plant. Violet-colored flowers about ½ inch long are borne singly on short leafless stems. June to August.

THE BLADDERWORTS (UTRICULARIA)

Small plants, many with underwater leaves divided into hairlike segments. Bladders attached to these trap and digest insects. All bloom into September.

U. SUBULATA has flowers of yellow, bladders on separate stalks..... U. JUNCEA is similar, but with the lower lip of the corolla consisting mainly of the high-arched palate..... U. VULGARIS has floating stems with much-divided leaves bearing bladders. The flowering stems may bear twenty or more yellow flowers..... U. PURPUREA has flowers on stems to 6 inches tall. Long-stalked leaves of many hairlike segments are borne in circles just beneath the surface of the water, bladders at the tips of some of them..... U. RESUPINATA grows in shallow water, bearing mostly undivided narrow leaves and tiny traps. The flowering branches, to 6 inches tall, each bear one purple or pink flower up to ½ inch long.

THE LOBELIA FAMILY – LOBELIACEAE

Placed in a family by itself, instead of with the bluebells (*Campanula*), because of the bilateral form of the flower.

LOBELIA

The flowers are bilaterally symmetric, the lower lip with three lobes, the upper lip split in two, a pointed lobe on either side. Through the split emerges a "rod" consisting of stamens joined around the style. At its tip is a "beard." The juice of the plants is milky and more or less poisonous.

CARDINAL-FLOWER, L. CARDINALIS, is a tall slender spike of brilliant dark red, the "beard" of the stamens a glistening white, the corolla-tube about 1½ inches long. Plants grow in damp soil, from 1¼ to 6 feet high. July to September.

GREAT BLUE LOBELIA, L. SIPHILITICA, bears heavy spikes of brilliant blue flowers to 1¼ inches long. The plants stand from 8 inches to 5 feet tall, and bear toothed, lanceolate leaves. August and September.

PALE-SPIKE LOBELIA, L. SPICATA, has pale blue or white flowers ½ inch long. Leaves vary from ovate to lanceolate, often broadest above middle. June to August..... INDIAN TOBACCO, L. INFLATA, is similar, but the flower's lower part (receptacle) "inflates" as the corolla falls. The leaves are rather bluntly toothed. The plant can give violent emetic effects if chewed. June to October. .... L. KALMII has a slender stem bearing almost hairlike leaves. The flowers, blue with a white center, appear at rather wide intervals July to September..... WATER LOBELIA, L. DORTMANNA, grows mainly under water. The narrow leaves form a rosette at the base. Flowers are few, pale violet or white, and slender. July to October..... L. NUTTALLII has a thread-like stem and leaves growing in sandy or limy soil. Flowers are blue with a white center. July to October.

Lobelia cardinalis   *Justice*

cularia subulata   *Johnson*

elia spicata   *Johnson*

Lobelia siphilitica   *Rickett*

THE MILKWORT FAMILY – POLYGALACEAE
Polygala is the only genus in the family among our wild flowers.

THE MILKWORTS (POLYGALA)

The name "milkwort" comes from an old belief that certain kinds, if eaten by cattle, would increase the flow of milk. The flowers have an intricate structure, best seen in *P. paucifolia*. In many species the flower-cluster looks like a head of clover. The flower-parts are five sepals, two of them larger and colored like petals; these are the "wings"; three petals, partly joined with each other and with the eight (or six) stamens, and a small capsule which is the fruit. The lower petal generally carries a fringe. Many species also form smaller flowers (some even underground) which do not open but which form fruits.

FRINGED MILKWORT or FLOWERING-WINTERGREEN, P. PAUCIFOLIA, has creeping stems (both above and underground) from which erect branches to 4 inches tall arise. Several leaves with short stalks and ovate blades expand near their summit. In their axils, on long stalks, are the plant's handsome rose-magenta flowers, up to an inch long, with conspicuous wings and fringe. A woodland plant. May to July.

P. POLYGAMA has small rose-pink or white flowers in a short, open raceme. The stem-leaves are short and narrow, slightly wider toward the tip. There are also narrow rosette-leaves at the base, $\frac{1}{4}$–$1\frac{1}{2}$ inches long. The plants grow to 18 inches tall. June and July..... WHORLED MILKWORT, P. VERTICILLATA, carries its narrow, pointed leaves – at least the lower ones – in circles, from three to seven at each level. The white or greenish (or purplish) flowers appear in slender, tapering spikes. June to October.

CROSS MILKWORT, P. CRUCIATA, from 4 to 20 inches tall, has four (sometimes three) narrow leaves in each circle. Branches may spring in pairs from the axils of the upper leaves. The flowers, from rose-purplish to greenish or whitish, occur at their tips in dense heads a little longer than wide. The sharp-pointed wings of each flower spread, disclosing the small petals within. July to October..... SHORTLEAF MILKWORT, P. BREVIFOLIA, is similar but commonly shorter with the leaves in circles of four or five. Flowers are pale purplish-rose. July to September.

P. INCARNATA has pale rose-pink flowers in spikes two or three times as long as thick. The petals form a tube which projects beyond the wings. The stem grows to 2 feet tall, bearing scattered, narrow leaves. June to November..... P. MARIANA resembles *P. incarnata*, but the flower-heads may taper to their tips, the flowers are less tightly packed, and the petals do not project beyond the wings. The petals and wings may be purplish, rose, or greenish. June to October..... P. SANGUINEA has flowers in short, dense spikes or long heads, from rose-purplish to pink, white, or greenish. When the flowers fall, small bracts are revealed. The leaves are very narrow; the stem grows to a foot or more tall. June to October..... P. NUTTALLII is similar to *P. sanguinea*, but not more than 10 inches tall. The flowers are greenish-white or dull purplish. June to October.

YELLOW MILKWORT or YELLOW BACHELOR'S-BUTTONS, P. LUTEA, a bog plant, grows from a rosette of blunt-tipped leaves, from 3 to 18 inches tall. The stem-leaves are lanceolate, often broadest toward the tip. The flower-stalks are frequently leafless, the flower-heads almost spherical. May to October.

Polygala incarnata   *Johnson*

Polygala lutea   *Johnson*

ygala paucifolia   *Gottscho*

Polygala cruciata   *V. Richard*

THE TEASEL FAMILY – DIPSACACEAE

Flowers minute, packed into heads. Petals four and joined; stamens four and separate.

DIPSACUS

TEASEL, D. SYLVESTRIS, 20–80 inches tall, carries its large lanceolate leaves in pairs. The small lavender flowers, crowded into a spiny head, have a tubular, four-lobed, radially symmetric corolla. July to October.

KNAUTIA

BLUEBUTTONS, K. ARVENSIS, has hemispherical flower-heads, in which the blue or lilac corollas are four-lobed. The paired leaves are pinnately divided into numerous segments. June to September.

THE DAISY FAMILY – COMPOSITAE

Flowers mostly numerous and small, many crowded together in a "head," which may resemble a single flower of other families. Flowers of two types: tubular four- or five-toothed "disk-flowers" in the center and strap-shaped "ray-flowers" surrounding them like petals. In some genera only disk *or* ray-flowers present, not both types. Each fruit an "achene" – a single hard-shelled seed that does not split open at maturity. The calyx represented by a "pappus" – seen in most genera as a circle or a pair of scales, teeth, fine hairs, bristles, or spines at the base of the corolla, generally best seen at the tip of the achene in the fruiting stage. In some genera, "chaff" – narrow green, papery, spiny, or bristly bracts – present among the disk-flowers. Each flower-head surrounded by one or several circles of bracts, somewhat resembling the calyx of other flowers.

THE GOLDENRODS (SOLIDAGO)

Except for one species (and occasional forms of other species) in which the rays are white, all the flowers of goldenrods are yellow, rays and disk-flowers alike. Mostly the rays are very small and there are seldom more than ten to a head. But the flower-heads themselves, being individually small, run into the hundreds in a single spray. The species are many and difficult to identify.

I. *Species with flower-heads on upper side of branches that curve outward.*

    A. Of these, the three mentioned on this page have three prominent veins running lengthwise in at least the lower leaves, all of which are stalkless.

S. GIGANTEA, which grows from 2 to more than 8 feet tall, is generally covered with a whitish bloom. Teeth on the leaves are found chiefly near the tips of the blades.

S. ALTISSIMA is similar, with a height to nearly 7 feet, a fine grayish down on the stem, and teeth toward the tips of the leaf-blades, if present at all..... S. CANADENSIS, up to 5 feet tall, has narrow, sharp-toothed leaves and an involucre of only $\frac{1}{12}$ inch.

By some botanists these three species are looked upon as one.

Solidago gigantea *Johnson*

dago altissima *Johnson*

Dipsacus sylvestris *Murray*

utia arvensis *Elbert*

SOLIDAGO (*continued*)

B. The leaves have one principal vein in the following group and in most of them (all except the last three) the blade tapers gradually into the stalk.

SEASIDE GOLDENROD, S. SEMPERVIRENS, has thick, succulent foliage, the basal leaves on long stalks, the stem-leaves stalkless. It grows 8–100 inches tall..... S. NEMORALIS is one of the earliest and commonest of the goldenrods of this region. The cluster of flower-heads is generally narrow and one-sided, but may be composed of several erect branches curving outwards. The lower leaves are generally broader toward their tips, and often toothed or scalloped there. The upper leaves may be narrow and pointed. The stem, which may become 4 feet tall, is finely downy..... S. ULMIFOLIA, which grows to 5 feet tall, has coarsely toothed or jagged leaves, elliptic and sharp-pointed. Through a magnifier one can see hairs on the under surface along the veins. The leaves diminish in size from the base to the tip of the stem, those among the flowers being mere bracts. The stem is smooth..... S. JUNCEA has finely toothed or scalloped lower leaves, with long stalks on the basal ones; their blades are broader toward the tip. Upper leaves are much smaller than the lower. The plant is smooth except for the leaf margins, and may grow to 4 feet in height. It is an early-flowering species..... S. ULIGINOSA used to be occasionally seen in this vicinity, but it is doubtful if it has survived the inroads of urbanization. It has wings on the leaf-stalks..... S. PATULA, another rarity for this region, has a stem which may be square or may bear several lengthwise ridges. The leaves are rough on the upper surface, with teeth often prominent and sharp. The plant will grow from less than 2 to more than 6 feet tall.

S. RUGOSA is a variable species, characterized by the flowering branches which spread widely from near the tip of the main stem. Some forms of the species resemble *S. juncea*, but are likely to be taller – sometimes close to 7 feet in height. It too is a goldenrod not certainly found within the New York area..... S. ARGUTA, only possibly found in this vicinity, has basal leaves with distinct stalks and carries a row of short hairs on the wings of these leaf-stalks.

S. ODORA, 20–40 inches tall, has narrow leaves without marginal teeth and without stalks, the upper ones very small. When crushed, the plant emits the odor of anise. .... S. ELLIOTTII, 20–80 inches tall, has smooth, elliptic, also stalkless leaves, mostly without teeth, often crowded on the stem.

II. *Flower-heads are borne in the axils of the leaves or in a long, cylindric, terminal cluster, or both.*

SILVER-ROD, S. BICOLOR, is almost unique among species of *Solidago* in having white instead of yellow rays. The disk-flowers are yellow. The stems are whitened with a very fine down. The leaf-blades taper into their stalks.

S. SQUARROSA, which may become almost 6 feet tall, has lower leaves whose blades taper down into stalks; the upper leaves mostly lack stalks. All are more or less sharply toothed. The bracts in each flower-head are bent sharply outward and downward (*i.e.* "squarrose").

S. FLEXICAULIS has long-stalked leaves on the stem as well as at the base. The leaf-blades are coarsely and sharply toothed. The stem, which may grow to more than 3 feet tall, is generally more or less zigzag. The flower-heads are partly in a terminal spike but also in the leaf-axils.

lidago sempervirens *Ryker*   Solidago squarrosa *Rhein*

Solidago bicolor *Rickett*   Solidago nemoralis *Johnson*

BLUE-STEM or WREATH GOLDENROD, SOLI-DAGO CAESIA, has purplish stems covered with a waxy bloom. The flower-heads are all distributed along the stem in leaf-axils. The stems are apt to arch and grow horizontally, whence the name "wreath goldenrod." The leaf-blades taper to sharp points and often are sharp-toothed. They almost never have stalks.

S. SPECIOSA is a beautiful species (*speciosa* means "beautiful") with a large terminal inflorescence made up of many cylindrical clusters, each head usually with five large rays. The stem bears from twenty to forty leaves with tapering blades and grows 2–7 feet tall..... S. PUBERULA grows 8–40 inches tall and has large rays of deep yellow. From twelve to sixty leaves are crowded onto the stem, all tapering into their stalks..... S. ERECTA, a rarity here, has leaves that may be blunt-toothed, scalloped, or plain-edged, but that taper at the base. The flower-cluster is loose and the bracts around each flower-head have broad midribs and round ends. The plant grows from 1 to more than 4 feet tall.

III. *Flower-heads are at the ends of more or less erect branches, where they form a flat-topped or dome-shaped inflorescence.*

The leaves are grasslike in all but the first species.

S. RIGIDA, up to 5 feet tall, has elliptic leaf-blades, the basal ones large and bluntly toothed and on long stalks, the upper ones stalkless, toothless and much smaller. Both leaves and stem are rough, generally with a harsh covering of short gray hairs (visible with a magnifier). The outer branches of the inflorescence are often bent outward to a horizontal position. The round-ended bracts of the flower-heads are easily seen.

S. GRAMINIFOLIA, 1–5 feet tall, is the most widespread of the grass-leaved species. The foliage may be smooth or it may bear short hairs best seen with a magnifier. The lower leaves are generally broader than the upper and tend to have from three to five ribs running lengthwise..... S. TENUIFOLIA has very narrow leaves on a plant that grows not more than 30 inches tall. The flower-heads are small and numerous, the ray-flowers are minute, and there are only from five to seven disk-flowers in a head. It is a plant of sandy soil..... S. MICROCEPHALA, 16–36 inches tall, resembles *S. tenuifolia*, but its leaves, folded lengthwise, are almost bristle-like, and there are only three or four disk-flowers in a head. The plant ranges southward from New York.

SOLIDAGO RIGIDA
MIDDLE LEAVES

Solidago caesia

Solidago graminifolia

dago rigida

THE GOLDEN-ASTERS (CHRYSOPSIS)

Except in color, the golden-asters are very much like the true asters. They are also close to the goldenrods, but their rays are longer and their disks are broader; furthermore, there are two circles of pappus in the flower-heads, the outer one of minute bristles or scales, the inner of long bristles or hairs. The golden-asters are largely plants of dry or sandy areas.

C. MARIANA has silky stems 8–28 inches tall. The leaves, at least when fully grown, are smooth. Branches given off by the midrib form a network of veins. Leaves along the stem are lanceolate; those at the base are widest between middle and tip. August to October..... C. FALCATA has stems 4–16 inches tall, covered with white wool, at least when young. The leaves are sickle-shaped. They have a central vein with no visible side-branches. July to October.

THE RAGWORTS and GROUNDSELS (SENECIO)

Yellow ray- and disk-flowers mark *Senecio*; but in some species there are no rays. This genus bears no relationship to ragweed (*Ambrosia*), an unpleasant weed that causes hayfever.

I. *Principal leaves in a tuft at the base of the stem, those on the stem being smaller and different in shape.*

GOLDEN RAGWORT or SQUAW-WEED, S. AUREUS, has blunt, heart-shaped basal leaves on slender stalks; they are usually edged with blunt teeth. Along the stem, from 1 to 4 feet tall, the leaves are much smaller, often pinnately cleft, and mostly without stalks. The whole plant is smooth when mature, though it may have loose tufts of wool on

stem and leaves when young. The flowering stems rise from creeping branches. The flower-heads are about an inch across. April to August.

S. OBOVATUS, from 6 inches to 2 feet tall, grows upward from slender runners. The basal leaves have narrow blades that are widest above the middle and taper downward to the stalks. They may bear tufts of wool when young. The stem-leaves are pinnately cleft. The plant grows largely in rocky woods, flowering from April to June. .... S. PAUPERCULUS grows chiefly in wet places and somewhat resembles *S. obovatus*, with small tufts of wool on its stems. The basal leaves, however, are smaller, rarely over 4 inches long. The leaves on the stem are narrow, pointed, and pinnately lobed or cleft. The flowers are nearly an inch across, but are sometimes without rays. May to August.

II. *Principal leaves borne along the flowering stems.*

GROUNDSEL, S. VULGARIS, is an Old-World plant that has become established as a weed throughout most of North America. It has leaves that are rather soft and thick and may be either wavy-edged, coarsely toothed, or pinnately lobed or cleft. Both stem and leaves are smooth or nearly so. The flowers are small and have no rays. March to October..... S. VISCOSUS, another weed from the Old World, is similar, but is noticeably sticky ("viscous"), has a fetid odor, and has floral rays which are short, curved, and inconspicuous. July to September..... S. JACOBAEA, a tall, coarse, leafy weed with rays at least ¼ inch long and leaves 2–9 inches long is a northern species that might reach this area. It is known as "stinking Willie" and is avoided by grazing animals.

necio vulgaris *Fischer* Chrysopsis mariana *V. Richard*

Senecio obovatus *Core*

Senecio aureus
Rickett

INULA

This is an Old-World genus, one species of which has become established in this country, having been brought here by early colonists.

ELECAMPANE, I. HELENIUM, has yellow disk- and ray-flowers, the rays both numerous and narrow. The plant grows 3–5 feet tall and has large, toothed, and mostly ovate leaves, woolly on the under surface, the lower ones with stalks. Largely a roadside plant. May to September.

TUSSILAGO

Here is an Old-World genus claiming only a single species, and this has become widespread in the northeastern United States.

COLTSFOOT, T. FARFARA, has a horizontal underground stem (a rhizome) which in spring sends up a bare but scaly stem 2–20 inches high, bearing a single flower-head with a yellow disk and narrow yellow rays. After the flowers have gone several leaves develop, each on a long stalk. The blade is large, round, indented, and toothed. The flowers appear from March to June.

THE TICKSEEDS and BEGGAR-TICKS (COREOPSIS and BIDENS)

Both of these genera have two distinct circles of bracts around each head, the bracts in the outer circle generally green, like small leaves; those in the inner circle broader and thinner and often yellowish. The seedlike fruits (achenes) of our species of both genera are tipped with rigid spines (the pappus); these are barbed, with minute hooks along their sides, generally pointing upwards in *Coreopsis* and downwards in *Bidens* (but there are exceptions). The achenes of *Coreopsis* are generally flat, with two spines and a thin marginal flange, or "wing." The achenes of *Bidens* generally have two or four spines but may have from one to eight. Their backward-pointing barbs make them adhere to clothing; they become the "beggar-ticks" that decorate the outfits of autumn hikers. *Coreopsis* flowers generally have eight showy rays, toothed in some species. *Bidens* flowers may have no rays. Some, however, are as worthy of cultivation as are the tickseeds.

TALL TICKSEED, COREOPSIS TRIPTERIS, grows to 8 feet tall or taller. The leaf-blades have three or five narrow, palmate segments on a stalk about an inch long. The ray-flowers are bright yellow, the disks brown. The flower-heads are anise-scented. July to September..... C. LANCEOLATA has long narrow leaves growing mainly from the lower few inches of the stem, which may be 8–30 inches tall. The broad yellow rays are toothed or lobed at the outer edge, dark-colored toward the center. The disk-flowers are brown. The flower-heads are borne on long leafless stalks. May to July..... C. ROSEA is unique here in having pink or white, instead of yellow, rays. The disk-flowers are yellow. The plant grows to 30 inches, bearing narrow leaves, sometimes two- or three-cleft. July to September.

B. CORONATA, up to 5 feet tall, has leaves divided pinnately into from three to seven narrow, sharply toothed segments. The ray-flowers (usually eight) are broad; each is terminated with a sharp point. Moist places. August to October.

eopsis tripteris   *Gerard*

Actinomeris alternifolia   *Rickett*

la ·helenium   *Johnson*

Tussilago farfara   *Rhein*

BIDENS (*continued*)

BIDENS CERNUA has flower-heads with broad yellow disks ($\frac{1}{2}$–1 inch across) and six or eight yellow rays up to $\frac{3}{4}$ inch long (or lacking altogether). The heads are directed sideways or slightly downward by a bend in the stalk. The plants grow from 4 inches to 6 feet tall, chiefly in wet places. August to October..... B. LAEVIS is similar to *B. cernua* but only half as tall and it holds its flower-heads more or less erect. The rays may reach an inch or more in length. Also a resident of wet regions. August to November.

BIDENS FRONDOSA usually displays no rays, merely disk-flowers, these surrounded by about eight leaflike bracts (therefore "frondose"), often unequal in size. The leaves are pinnately divided, the end-segment long-stalked. The plant grows up to 3 feet tall. August to October..... B. COMOSA also has no ray-flowers. Its leaves are coarsely toothed but not further lobed or divided.

SPANISH NEEDLES, B. BIPINNATA, have leaf-segments which are twice ("bi-") divided or cleft pinnately. The "needles" are the very narrow four-angled achenes which carry spines (from two to four) by which they cling to clothing. This and all but one of the remaining species of this area usually appear without ray-flowers. They bloom largely in late summer and autumn..... B. VULGATA has pinnately divided leaves, the segments sometimes cleft. The outer bracts of the flower-heads number more than ten; they are unequal and are edged with short, stiff hairs..... B. DISCOIDEA is a slim plant with a red stem bearing three-parted leaves. The smooth, narrow bracts on the flower-head number from two to five..... B. BIDENTOIDES, with stem either purplish or green, has a toothed but undivided leaf-blade tapering into a long stalk. There are from three to five narrow, 2-inch outer bracts on the flower-head. The achenes are long and narrow and two-horned..... WATER-MARIGOLD, B. BECKII (seldom seen), grows in water. The flower-head is handsome, with broad, $\frac{1}{2}$-inch yellow rays surrounding the large yellow disk. Aerial leaves are undivided; under-water ones have hairlike segments. July to October.

WINGSTEM (ACTINOMERIS)

A. ALTERNIFOLIA, the only species, grows up to 6 feet tall or more. The edges of each leaf are continuous with two narrow "wings" that extend vertically downward along the stem. The few yellow rays in the flower-head are of unequal size and they point downward. The disk-flowers point in all directions. The achenes are flat, usually margined, and furnished with two or three spines each. August and September.

SUNFLOWERS (HELIANTHUS)

The very tall plants with enormous flat heads of yellow bloom borne singly, from which we derive our "sunflower seed" for feeding birds, are but one of many different species of *Helianthus* seen in the northeast, a number of them around New York. While the flowers in the other kinds are smaller, they all have long yellow (occasionally reddish) rays and yellow or brownish-purple disks. The pappus at the base of each corolla consists of a pair of scales or bristles or scales tapering into bristles. Alongside each flower is a thin bract, constituting the "chaff." The bracts outside each flower-head are leaflike, in many overlapping rows. The leaves in different species may be borne singly or paired, stalked or stalkless. They are mostly ovate or lanceolate, and generally have a pair of veins branching from the midrib at the base of the blade. Many species are rough-hairy plants.

COMMON SUNFLOWER, H. ANNUUS, which in the east has spread from cultivation, grows up to 10 feet tall or more each year from seed. The whole plant is rough with bristly hairs. The leaves are mostly single and stalked, with broad ovate blades. The bracts

ens frondosa *Rickett*

Helianthus annuus
Johnson

ens laevis *Gottscho*

Bidens cernua *Johnson*

are long-pointed and edged with bristles. The "seed" is the seedlike fruit, the achene, a single true seed within each one. July to November.

The remaining sunflowers of the New York area are mostly woodland plants. All have yellow/rays and all except *H. angustifolius* have yellow disks. Most of them grow from a horizontal underground stem – a rhizome. The leaves of all except *H. decapetalus* are rough on the upper surface, and that is occasionally very slightly rough.

H. DECAPETALUS carries flowers which bear from eight to fifteen rather pale rays an inch or more in length, surrounding a half-inch disk. The leaves are lanceolate or ovate, sharply toothed, more or less three-ribbed, mostly smooth on the upper surface, distinctly stalked, and generally paired. The smooth stem grows from 2 to 5 feet tall. August to October.

H. DIVARICATUS has flowers of a more intense color than *H. decapetalus*. The eight to fifteen rays average close to an inch in length; the disk $\frac{1}{2}$ inch in diameter. The leaves are mainly lanceolate with a broad base and usually with no stalk; also rough, three-nerved, and generally paired. The stem is smooth and grows from 2 to 5 feet tall, the flowers on short stalks at the summit. July to October.

H. GIGANTEUS earns its name by growing up to 10 feet tall. Its flowers, in comparison, are small, the ten to twenty rays being not more than 1 inch long, the disk less than an inch across. The leaves, which are mostly borne singly, have a short stalk or none. They are rather narrow, and either toothed or plain. The plants often grow in damp thickets. July to October.

JERUSALEM-ARTICHOKE, H. TUBEROSUS, grows from an edible tuber, for which it was cultivated by the American Indians. Its common name has nothing to do with Jerusalem; it is a corruption of the Italian *girasole*, meaning sunflower, or "turning to the sun." It is a tall, rough plant with broad, ovate leaf-blades on distinct stalks, mostly carried singly. The floral rays (from ten to twenty) are up to $1\frac{3}{8}$ inches long; the disk is often an inch across. The plant grows largely in damp areas. August to October..... H. STRUMOSUS is a harsh-feeling plant, the leaves of which are covered with stiff, pointed hairs with swollen bases. The leaf-blades are lanceolate or ovate and are on short stalks. The flower-heads bear from eight to fifteen rays from $\frac{2}{3}$ to $1\frac{3}{4}$ inches long around a disk less than an inch across. The plant grows from 3 to 6 feet tall from a long, thin rhizome, the branches of which may bear small, slender tubers. July to September..... H. ANGUSTIFOLIUS has flower-heads with a dark-purple disk about $\frac{2}{3}$ inch broad. The leaves are narrow and rough and are mostly borne singly. The stem is also rough; it grows from 2 to 6 feet tall. The plant is found mainly in wet areas near the coast. August to October.

Helianthus giganteus   *Johnson*

anthus decapetalus   *Rickett*

anthus divaricatus   *Rickett*   Helianthus tuberosus   *Johnson*

CONEFLOWERS (RUDBECKIA)

The showy flower-heads of *Rudbeckia* species have "disks" that form a hemisphere or cone. The rays are yellow or orange.

BLACK-EYED- (or BROWN-EYED-) SUSAN, R. HIRTA, is a familiar plant of fields, open woods, and roadsides over a long season. Its dark-brown hemispherical (or conical) disk is surrounded by rays of rich yellow, $\frac{3}{4}$–$1\frac{3}{4}$ inches long and tending to turn downward. The entire plant is rough-hairy. The leaves are more or less ovate, those at the base of the stem coarsely toothed and tapering into their stalks. The plant grows from 1 to 3 or more feet tall. June to October.

R. SEROTINA, also called Black-eyed-Susan, as well as niggerheads, from the color of the disk, is an invader into our area from the west. While many botanists consider it a form of *R. hirta*, it does have distinctive characteristics, such as narrow (instead of ovate) leaves, mostly without teeth. The orange-yellow ray flowers, $\frac{1}{2}$ to $1\frac{1}{4}$ inches long and commonly bent downward, may occasionally verge into red or green forms.

Numerous other variations in the flowers, leaves, and growth pattern have been noted. The plant grows from 1 to 3 feet tall. June to October.

R. TRILOBA can usually be recognized by the presence of three (occasionally five or more) pointed lobes on some of the leaves. Most of the leaves, however, range from ovate to lanceolate, those at the base having heart-shaped blades on long stalks. The rays of the flower-heads are orange or orange-yellow, often darker at the base, and not much longer than the breadth of the dark-brownish-purple dome that is the disk. June to October.

R. LACINIATA is generally the tallest of the coneflowers, with a potential 10-foot height. It is a coarse plant with leaves irregularly and jaggedly divided, cleft, lobed, and toothed (*i.e.*, "laciniate"). Both stem and leaves are smooth. In the flower-heads the yellow rays, 1–$2\frac{1}{2}$ inches long, turn downward. The conical disk is yellow or greenish. The plant is found in wet places such as roadside ditches. July to September.

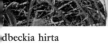dbeckia hirta   *Rickett*   Rudbeckia laciniata   *Rickett*

Rudbeckia triloba
Johnson

SNEEZEWEEDS (HELENIUM)

The sneezeweeds are characterized by broad, fan-shaped rays with three or more lobes at the end; they are usually directed downwards in varying degrees, the nearly globular dome which is the "disk" thus being made conspicuous. The leaves are borne singly; they are narrow and their edges are continued down the stem as narrow flanges. The pappus, which clings to the "seed" (achene) of a sneezeweed, consists of a few small scales, each often tipped with a bristle.

H. NUDIFLORUM (8–40 inches) has a brown or purplish disk about ⅜ inch in diameter. The rays, which are about that length, are directed sharply downward. They are often purple-tinged at the base. June to October.

H. AUTUMNALE (1–5 feet) has a yellow disk averaging ⅝ inch in diameter. The rays are about the same length or slightly longer and about ⅛ inch broad at the tip. They slope downward only slightly. July to October.

SILPHIUM

Most species of *Silphium* are known as rosinweed because their stems contain so much resin ("rosin"). They are found mainly in the middle-west and south; one species, however, has drifted eastward to New York. All are tall, coarse plants. A peculiarity of their flower-heads is that the disk-flowers are sterile; they yield no fruit. The ray-flowers (which are numerous) leave several rows of broad, flat achenes (the "seeds") around the base of the disk.

CUP-PLANT, INDIAN-CUP, or CARPENTER-WEED, S. PERFOLIATUM, is distinctive with its paired leaves (except the lower ones) united at the base to form a series of cups around the stem. It has a four-angled stem 3–8 feet tall. The leaf-blades are somewhat ovate with elongate tips, rough, coarsely toothed, and from 6 to 14 inches long. The lower leaves are stalked. The pale-yellow rays are generally an inch or more in length. The disk also is yellow. July to September.

HELIOPSIS

We have one species.

OX-EYE, H. HELIANTHOIDES, has a smooth stem from 1 to 5 feet tall bearing pairs of stalked leaves with toothed, ovate blades. Both the generic and specific names of this plant refer to its resemblance to the sunflower (*Helianthus*). The all-yellow flower-head is close to 3 inches across, the conical disk being ¾–1 inch in diameter and the rays (about ³⁄₁₆ inch wide) about an inch in length. June to October.

enium nudeflorum *Gottscho*

Silphium perfoliatum *Johnson*

Helenium autumnale
Johnson

THE WILD ASTERS (ASTER)

There are so many asters and the differences between them are frequently so slight that it is sometimes difficult even for the botanist to distinguish species. The genus *Aster*, however is easily recognized. The rays are narrow and are purple, lavender pink, blue or white. The disk is in general rather small, and contains yellow flowers which in many species turn reddish. The pappus, which clings to the achene (the "seed"), consists of a tuft of fine bristles. The bracts (the leaflike parts around a flower-head), usually green-tipped, overlap in several circles. Their exact shape, texture, or hairiness may distinguish a species. To determine these, at least a hand magnifier is usually required. Under cultivation, particularly in England, our wild asters and their hybrids are known as "Michaelmas daisies." They bear only remote family relationship to the China-aster (*Callistephus*) of our gardens. A preliminary classification of asters may be made on the basis of the shape of their leaves and the presence or absence of a leaf-stalk.

I. *Species in which the lower leaves, at least, have heart-shaped blades on distinct stalks.*

A. CORDIFOLIUS (1–6 feet), has a nearly smooth stem with thin, ovate, sharply toothed leaf-blades on slender stalks. The bracts are smooth and rather narrow, with blunt tips. The rays, less than ½ inch long, are pale blue or violet or white. The disk

tends to turn red early. August to October. .... A. SAGITTIFOLIUS is similar to *A. cordifolius*, but the leaf-blades are narrower and also are rough, and the leaf-stalks are broad and flat. The rays vary from pale blue to pink or white and are up to ½ inch long..... A. LOWRIEANUS also resembles *A. cordifolius* except that the leaf-blades are smooth and soft, they display a whitish bloom, and generally have no marginal teeth..... A. SCHREBERI is a white-flowered species in the same group – the leaves with heart-shaped blades on distinct stalks. It is, however, more like *A. macrophyllus* (below), but may be distinguished by its smooth bracts. The whole plant is generally rather smooth and the leaves are thin. July to October..... A. MACROPHYLLUS (1–5 feet) has thick, coarsely toothed leaf-blades tapering to a sharp point. The flowering branches are glandular. The bracts are downy with broad, blunt tips. The rays are violet or blue.

A. UNDULATUS (1–4 feet) is a hairy plant with downy bracts. The leaf-stalks have two lobes at their base and with these they "clasp" the stem. The leaf-blades seldom have teeth. The rays are pale blue or violet. August to November.

A. DIVARICATUS (1–3 feet), a common and variable species, has thin, sharply toothed leaf-blades on slender stalks, attached to a stem that is frequently zigzag. The bracts are rather broad and blunt. The rays, ½ inch long, usually number about ten. July to October.

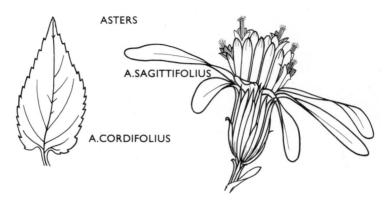

ASTERS

A.SAGITTIFOLIUS

A.CORDIFOLIUS

Aster divaricatus
Gottscho

ter undulatus   *Rhein*   Aster cordifolius   *Rickett*

ASTER (*continued*)

II. *Species that have no leaf-stalks; the leaf-blades themselves are attached to the stem.*

NEW ENGLAND ASTER, A. NOVAE-ANGLIAE (1–8 feet tall), is the handsomest of our wild asters, with forty or fifty rays of deep purple, pale lavender, pink, or white in each flower-head. The stalks and bracts of the flower-heads are covered with stalked glands. The rest of the plant is hairy and perhaps glandular. The leaves, which are lance-shaped, have two downward-pointing basal lobes which partly surround the stem. July to October.

NEW YORK ASTER, A. NOVI-BELGII (1–4 feet), often rivals the New England aster (above) in color but the stem is finely downy or nearly smooth, not hairy, and the generally lanceolate leaves are sharply toothed and smooth. The tips on the bracts beneath the flower-heads tend to turn outwards or downwards. July to October..... A. PUNICEUS is another handsome species, and an extremely variable one. The stem and leaves may be bristly, hairy, or almost smooth. The leaves vary greatly in shape, but characteristically, at the base they appear to surround the stem. The bracts beneath the flower-heads are narrow and sharp-pointed. The rays, which may be blue-violet, lilac, pink, or white, are about ½ inch long and number from twenty to forty. August to November.

A. PRENANTHOIDES (1–3 feet) has a rough, ovate or lanceolate leaf-blade which tapers sharply to a broad, flat base with two long lobes which more or less surround the stem. The bracts beneath the flower-head are very narrow and translucent. The rays are pale. August to October.

A. PATENS (1–3 feet) has rather small, blunt leaves with no teeth and no stalks, but with lobes at the base which almost encircle the stem. The bracts are often glandular and downy, with spreading green tips. The rays vary from violet to pink. August to October. .... A. LAEVIS (1–3 feet) has a smooth surface that is often whitened with a bloom. The leaf-blades are mostly lanceolate or elliptic, the lower ones with stalks, the upper stalkless and "clasping" the stem. The bracts are narrow and whitish with green tips. August to October.

ASTERS

A.PRENANTHOIDES
DISK-FLOWER

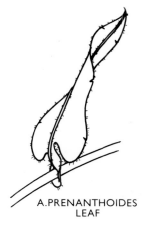

A.PRENANTHOIDES
LEAF

er-novi-belgii   *Elbert*

Aster novae-angliae   *Rickett*

Aster patens   *Elbert*

Aster prenanthoides   *Rhein*

ASTER (*continued*)

III. *Species whose leaves are not heart-shaped at the base and do not appear to encircle the stem. All on this page have colored rays.*

A. In the first four species the leaf-blades are ten or more times as long as wide.

A. LINARIIFOLIUS has a more or less downy stem and rarely grows more than 2 feet tall. It is beset with numerous stiff, rough needle-like leaves; there is often only a single flower-head at the summit of a stem. July to October.

A. DUMOSUS somewhat resembles *A. linariifolius* except that the stem is smooth and often branched; the leaves, which are rough, vary from very narrow to lanceolate or elliptic, and the flower-heads occur on stems which bear many small bracts. The rays are short and pale. August to October.

A. SUBULATUS is a smooth and fleshy, bushy-branched plant up to 3 feet tall with very narrow leaves. The flower-heads are borne in a raceme; the rays are purplish; the disk-flowers are relatively few. Found mostly in coastal marshes. August to October.

A. TENUIFOLIUS, another plant of coastal marshes, seldom grows more than 2 feet tall. The few leaves are fleshy and extremely narrow, and the upper ones are shorter than the lower. The rays are numerous and short and usually pale purple. August to October.

B. In the remaining species on this page the leaves are less than ten times as long as wide.

A. SPECTABILIS has violet floral rays up to $\frac{2}{3}$ inch long. The leaf-blades range from lanceolate to ovate and the lower ones taper into their stalks. The plant is occasionally glandular. It spreads by slender runners through dry northeastern woods. August to October..... A. RADULA is a plant of wet woods and bogs which also spreads by slender runners. Its smooth stem bears numerous narrow, rough, veiny, toothed, stalkless leaves. The floral rays are pale violet and about $\frac{2}{3}$ inch long. July to September..... A. CONCOLOR has a rather silky stem and leaves, and the leaves are stalkless, elliptic-oblong to lanceolate, and also rather crowded. The flower-heads are in a spikelike raceme. The rays are about $\frac{1}{4}$ inch long and lavender. It is a plant of dry sandy soil, often in pine woods. August to November.

ASTER ACUMINATUS

ter subulatus   *Gottscho*

Aster dumosus   *Rickett*

er tenuifolius   *Johnson*

Aster linariifolius   *Justice*

ASTER (*continued*)

C. All species mentioned on this page have flower-heads with white rays. Those in the first group described have leaves that are more than ten times as long as wide.

A. ERICOIDES (1–4 feet) is usually covered with minute gray hairs. The leaves are narrow, stiff, and crowded, as on a heath-plant (*Erica*). The flower-heads are numerous and small. The bracts beneath them, seen through a hand magnifier, have broad green tips with a minute spine on the end. July to October.

A. VIMINEUS (1–5 feet) is smooth or nearly so. The long, narrow leaves may have a few marginal teeth. The stem is often purplish and may arch, with the tiny flower-heads standing along one side of the branches. In the disk-flowers the corolla-lobes are nearly as long as the expanded part below. August to October..... A. PILOSUS does not always live up to its name, for "pilose" means "with long hairs" and plants of this species are often smooth. The stem bears numerous short, narrow leaves, those on the flowering branches being so small as to be called bracts. The bracts directly beneath the flower-heads are narrow and sharp-pointed. A highly variable species of dry areas, sometimes confused with *A. ericoides*. August–October.

D. In the remaining species the leaves are less than ten times as long as wide.

A. ACUMINATUS (8–40 inches) has easily recognizable leaves. They are sharply toothed and generally elliptic or lanceolate and they taper to a narrow base without a stalk. The heads are quite large (see page 272), with rays up to ⅜ inch long. July to October.

A. UMBELLATUS (1–8 feet) is a bushy plant with narrow, lanceolate or elliptic leaves borne all the way up to the inflorescence. The flower-heads are numerous, forming a flat or rounded array on many rather erect branches (but *not* in an umbel). The rays are relatively wide, about ¼ inch long and few (six or eight) in number. July to September..... A. SIMPLEX (2–5 feet) has narrowly lanceolate or elliptic leaves on the main stem and branches and many much smaller leaves on the flowering branches. The flower-heads are scattered all over the plant. The rays (which may sometimes be lavender) are about ½ inch long. The distinguishing feature of the species lies in the disk-flowers: the corolla begins as a slender tube, then expands suddenly into a wider tube; this ends in five erect teeth which are shorter than the wide tube below them. August to October..... A. LATERIFLORUS (1–4 feet) is similar to *A. simplex* but the rays are shorter and in the disk-flowers the teeth are as long as or longer than the wide part of the corolla-tube. August to October..... A. INFIRMUS (1–4 feet) has veiny leaves that may be either elliptic or ovate. The flower-heads are in a widely branched cluster. The rays are wide and up to ⅜ inch long. July to September.

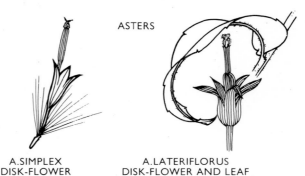

ASTERS

A.SIMPLEX
DISK-FLOWER

A.LATERIFLORUS
DISK-FLOWER AND LEAF

Aster vimineus   *Rhein*

er umbellatus   *Johnson*

er acuminatus   *Uttal*

Aster ericoides   *Johnson*

WHITE-TOPPED ASTER (SERICOCARPUS)

This genus is readily distinguished from the genus *Aster* by its few short, broad, white rays, its cream-colored disk-flowers, its whitish, green-tipped bracts beneath the flower-head, and the silky hairs with which the achenes (the "seeds") are covered. The achenes have a pappus of white bristles. The flower-heads are in flat clusters.

S. ASTEROIDES (6 inches–2 feet) has veiny leaves of various shapes, often toothed at the edges, and sometimes (not always) stalked. Dry woods. June to September.

THE FLEABANES (ERIGERON)

As distinct from *Aster*, the bracts around the flower-head in our species of *Erigeron* are in a single circle of uniform length, and most of them bloom in spring. The flower-heads are generally small, the rays numerous (in some species 100 or more), and very fine.

ROBIN'S-PLANTAIN, E. PULCHELLUS, has flower-heads an inch or more across, the largest of any of the fleabanes. A small group of long-stalked heads may top the hairy stem, 6–24 inches tall. The rays are generally tinted pink or lavender; the disk is yellow. The basal leaves are toothed and are widest in their outer half. The few stem-leaves are either toothed or plain and lanceolate or ovate. April to July.

DAISY FLEABANE, E. PHILADELPHICUS, grows slightly taller than *E. pulchellus*, and has one or many flower-heads up to an inch across, each with many rays, generally tinted pink or lavender. The stem is hairy. The basal leaves are narrow and may be toothed or scalloped. The upper leaves have two basal lobes which extend on either side of the stem. April to August.

DAISY FLEABANE, E. STRIGOSUS (1–4 feet), is the commonest of the northeastern fleabanes. This and the two remaining species of our region have white more often than tinted rays. The yellow disk, containing more than 20 flowers, is ⅓–⅔ inch across. The plant's slender stem breaks into a branching inflorescence at the top. The leaves on the stem are more or less lanceolate and mostly without teeth..... DAISY FLEABANE, E. ANNUUS (1–5 feet), is somewhat like *E. strigosus* but coarser. The stem-leaves are commonly ovate and sharply toothed. June to October..... MULE-TAIL or HORSE-WEED, E. CANADENSIS (1–6 feet), is an unattractive and abundant weed. The hairy stem bears numerous bristly leaves. Many minute flower-heads are crowded in crude inflorescences. June to November.

GALLANT SOLDIERS (GALINSOGA)

These are small weeds with inconspicuous flowers. Ovate, toothed leaves on short stalks come in pairs (occasionally threes) with stalked clusters of flower-heads in their axils. The small yellow disk is surrounded by four or five bracts and the same number of small, white, three-toothed rays.

G. PARVIFLORA has hairs lying flat on the surface of the stem. The pappus of the disk-flowers appears as fine, short bristles. The achenes (the "seeds") of the ray-flowers have no pappus..... G. CILIATA, the commoner species, is roughly hairy. A hand magnifier is required to see the sharp tips of the pappus on its achenes.

BOLTONIA

Plants of *Boltonia* have the general appearance of asters, but the yellow disk is dome-shaped or conical instead of flat. Two or four spines on the achene constitute the pappus. Ray-flowers are white, lilac, or pink.

B. ASTEROIDES carries its flower-heads generally in a broad, flat cluster. Its leaves are lanceolate or narrower. July to October.

Erigeron philadelphicus *Johnson*

geron pulchellus *V. Richard*

Sericocarpus asteroides *Scribner*

geron strigosus *Scribner*   Galinsoga parviflora *D. Richards*

CHRYSANTHEMUM

The chrysanthemums of autumn flower gardens are represented in the wild all summer long by the familiar ox-eye daisy, which has come to us from across the Atlantic.

OX-EYE DAISY or MARGUERITE, C. LEUCAN-THEMUM, produces handsome white-rayed flower-heads 2 inches across at the tips of stem and branches on plants that grow 1–3 or more feet tall. The leaves are all unevenly toothed or lobed, the lower ones ovate with the broader part outward, the upper ones much narrower, perhaps with parallel sides, sometimes "clasping" the stem with the lowest lobes. May to October..... FEVER-FEW, C. PARTHENIUM, is a daisy-like plant that has escaped from cultivation. It bears many heads ⅜–¾ inch across with a yellow disk and white rays about ¼ inch long. The leaves are twice divided pinnately. The plant grows 1–3 feet tall. June to September.

CHAMOMILE (ANTHEMIS)

In the flower-heads of chamomile the rays are white (in one seldom-seen species, yellow) and the disk is yellow. The bracts of the flower-head have papery, translucent margins. There is practically no pappus on the achenes (the "seeds"). The disk-flowers are mingled with the sort of bracts known as chaff. The leaves are pinnately cleft into many threadlike parts. In at least one species they are irritating to the touch.

STINKING MAYWEED, STINKING CHAMO-MILE or DOG-FENNEL, A. COTULA, has foliage that not only has a disagreeable odor but that raises blisters on the skin of those who handle it. Farm workers particularly hate it.

May to October..... CORN CHAMOMILE, A. ARVENSIS, resembles *A. cotula*, but lacks the ill scent of that species. It is less common.

MATRICARIA

Our species of *Matricaria* closely resemble *Anthemis*, the foliage in both being very finely divided pinnately and the rays of *Matricaria*, when present, being white, the disk yellow.

PINEAPPLE-WEED, M. MATRICARIOIDES, has a conical disk but no rays. The foliage when crushed emits the fragrance of pineapple. .... WILD-CHAMOMILE, M. MARITIMA, is a spreading, branching herb up to 2 feet tall. The disk is ¼–⅜ inch across. There are from twelve to twenty-five rays. June to October.

ACHILLEA

The flat-topped inflorescences of *Achillea* consist of many small and tightly packed flower-heads, each possessing only a few short, white (or occasionally pink) rays. There is no pappus on the achenes (the "seeds").

YARROW or MILFOIL, A. LANULOSA, stands 1–3 feet tall. The leaves, borne singly, are narrow, without stalks, and cut into innumerable fine divisions. The plant has a characteristic odor. June to November..... A. MILLEFOLIUM, the European species of yarrow, is almost identical and generally confused with the American species..... SNEEZEWEED, A. PTARMICA, sometimes escapes from cultivation. The ray-flowers are numerous and conspicuous. The leaves are narrow but not finely cleft.

hillea lanulosa   *Gottscho*

Chrysanthemum leucanthemum   *Johnson*

hemis cotula   *Johnson*

Matricaria matricarioides   *D. Richards*

ANTENNARIA

The species of *Antennaria* (and there are many of them) go by the various common names of "everlasting," "pussy-toes," and "ladies'-tobacco." None of them have ray-flowers. The differences among certain of them are exceedingly minute. In the genus as a whole, the principal leaves are at the base of the plant. Pistillate and staminate flowers appear on separate plants. Staminate flowers, however, may have a style such as belongs in a pistillate flower, but it will be nonfunctional.

A. PLANTAGINIFOLIA has rather large long-stalked basal leaves with from three to seven conspicuous veins, somewhat like the leaves of plantain (*Plantago*). The flowering stem that rises about a foot tall from this rosette bears several stalkless, narrow leaves and a tight cluster of flower-heads. Runners that grow out from the basal rosette form new rosettes at their tips. These basal leaves are hairy when young but smooth when mature. April to June..... A. NEGLECTA, which also spreads by runners, has basal leaves that are broadest near the tip, and there about ½ inch across. They have one main vein. The flowering stem rises about a foot (that of staminate flowers less), bearing very narrow leaves and several crowded flower-heads. The bracts have rather showy white tips. In one form only one flower-head develops. April to July..... A. NEODIOICA is similar but variable, and it forms offshoots instead of runners, so that a dense mat of leaves occurs. May to July.

GNAPHALIUM

Generally called "cudweed" or "catfoot," species of *Gnaphalium* are also known as "everlasting" because the white or colored bracts around the flower-heads are dry and keep their looks long after they are picked.

Two kinds of flowers appear in the same head: the central ones have both stamens and pistil; the outer ones lack stamens. The leaves are distributed over the stem, seldom clustered at the base in a rosette. The plants are generally covered with a white or dingy wool.

CATFOOT, G. OBTUSIFOLIUM, has flattish clusters of flower-heads at the tips of branches on stems that stand from 4 inches to 3 feet tall. The leaves are stalkless, narrow, and sharp-pointed. August to November..... G. VISCOSUM is similar but has glandular hairs on the stem and ridges that run down the stem from the edges of the leaves. July to October.

CUDWEED, G. PURPUREUM (2–20 inches) bears rather blunt leaves that are mostly wider toward the tip. The flower-heads, clustered in the axils of the upper, smaller leaves, form a rather tall, narrow inflorescence. The bracts are brown or purplish. April to October..... LOW CATFOOT, G. ULIGINOSUM, is widely branched, very leafy, and not more than a foot tall. The uppermost leaves extend above the flower-heads, which are closely clustered and enveloped in wool. July to October.

ANAPHALIS

We have a single species of this mainly Asian genus.

PEARLY EVERLASTING, A. MARGARITACEA, grows up to 3 feet tall with long narrow leaves projecting from the stem, all covered with white wool. The flower-heads, with pearl-white bracts, are clustered at the tip of the stem. Pistils and stamens usually occupy flowers on separate plants, though pistillate flower-heads may hold a few stamens. July to September.

aphalium purpureum   *Johnson*

Gnaphalium obtusifolium   *Johnson*

phalis margaritacea   *Ryker*

Antennaria plantaginifolia (female)   *Johnson*

THE THISTLES (CIRSIUM)

Thistles are known for their prickles – on stem, leaves, and the bracts around the flower-heads. They are further distinguished from other composites by the feathery pappus and by the hairs or bristles (instead of scales) with which the flowers are mixed. The flowers are very narrow and all alike – there are no rays. They are usually blue-purple.

BULL THISTLE, C. VULGARE, forms a flat rosette of leaves the first year; the second year it sends up a flowering stem to 5 feet or more. The leaves on this are coarsely toothed or pinnately lobed and thoroughly armed with prickles. On the under surface they are usually woolly or webby. From each leaf a prickly flange or "wing" runs down the stem. The flower-heads are 2 or 3 inches tall; the bracts are all tipped with spines. June to October

The remaining species of Cirsium *do not have prickly stems.*

C. DISCOLOR has numerous leaves deeply cleft pinnately and bearing a felt of white wool on the under surface. The uppermost leaves on each stem are close around the flower-head, on which the outer bracts have a weak prickle bent downward. The inner bracts have a long, colorless, soft tip. The plant may grow up to 10 feet. July to October..... C. ALTISSIMUM is similar but taller (to 12 feet), and the leaves are less deeply cleft or lobed (sometimes unlobed). July to October..... PASTURE THISTLE, C. PUMILUM, has a hairy stem 8–36 inches tall, rising from a rosette of pinnately cleft leaves. The stem-leaves are very prickly and most of the bracts are also prickle-tipped. The flower-heads

are sometimes 4 inches tall. Often they are directly surrounded by leaves or leaflike bracts. June to September..... C. VIRGINIANUM reaches 4 feet or more in height and may bear forty or more felt-lined, prickly-edged leaves along its stem. The long stalks which carry the flower-heads bear additional small leaves. The outer bracts are prickle-tipped, the inner bracts soft-tipped. The flowers are red-purple. August to October.

SWAMP THISTLE, C. MUTICUM, blooms on a hollow stem up to 10 feet tall, usually branched, and rising from a rosette of long-stalked leaves. On the stem the leaves are rather thin and deeply cleft pinnately. The bracts surrounding the flower-heads are covered with a web of hairs; the outer bracts have minute spines at the tip. The flowers are purple. July to September.

YELLOW THISTLE, C. HORRIDULUM (1–5 feet tall), has very prickly, pinnately cleft leaves and a circle of prickly, leaflike bracts surrounding the flower-head. The bracts beneath this are soft-tipped. The flowers are yellow (pale purple in one form). May to August.

ONOPORDON

One species has reached the United States.

SCOTCH or COTTON THISTLE, O. ACANTHIUM (3–10 feet), has a prickly-winged stem like that of *Cirsium vulgare* (above). It differs from *Cirsium*, however, in having unbranched pappus-hairs (those of *Cirsium* are feathery). The flower-heads are 1–2 inches across with purple or crimson flowers and spine-tipped bracts. July to October.

sium horridulum   *Johnson*

Cirsium discolor   *Rickett*

sium muticum   *Scribner*

Cirsium vulgare   *V. Richard*

BURDOCKS (ARCTIUM)

The coarse weeds that we know as burdocks bear purple or pink flowers which are all alike. They are tubular, and each small flower contains both stamens and a pistil. They are in large part enclosed by the bracts, which form a ball around the mass of them, each individual bract tipped by a hooked bristle. Both local kinds bloom from July to October.

COMMON BURDOCK, A. MINUS, is a bushy-branched plant to 5 feet tall. The leaves have ovate blades on distinct stalks. The flower-heads have very short stalks or none. .... A. LAPPA is a less common species with its flower-heads on definite stalks.

MIKANIA

A single species of this warm-climate genus has spread into our area.

CLIMBING HEMPWEED, M. SCANDENS, is the only vine among our composites. It clambers over other plants in wet areas. Its leaves are paired and stalked, the blades ovate. The flower-heads are in compact clusters, each head containing just four flowers surrounded by four bracts; there are no rays. July to October.

EUPATORIUM

Among the handsome composites of late summer and autumn are members of the genus *Eupatorium*, some of which are known as "Joe-Pye-weed" after an Indian medicine-man, one or more others as "boneset." The heads, many of which are clustered together to form a flat or round-topped inflorescence, contain no rays, only tubular flowers of the "disk" type. The leaves of most species are mainly in circles or pairs, and they are separated here accordingly.

I. *Species in which the leaves are mainly in circles of three or more.* These are all known as Joe-Pye-weed. The flowers are all in some shade of old-rose or lavender, and they appear from July to September.

SWEET JOE-PYE-WEED, E. PURPUREUM (to 7 feet), smells of vanilla when bruised. The leaves are mostly in threes and fours, with short stalks and lanceolate or ovate, sharply toothed blades with one main vein. From three to seven flowers are in each head.

E. FISTULOSUM (to 7 feet) has a hollow stem carrying leaves in circles of from four to seven. They have rather narrow elliptic or lanceolate blades, and rough, on short stalks. In each there is a single main vein. Each flower-head contains from five to eight flowers..... E. DUBIUM (to 5 feet) carries its leaves in threes and fours. The ovate blades are coarsely toothed and on short stalks. There are often three main veins. Each flower-head contains from five to twelve flowers.

kania scandens　　　　　　　　　　*Uttal*

Eupatorium fistulosum　　　　　　　　*Rickett*

patorium purpureum　　　　　　　*Rickett*

Arctium minus　　　　　　　　　　*Gottscho*

EUPATORIUM (*continued*)

E. MACULATUM grows 2–7 feet tall. This Joe-Pye-weed bears its leaves mostly in circles of fours and fives. The blades are lanceolate or narrowly ovate with one main vein, the teeth either sharp or blunt, the stalk short. Each flower-head contains from eight to twenty or more flowers. The inflorescence is rather roughly flat-topped.

II. *Species in which the leaves are not in circles; they are mostly paired.* The flowers are white in all these species in our area.

WHITE SNAKEROOT, E. RUGOSUM (1–5 feet) has ovate leaf-blades with large teeth, the larger leaves on stalks an inch or more long. The bracts surrounding the flower-head are sharp-pointed and nearly all of the same length. The plant is poisonous to cows who eat it and to persons who drink their milk. July to October..... E. AROMATICUM is similar but the leaf-blades are thicker, less sharply toothed, and have stalks less than an inch long; no stalks on the upper leaves.

The bracts of the flower-heads are of several lengths and tend to be broader towards the tip. August to October.

THOROUGHWORT or BONESET, E. PERFOLIATUM (1–5 feet) has distinctive leaves that are long, narrow, tapering, wrinkled, toothed, rather light green, and joined in pairs so that the stem seems to grow right through (*per*) them. The whole plant is hairy. July to October..... E. ALBUM (to 3 feet or taller) has narrow leaves of various shapes, all edged with large blunt teeth. In each head there are about five flowers. July to October.

E. ROTUNDIFOLIUM (1–5 feet) is a hairy plant with stalkless leaves otherwise much like those of *E. rugosum* (at left). They are more nearly ovate than round, despite the name. There are from five to seven flowers in each head. July to October..... E. SESSILIFOLIUM (2–5 feet) has smooth, narrow, toothed leaves that are broadest at their rounded base. They have no stalks. In each head there are five or six white flowers. July to September.

Eupatorium rugosum   *Johnson*

Eupatorium rotundifolium   *Scribner*

Eupatorium maculatum   *Johnson*

Eupatorium perfoliatum   *Johnson*

THE IRONWEEDS (VERNONIA)

While there are numerous ironweeds across North America, as well as on at least three other continents, only one species of *Vernonia* is likely to be found in the vicinity of New York, and that one is named for the city (or state).

NEW YORK IRONWEED, V. NOVEBORACENSIS, is a tall and handsome plant with vivid purple flowers, assembled in a branching inflorescence at the summit of a leafy stem. In each head there are between thirty and fifty flowers, all tubular; there are no rays. The bracts around each flower-head narrow rather abruptly into a hairlike tip. The leaves are lanceolate, their edges toothed or plain. The stems reach a height of 6 or 7 feet. The plants often grow in marshy places. July to October.

THE BLAZING-STARS (LIATRIS)

The "blazing-stars" that belong in the genus *Liatris* (another is in *Chamaelirium* in the lily family) are slender, unbranched plants, generally 3 or 4 feet tall, with mostly narrow leaves in a close spiral and a spike of rose-purple flower-heads. The leaves are usually marked with resinous dots. To distinguish species a hand magnifier usually is necessary; the pappus must be closely examined and the flowers in several heads must frequently be counted. All species growing in this area have pappus-bristles with no branch-hairs, and all blossom between July and October.

L. PYCNOSTACHYA (2–5 feet tall) is a midwestern species that has escaped from cultivation on Long Island, where it fills wide fields with tall and crowded purple spikes of bloom (*pycnostachya* means "with crowded spike"). The very narrow leaves are similarly crowded lower down on the tall, straight stem. The bracts beneath the flower-head are oblong with sharp tips which either spread outward or bend downward; they are ridged on the back. There are from five to twelve flowers in a head..... L. GRAMINIFOLIA (8–48 inches tall) has grasslike leaves (which is the meaning of *graminifolia*) on its stem. Before flowering time it may have narrow-bladed, flat-stalked basal leaves, their stalks edged with hairs. The heads have from five to fifteen flowers apiece. The bracts beneath each head, which are oblong, blunt, and rather narrow, are also edged with hairs and ridged or striped on the back..... L. SPICATA (1–6 feet) is the species most often seen in gardens, as well as in damp places in the wild. The leaves are numerous and narrow, except for the lowest ones, which may be nearly an inch wide. The upper leaves merge gradually into tall bracts which are sometimes mingled with the lower part of the dense spike of flower-heads. Most of the bracts beneath the heads are oblong and blunt, either green or purple, with a thin red margin, ridged on the back, and closely pressed together. Each head is likely to contain an average of about ten flowers..... L. BOREALIS (1–4 feet) has broader leaves than most blazing-stars, the lower ones often an inch or more wide. There are from thirty to sixty or more flowers in a head. The bracts are often reddish with a narrow, red, petal-like margin; they are roundish, and lie close around the flower-head.

Liatris pycnostachya   *Gottscho*

Vernonia noveboracensis   *V. Richard*

KUHNIA

One species of this genus occurs in our range.

FALSE BONESET, K. EUPATORIOIDES (1–5 feet), somewhat resembles one of the "true" bonesets in the genus *Eupatorium*. It bears a branching, terminal inflorescence of cream-colored, tubular disk-flowers, up to thirty flowers in a head. The pappus is feathery; the bracts beneath the flower-heads are narrow and blunt but somewhat variable. The leaves are lanceolate and paired, and may be either toothed or plain on the edges. The plant grows mainly in dry, open places. July to October.

ERECHTITES

The species that we find most commonly in our area is widespread as a weed over much of the United States.

FIREWEED or PILEWORT, E. HIERACIFOLIA, may grow from a few inches up to 10 feet tall, bearing its tubular, whitish flowers in many small heads, each surrounded by a ring of bracts of equal length with a few smaller bracts at the base. The outer flowers in the head lack stamens. The pappus on the achenes (the "seeds") is composed of many white bristles. The leaves, borne singly, are narrow, lanceolate, and toothed, and they have only a short stalk, if any. July to October. This plant bears no relationship to the other "fireweed" (*Epilobium angustifolium* in the evening-primrose family). Both are so named because they are especially abundant after fires..... E. MEGALOCARPA, a similar but fleshier plant with green, brown-edged flowers, may be found along the seashore and in marshes on Long Island.

TANACETUM

The European species that has made itself at home along roadsides in the United States is a well-known, strong-scented, bitter-tasting herb that has had cooking, dyeing, and medicinal uses.

TANSY, T. VULGARE, has escaped from cultivation. It grows up to 5 feet and bears a flat-topped cluster of small, bright-yellow flower-heads (⅜ inch wide or narrower). All the flowers are tubular. There is no evident pappus on the achenes (the "seeds"). The leaves are smooth and are divided pinnately into segments which in turn are cut into many fine lobes. July to October.

Kuhnia eupatorioides   *Johnson*

macetum vulgare   *Elbert*   Erechtites hieracifolia   *Elbert*

STAR-THISTLES and KNAPWEEDS (CENTAUREA)

All species of *Centaurea* found in this vicinity – in fact, with few exceptions, all in the United States – have come to us from Europe and have spread either as weeds or as garden escapes. The flowers are generally blue or purple (sometimes pink or white) and all are tubular, but the outer ones are larger and not quite radially symmetric, their larger corolla-lobes sometimes simulating rays. The bracts beneath the head are distinctive and require a hand magnifier for certain identification of the species. Each has a terminal appendage, in most species at least partly brown and bearing a characteristic fringe. The nature of the pappus on the achenes (the "seeds") is sometimes a further guide to the species, for if present it may consist of bristles or perhaps of scales.

BROWN KNAPWEED, C. JACEA (1–3 feet tall) carries rather jagged brown appendages on the bracts. There is no pappus on the achenes. The basal leaves, which are stalked, may be lanceolate or ovate and are sometimes toothed. The stem-leaves are slender and stalkless. The flowers, terminating stem and branches, are light rose-purple. June to September.

BLACK KNAPWEED or SPANISH-BUTTONS, C. NIGRA (1–nearly 3 feet tall), bears almost black triangular appendages with long fringes on its outer bracts. There is a minute pappus. The lowest leaves are lanceolate and sometimes toothed or wavy-edged; the upper leaves are narrow and pointed. The entire plant is rough. The rose-purple flower somewhat resembles that of *C. jacea*. July to October.

C. MACULOSA (1–4 feet tall) has a wiry stem whose many branches end in heads of flowers ½–1 inch broad. The bracts beneath these flower-heads are pale and ribbed, and each outer one bears a short, dark appendage with a fringe on each side of from five to seven hairs. The lowest leaves are pinnately divided; the upper leaves are simpler. June to October..... CALTROPS or STAR-THISTLE, C. CALCITRAPA (8–20 inches tall) carries only a few tubular purple flowers in each head. The bracts on the flower-heads end in stiff spines which spread in all directions. The lower leaves are deeply pinnately cleft or divided, the lobes or segments more or less toothed. June to October..... CORN-FLOWER, BLUE-BOTTLE, or BACHELOR'S-BUTTONS, C. CYANUS (1–4 feet tall) is a familiar garden flower that has spread into the wild. Its long loose branches end in single heads of flowers. The outer bracts have a toothed, whitish margin, the inner ones often a jagged and colored tip. While the flowers are most frequently blue, they may also be violet, pink, or white, and the marginal flowers in the head are large and may become ray-like. The lower leaves may be either toothed or pinnately cleft; the upper ones are linear. The plant is woolly-white when young. July to September.

Centaurea nigra   *Gottscho*

ntaurea maculosa   *Johnson*

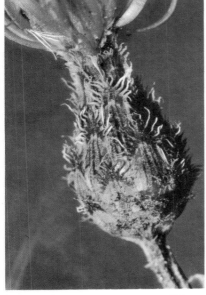

Centaurea maculosa   *Rickett*

Centaurea jacea   *Johnson*

CICHORIUM

This European genus, one species of which has become a roadside weed in North America, belongs in the group of composites that have only ray (or raylike) flowers.

CHICORY, C. INTYBUS, which may grow up to 5 feet tall, displays its flower-heads close-set along its erect stem. These are flattish, about 1½ inches across, and they have practically no stalks. They are usually of clear, light blue (though occasionally pink or white) and the flowers are solely strap-shaped. The leaves on the stem are small, oblong or lanceolate, often toothed, stalkless, and sometimes appearing to surround the stem. The basal leaves are generally pinnately cleft. June to October.

THE RATTLESNAKE-ROOTS (PRENANTHES)

The intensely bitter roots found on plants in this genus were once thought to furnish a remedy for snake-bite. The plants on the whole are tall and contain milky juice. They bear their leaves singly. Slender heads consisting entirely of ray-flowers hang in small clusters near the tip of the stem. The bracts around each flower-head are of two sizes, the longer ones forming a cylinder around the flowers, the shorter ones outside and at the base. The pappus on the achenes (the "seeds") is composed of numerous bristles.

P. ALTISSIMA (2–7 feet tall) has leaves with ovate or triangular blades, sometimes indented at the base, often deeply lobed or cleft palmately, sometimes toothed, and occasionally stalked. In each flower-head there are five of the long bracts and five or six greenish-white ray-flowers. The pappus is generally creamy-white. July to October.

GALL-OF-THE-EARTH, P. TRIFOLIOLATA (6 inches—5 feet tall), has leaves that vary greatly in shape, being lobed, cleft, or divided palmately into three, and mostly stalked. In each flower-head there are about eight long bracts, about ten whitish or pink ray-flowers. The pappus is cream-colored. In these floral details, though essentially not in leaf form, the species closely resembles the more southern P. serpentaria, which may reach New York. July to September.

P. RACEMOSA has up to twenty-five pink or white ray-flowers in a head. The pappus on the achenes is yellowish. The plant grows up to 5 feet tall and is very smooth and pale. Only the lowermost leaves are stalked; they have more or less elliptic blades. The stem-leaves mostly appear to encircle the stem with the lobes at the base of the blade. August and September.

WILD LETTUCE (LACTUCA)

As distinct from cultivated lettuce (*Lactuca sativa*), the several species of wild lettuce, both native and introduced, that have entered our area are scarcely deserving of attention as wild flowers. They are tall (some up to 10 feet), leafy-stemmed plants bearing many very small flower-heads, mainly yellow or blue. The individual flowers are all of the ray type. The pappus is a mass of numerous soft bristles, in most species at the summit of a long narrow beak which extends from the achene (the "seed"). The leaves are sharply toothed, often pinnately lobed.

L. CANADENSIS is the tallest one. Its leaves are mainly lanceolate, clasping the stem at the base. The minute flowers are yellow, sometimes becoming purplish in age. July to September..... L. FLORIDANA (to 6 feet) has small bluish flowers with a bright white pappus. The leaves are generally lobed. August to October.

Prenanthes altissima *Rickett*

nanthes trifoliata *Ryker*

horium intybus *Johnson*

Prenanthes racemosa *Johnson*

TRAGOPOGON

Three species of *Tragopogon* grow and bloom in North America, but none is native here. They resemble each other in having smooth stems bearing single large flower-heads and long grasslike leaves which sheathe the stem at their bases. The flowers are all of the ray type. The bracts beneath each flower-head are equal in length. The pappus on the achenes is of feathery bristles; it stands at the summit of a slender beak and makes a conspicuous, fluffy globe when the plant is in fruit.

SALSIFY or OYSTER-PLANT, T. PORRIFOLIUS, is an escape from vegetable gardens. The flowers are purple. Their bracts are an inch or more long. When in fruit their pappus makes a globe at least 2 inches across. Just below the flower-head the stem, which reaches about 3 feet in height, is swollen and hollow. April to August. (The plant illustrated opposite is a hybrid with different coloring from the species.)

GOAT'S-BEARD, T. PRATENSIS, has yellow flowers which close at midday. The bracts are mostly less than an inch long. The stem is not swollen below the flower-head. The leaves are slightly broader at the base than those of *T. porrifolius*. May to August.

T. MAJOR (sometimes called *T. dubius*) has yellow flowers like those of *T. pratensis* but with bracts 2 inches long or longer and a stem swollen below the flower-head like that of *T. porrifolius*. May to July.

HYPOCHOERIS

One species of this Old-World genus has become naturalized in North America.

CAT'S-EAR, H. RADICATA, bears a head of yellow ray-flowers much like that of a dandelion (*Taraxacum*, Plate 149), 1–1½ inches

broad, and on each achene there is a long, slim beak which bears a feathery pappus. Overlapping bracts beneath the flower-heads are of several lengths. Additional bracts, as chaff, are mixed with the flowers. The flowering stem, 8–16 inches tall, is virtually naked except for a possible branch or two bearing flower-buds. The basal rosette consists of evenly lobed, hairy, ovate leaves. May to September.

DWARF-DANDELION (KRIGIA)

This is one of the relatively few genera of composites to bloom in spring.

K. VIRGINICA has a cluster of narrow, pointed, pinnately lobed leaves from which arises one or more leafless stems up to a foot tall, each bearing a single head of yellow ray flowers. The bracts are all approximately equal in length. The pappus, of a few long bristles (not more than ten), is surrounded by a ring of scales. A plant of dry soils. March to August.

HAWKBITS (LEONTODON)

The hawkbits are also like small-flowered dandelions, sending up naked stalks of yellow flower-heads from a basal leaf rosette.

FALL-DANDELION (L. AUTUMNALIS) has blooms on scaly stems about a foot tall; these sometimes branch near the tip. The plant's basal leaves are deeply cleft pinnately into narrow lobes. The principal bracts beneath the flower-heads are more or less equal in length, with a few smaller ones at the base. The pappus is feathery and tawny. May to November..... L. LEYSSERI, 8 inches tall and with basal leaves less deeply cut, and L. HASTILIS, with bristly stem and leaves, may occasionally be found in the New York area.

Tragopogon porrofolius   *Voss*

...igia virginica   *Johnson*

...ypochoeris radicata   *Johnson*

Tragopogon major   *Williamson*

LAPSANA

The Old-World genus *Lapsana* has one species naturalized in America.

NIPPLEWORT, L. COMMUNIS, is a slender, branching plant 6–60 inches tall. The toothed, ovate leaves are borne singly; the lower ones have stalks. The yellow flower-heads are small, with only about ten rays to a head; there are no disk-flowers, and there is no pappus on the achenes. June to September.

SOW-THISTLES (SONCHUS)

The sow-thistles are common and rather ugly plants, with prickle-edged leaves and small heads of yellow ray-flowers; the pappus in all species of coarse, white bristles. The various kinds grow from 1 to 6 or more feet tall and flower from June or July to October. All are native European plants.

S. ASPER, the earliest to bloom, is also the spiniest of leaf. The lobes of the leaves which extend on either side of the stem are large and rounded.

S. OLERACEUS has paler yellow flowers. Its leaves have a few deep, sharply pointed lobes, including those which more or less surround the stem, edged with soft spiny teeth. The achenes are wrinkled crosswise. .... S. ARVENSIS has flower-heads 1½–2 inches across, with bracts in about three lengths. The achenes are wrinkled across their ribs. The leaves are pinnately lobed or cleft, with pointed lobes extending on either side of the stem. This species is most common in cultivated ground.

TARAXACUM

The genus which includes the common dandelion of lawns contains a great many other species too, but very few of these are known in North America, and only the one is generally recognized in the region of New York.

COMMON DANDELION, T. OFFICINALE, is the well-known weed from the Old World that is found here wherever grass is growing. The pinnately lobed or cleft leaves which form a flat rosette on the ground taper into a flat stalk. The achenes ("seeds") are olive-brown and they taper up into a long thin beak that bears the pappus, which is hairy but not feathery. The flower-head is borne at the summit of a bare and hollow stem that carries a milky sap. It consists of many tightly packed, bright-yellow raylike flowers. Beneath them are long green bracts with a circle of smaller bracts at their base. These long bracts grow together and enclose the achenes during their development. When the seeds inside the achenes are mature, the long bracts open and turn downward around the stem, and the pappus on the achenes expands into a ball of fluff. March to December.

HAWK'S-BEARD (CREPIS)

Crepis is a genus of weedy plants, mostly native in Europe. One species has become established in the vicinity of New York.

C. CAPILLARIS bears small heads of yellow ray-flowers on stems 1–2 feet tall, usually branching. The leaves, which are more or less lanceolate, though generally wider towards the tip, may take on almost any marginal design – even-edged, toothed, or pinnately cut into narrow, pointed lobes, and the lobes themselves sometimes cut. Most of them are at the base of the plant. The few others have pointed "ears" by which they seem to "grasp" the stem. The bracts around the flower-head are of equal length (about ¼ inch) in a single circle, with a few shorter bracts at the base. The pappus is of soft white bristles. The achenes are ten-ribbed, smooth, and slightly narrowed at both ends. July to October.

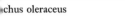

chus oleraceus   *Johnson*   Lapsana communis   *Fischer*

Taraxacum officinale   *Rickett*

chus asper   *Johnson*

THE HAWKWEEDS
(HIERACIUM)

The hawkweeds, which are also known by several other common names, are a large group of mostly weedy plants with generally small heads of mainly yellow flowers, all of the ray type. The bracts around each head are in several overlapping circles, often with much shorter basal bracts. The pappus consists of a circle of bristles.

I. *Species in which stem-leaves are missing or, if present, are much smaller than the leaves in the basal rosette.*

    A. Several of these have flower-heads in a rather small or tight cluster at the tip of the stem. These generally spread rapidly by runners.

DEVIL'S-PAINTBRUSH, H. AURANTIACUM (8–30 inches), is one of the few species of *Hieracium* that does not have yellow flowers. Its red-orange heads of bloom are well known in late summer. The plant is coarsely hairy. Its leaves, 2–8 inches long, are narrow but inclined to be broader towards the tip. June to October.

KING-DEVIL, H. PRATENSE (6–36 inches), nearly duplicates the devil's-paintbrush in its hairiness, leaves, and runners, but has yellow flower-heads. May to September..... H. FLORIBUNDUM, also known as KING-DEVIL, is similar, though the foliage is gray-green instead of hairy (except on the edges and midrib of the leaves) and the bracts are blackish. June to August..... H. FLOREN-TINUM, though not likely to be found within our area, is almost the same as *H. floribundum*, but with few if any hairs and likely without runners. May to September..... MOUSE-EAR, H. PILOSELLA, rarely exceeds 10 inches in height and may carry only one

flower-head. The stem and leaves bear scattered long hairs. The runners are slender and leafy. May to September.

    B. In the remaining species with the principal leaves at the base of the stem, the flower-heads are somewhat loosely disposed in a widely branching cluster. These have no runners.

RATTLESNAKE-WEED or POOR-ROBIN'S-PLANTAIN, H. VENOSUM (8–30 inches), generally has conspicuous red or purple veins in the leaf-blade. The plant bears long hairs. May to October.

H. VULGATUM (6–36 inches) bears sparse long hairs on its short-stalked basal leaves. The blades have long blunt teeth in their lower half. The heads are large, with from forty to eighty flowers in each. The bracts bear blackish hairs. May to September.

II. *Species with leaves on the flowering stem not much smaller than those at the base.*

H. PANICULATUM (to 4 feet) has long, slender stalks that spread in all directions, even downward, bearing flowers, from ten to twenty in each head. The plant is almost completely smooth. The leaves are lanceolate or elliptic, paler on the lower side. July to September..... H. CANADENSE (1–5 feet tall) is more or less hairy. The leaves are numerous and much alike: lanceolate, without stalks, variously toothed or plain along their edges. Forty or more flowers are in each head. July to September..... H. SCABRUM (1–5 feet) has a stem that is densely downy or is covered with short hairs, many of them tipped with glands. The leaves, 1½–8 inches long, are rather thick, sparsely hairy, and have few or no marginal teeth. The flower-heads are in a rather compact, cone-shaped cluster, each head composed of forty or more ray-flowers.

ieracium pratense and Hieracium venosum   *V. Richard*

Hieracium vulgatum   *Uttal*

ieracium auranticum   *White*

Hieracium paniculatum   *Rickett*

Index of Names

English and Botanical

English names of two or more words, not joined by a hyphen, that begin with Black, Blue, Common, Early, False, Field, Purple, Red, Tall, White, Wild, Yellow are indexed under the second (or subsequent) word: Mustard, Black; Violets, Early yellow; Foxgloves, False; Burdock, Common; Marjoram, Wild. Names consisting of hyphened words are generally indexed under the first word, some under both first and second words: Butterfly-weed; Five-fingers; Marigold, Marsh-, Marsh-marigold. Other names of two or more words may be indexed under the first or any subsequent names; many in both ways: Gentian, Fringed, Fringed Gentian.

Botanical names of species will be found under the names of their genera.

An effort has been made to correct in the index misspellings and mispunctuations discovered in the text or plates.

315